My Crazy Ride to IRONMAN!

One woman's triumph over ADHD, assault, and family dysfunction by crossing the finish line

By, Dana L. Shepard Cardwell

A story of perseverance and persistence.

This book is dedicated to the memory of Debra Zapata and all others who have lost their life doing what they love, cycling. God Bless You, Debra, and other cycling angels who protect us as we venture down the road.

For those who showed me guidance, love, and support along my journey, I love you and may God continue to bless you. For those few who were an obstacle in my road, you've helped me more than you'll ever know - thanks for making this book possible. My wish for you is to find your pot of gold at the end of your rainbow.

An extra special thank you to my wonderful husband and daughter. To Mr. Richard Paoli for his original guidance and direction on this memoir when all I had was vomit on 300 pages. To Dave Clark and his wife for being a part of my journey. God presented you at a much needed time. Thank you for taking on the editing and cleaning my book up. Our meeting was a "sign". To the lost souls who only want to be heard. To those who continue to guide me, love me, and have stood by my side when others jumped off my ship for writing a book. I love you for accepting me just the way I am; this one's for you. You guys are amazing.

"Be who you are and say what you feel because those who mind don't matter and those who matter don't mind." Dr. Suess

Chapter 1   Someday

"There's a journ' that leads to happiness, past the beaten path we know. It's on our list called one of these days, but we never stop..... to go." (www.nimblewillnomad.com)

Just as Navy Seals are a miniscule percentage of the U.S. Navy, Iron Chicks represent a minority of athletes. We are a select few. Years ago, I was perfectly happy doing my own thing: 5K runs, 10ks, half-marathons, and smaller triathlons. Never in my wildest dreams did I envision hearing the words from Mike Reilly, "Dana Cardwell, YOU are an **Ironman**!" Why would I want to? I wasn't one of those "hardcore" types. Like many people, I've worked through a lot in my life, but it wasn't until my Ironman journey that I realized why I shied away from the hardcore type. Why? Well, frankly, if you put a group of Ironmen in a small area, you get spontaneous combustion from all the competitive genes and energy.

Let me point out, this book is not just about my story of becoming an Ironman, it's about choosing to get healthy, working through issues, perseverance, persistence, and a plethora of facts (some more useful than others); however, one of those facts just might save your life. So hop on my crazy ass train and hold on, because we're in for a wild ride.

We'll start with a little history first. After completing a Half-Marathon one year in June, which, by the way was excruciatingly hot, I heard someone say, "I'm doing this in the extreme heat because *Someday* is not a day of the week!" Amen to that. That was alright with me. I've always agreed with Henry Beecher when he said "The difference between perseverance and obstinacy is that one comes from a strong will and the other from a strong won't." That pretty much sums up my philosophy of life right there.

> *"Many people have a dream of reaching the Ironman Triathlon finish line, but there are several reasons why many an aspiring Ironman will never reach it. The 2.4 mile open water swim is the first discipline in the Ironman Triathlon and many people are beat before they start as they feel there is no way they could ever swim that far. The distance is daunting and the thought of navigating the swim along with 2,500 or more other triathletes is enough to scare many people off of even trying."* (Ray Fautex, Examiner.com)

Relatively few people are Ironman finishers. Becoming one of the 1/1000th of 1% of the world who can say they have completed an Ironman Triathlon is quite an accomplishment. For most athletes, doing one part of the race would be a major effort. Swimming 2.4 miles or biking 112 miles *or* running a 26.2 mile marathon would be a fine accomplishment in its own rights. However, doing all three events, consecutively, in one day is borderline psychotic.

> "With the right mindset and dedication, it IS in fact possible to squeeze in your training, your work, your social life, your laundry, your naptime, etc. – but it all boils down to how badly do you want it? The sport of triathlon is not as elite as many people make it out to be. It's meant to be fun, it's meant to be a hard-core challenge, and there really is no better feeling than crossing that finish line for your first multi-sports race whether it's a short sprint, or an Ironman. "
> (www. Steeldirectory.com/travel_guide/42130/marathon_tips/ doing_an_ironman_triathlon.html)

My *someday*, Ironman journey started in 2007 when my husband, Eric, our buddy, Pat, and I trained for and then "killed" the Austin Ironman 70.3. When I say "killed" I should say... we almost died. We trained well, or so we thought, but not having a solid nutrition plan almost derailed our dreams of finishing a 70.3 Ironman.

As the "Dynamic Trio" we did a long ride once a week and either did spinning intervals with videos in our home on the other days or we did a short outdoor bike ride after work. There's a beautiful, long, straight stretch of the Guadalupe River about a mile from our home, so we swam one to two miles a week in the river. The race was in September and as is typical for Texas at that time of the year, it was hotter than Hades. We trained for the run with a weekly three miler and then one long run on the weekend. Training was in the summer and on really hot weekends we might do a long ride and save the long run for the following week. We were "flexible" with our schedule and when training started to get hard that's when we incorporated our favorite saying, "It's all about the stories, let's talk training over a glass of wine or cold brew."

To live life to the fullest, you need to get your priorities in place. The same thing goes with an Ironman. Most people don't train for an Ironman by themselves. It's a journey you share with one or more athletes. You need to decide who you let on your train. There are people who set off to accomplish personal records (PRs) or those who just want to stay healthy, or have fun, or add another successful notch to their bucket list. Getting healthy is hardly a piece of cake (pun intended). It takes hard work if you have been out of practice.

In a review of thirteen trials published in the *Journal of Clinical Psychiatry* in 2011, depressed patients participating in physical activities such as swimming, biking, running, and even walking saw more improvement in depression symptoms than those in the non-exercise groups. Think about it. When people are feeling sadness, anger, or even just frustration (all symptoms of depression) they are most likely not living active lifestyles. The tragedy is that a hard work-out can actually save that person with improved health and an improved mood.

The year of training for our first 70.3 (Half Ironman) was a blast. Couch potatoes couldn't even know going so long and so hard could actually be so exciting. We had so much fun and attended so many gatherings celebrating the events we did along the way. We were **weekend warriors**! We would train for a few weeks then suit up like a super-hero to compete in an Olympic or Sprint Triathlon around Texas. While I took on the personification of Superwoman, Eric was my Superman, and that left my friend Pat as Thor. Our moods where uplifted as we looked forward to the challenge ahead of us and the celebration of conquering the quest, afterwards.

I remember one trip to Austin where we all stayed at the Radisson Hotel near Town Lake. The Mexican Free-Tail Bats gather under the Congress Avenue Bridge just outside the Radisson. After our Olympic race, Eric, Pat, Sheri (Pat's wife) and I drank wine on the lawn overlooking the bridge and watched the one million bats take off for the evening. It was truly delightful. Many trips where just as exciting, but didn't include a million or so bats. That was a sight to see and add to our growing list of stories.

When I run triathlons, I like to stay at places that include breakfast, so I will be able to eat *something* besides a breakfast bar before the race. On the day of the 70.3 Ironman race, we stayed at the Embassy Suites Hotel just across Town Lake Bridge in Austin. As usual, we had to wake up well before dawn, which is one thing irritates me about racing.

You have to get up in the pitch black (before even the bats return home), but I do it, begrudgingly. Eric and I got up on race day, and the only thing set out at the breakfast bar at 5:30am was coffee and a little fruit. I failed to realize we would be heading out well before breakfast started—first mistake of the day. Since I'm hypoglycemic, I need to fuel accordingly for long races. So, I drank my normal two to three cups of coffee and grabbed a banana.

Pat, Eric, and I headed out to the car as I was eating my banana. What was my mistake? Well, when you leave for a race so early (to check in your supplies for the race like bike gear, run gear, towel, pump for your tires, etc.), by the time you actually start your race unless you've continued to eat a decent amount of food, you're likely to have used up the fueled-up energy prior to the race even starting.

I used the Port-a-potty right before the event and hastily ingested a goo (Goo or gels are small packets with carbs, sugar, and vitamins that give you a physical and mental boost during a race). Some gel packets come with caffeine; you have the nutrient boost and a shot of caffeine all in a little power packet to can tuck away on your bike or in your run supplies. Most gel energy packets can be taken every 45 to 60 minutes during a race or endurance training.

This time, I started off the race with an empty stomach. Not a great plan. The swim went really well, even though we had there had been the possibility the swim being cancelled due to high levels of E. Coli that year due to lack of rain. Fortunately, the swim went on as planned. And I rocked it! I felt strong coming out of the water and zipped through the massive crowd to get my gear and head out on the bike.

I usually wear a tri-suit type outfit, so all I have to do is put a bike jersey on with my gels in the pockets, my helmet, bike shoes, and sunglasses. I headed out on my 56-mile bike ride feeling strong and Ironwoman powerful. It wasn't until mile 35, with such little nutrition in me, that I realized I didn't plan well at all. Gel packets are not enough to hold you through a 1.2-mile swim, 56-mile bike ride, and 13.1-mile run. My body was begging for more protein.

Coincidentally, around mile 35 on the bike route, there was a guy offering hand-outs of power bars. But as fate would have it, I had already passed him and mentally registered him as just another spectator waving at us on the sideline. My mind took the path of least resistance and I chose not to take the time to circle back a mile or so because that would add up to extra miles. "This sucks," I thought. That was my second mistake. By the time I was coming in the transition area off the bike, I had lost so much performance and energy that it was amazing I still had power to take off on the run. I forced myself to eat a bar when I got off the bike, but it was too little, too late.

Your body needs to be liquefied (yes, that's my own word) well before it gets thirsty and nutritionalized well before you get hungry and / or you are about to faint. I headed out on my 13 mile run and mustered enough speed to hold a slow jog. At mile three I caught up to our buddy, Pat. I had beaten both Pat and Eric out of the water but Pat blew by me on the bike around mile 20. I caught back up to him at mile three on the run when the temperature outside was 95 degrees. He wasn't looking so good. To be exact, he looked putrid. Ashen skinned, with a droopy expression cemented on his face, he ran slumped over.

I asked him how he was doing, he said, "Not good, I keep cramping up. You want to walk with me?" My mind thought, "Hmm... I'm holding a slow jog, and I can keep going for as long as I can or just hang with a buddy and pass time in a more enjoyable speed." Misery does love company, so after a good two minutes of soul searching, I knew I was not going to be earning any top places in this race so I might as well join a friend for the ride, well, run. We talked about Pat's cramps as he did a fast limp/walk resembling the Hunch Back of Notre Dame.

Why do I compete through horrible temperatures and push my body through excruciating pain? Because I can, that's why. Because I don't take for granted one hellish moment that other people can't do what I do; don't have the legs to propel them forward or don't have the disease-free body that I have. God gave me the ability to see his beauty through a swim, bike, and run route with healthy legs, eyes, heart, and soul.

My theory is you have to get out of your comfort zone to work through issues and remove... wait for it........*obstacles in your road.* If you take time to think about it, you will notice when things aren't going well, many change the mission, which isn't always good. I can almost promise you a better life after you cross that finish line of completing an endurance challenge.

A report in the July 2010 issue of *Harvard Health Letter* states... "The outdoors beckons. Heed that call and you'll reap physical and mental health benefits. Here are five reasons to get outdoors:

- **Your Vitamin D levels rise.** Studies suggest this vitamin helps fight certain conditions, from osteoporosis and cancer to depression and heart attacks.

- **You'll get more exercise.** If you make getting outside a goal, that should mean less time in front of the television and computer.

- **You'll be happier.** Light tends to elevate people's mood. Physical activity has been shown to help people relax and cheer up.

- **Your concentration will improve.** Children with ADHD seem to focus better after being outdoors. It may be a stretch for adults, but if you have trouble concentrating, outdoor activity may help.

- **You may heal faster.** In one study, people recovering from spinal surgery experienced less pain and stress and took fewer pain medications when they were exposed to natural light."

If you've complained about weight issues and thought, "I gave up working-out because I gained all the weight back, anyway.", then know this; The January/ February 2011 edition of *Nutrition Action Healthletter* states, "Eating more protein and picking the right carbs may help dieters avoid regaining lost weight." Researchers studied nearly 800 overweight adults who had lost an average of 24 pounds on a low-calorie diet over the previous two months. Those who were then assigned to eat a lower protein diet with high glycemic carbs regained nearly four pounds over the few months. I will get into proper nutrition to become an active, sexy athlete later in this book, so keep reading.

Iron Nugget:

What keeps you from chasing a dream?

How can stepping out of your comfort zone lead to change in your life?

2 Attention Deficit Hyperactive Dana (ADHD)

"It is never too late to have a happy childhood." (Tom Robbins)   "Nobody can be uncheered with a balloon." (Winnie the Pooh)

In the beginning...
My mother knew she was in for a roller coaster ride with me when I was only 3 years old. One sunny afternoon, my mother was at home changing my new born brother's diaper and making sure my 1 year old sister was still napping, when she received a phone call. Mother claims that the manager of the local Kroger's grocery store, a mile or more from our house, was on the line.

He asked, "Mrs. Shepard? Do you have a little boy named, Dino?" My mother replied, "No, but I *do* have a little girl named, Dana." He then informed her that I was at the store helping myself to a candy smorgasbord (those weren't exactly his words, but you get the picture). My mother told the manager that was impossible, I was in the backyard playing. She proceeded to describe the newly added latch at the top of our privacy fence that my father had installed to prevent certain children from unlocking it.

The story ends where my mother loaded up the babies and upon retrieval of my happy little self, asked me, why I would walk so far from home and cross that very busy street in front of Kroger's. She tells me that my reply was, "'Cause I wanted some candy, Mama!" Needless to say with two little babies and one active toddler my poor mother was busy!

The *Diagnostic and Statistical Manual of Mental Disorders* (DSM-IV, 2004) states that Attention Deficit Hyperactivity Disorder, commonly known as ADHD, is classified as having symptoms more frequent and severe than other children characterized by poor concentration, distractibility, hyperactivity, impulsivity, and other symptoms which adversely affect a child's academic performance. It goes on to list three types of ADHD. The first is ADHD-IA with characteristics being primarily inattentive. The second type is ADHD-HI with characteristics being primarily hyperactive-impulsive (my type) and the third type, ADHD-C, having a combination of the first two, ADHD-IA and ADHD-HI.

Children with ADHD and Learning Disorders (LD) often experience difficulty making friends and maintaining appropriate relationships with peers (Henker & Whalen, 1999). The ADHD child may fidget frequently, have difficulty taking turns, interrupt and blurt out comments, have a hard time listening, talk excessively, lose things, act prior to thinking, and may shift quickly from one activity to another.

The positive note is that research has shown people with ADHD tend to have average or above average intelligence (Garguilo, 2008). They are often very creative and usually have a high energy level. These individuals are frequently very sensitive and highly affectionate. Yelling at those with ADHD doesn't work and can back fire. Among adolescents diagnosed with ADHD, the rate of incarceration is substantially high, with approximately 50 percent of "delinquent" youths being diagnosed with ADHD (Foley, Carlton & Howell, 1996).

I was conniving and manipulative at an early age. I remember my long, blonde locks that were down to my buttocks. I hated that long hair and felt like Rapunzel each time my mother wrestled with me to brush and braid it. I wanted to wake up and not have to worry about Mom pulling my hair as she tried to comb the knots out. So, I devised a scheme. I announced to my sister one Saturday morning while watching cartoons that we were going to play "booty pallor". My sister was age five, while I was seven. Sis asked me with a confused look, "Huh? What's that?"

OK, so I had two front teeth missing and it only sounded like "booty pallor", but what I was trying to tell her was "beauty parlor". I informed her that she was going to cut my hair and we were going to have fun! Sis immediately shook her head from side to side with cereal in her mouth, "Nuh UH! Mommy get mad!" My sister wasn't dumb, as I gave her the evil eye and stood over her with the scissors, she had a moment of silence and deep thought. Her thought was more like, "Should I take on Mommy or the evil sister?" The evil ADHD sister won and I ended up blaming the whole thing on my poor innocent sister. I became a boy for the next two years.

Prior to ADHD intervention, it's crucial that parents have a comprehensive medical review on their child to rule out other health issues. A recent report by Chan et. al (2005) noted in a survey of 2,000 primary care pediatricians and family physicians that approximately 70 percent of physicians reported administering ADHD specific rating scales to parents and teachers when ADHD associated complaints were presented. Many did not even bother submitting a blood panel. A child should be checked for Lead, Zinc, Magnesium exposure, allergies, diabetes, and Iron deficiencies, thyroid disorders, seizures, and even sleep disorders prior to being labeled as ADHD (Monastra, 2008). Also, what does their diet look like?

One of the problems with ADHD is that the individual can be depressed or *down*. I was a Debbie Downer when I trained for my first Ironman. On the other hand, if you go through life being told that everything needs to be perfect, i.e., your grades, athletic performance, musical skill then you most likely will live life with unrealistic expectations. We live in an imperfect world, with imperfect people. If you live your life trying to achieve perfection, you will live with disappointment, anger, and unhappiness. To quote a famous man, *"It is not our abilities that show who we are, but our choices"*, Dumbledore to Harry Potter.

Let's go back to my childhood. I lived my first 12 years in a very small South Texas town. I was born with a small silver spoon in my mouth. Not big, mind you, just a little, glowing spoon. Life was good. My father owned a couple of businesses in town, was a city council member, and was president of the local Chamber of Commerce.

Mom was president of the local women's church group and was involved with the Junior League. She loved to shop and get her hair done—a lot! Our family appeared to resemble the ideal nuclear family. My mother stayed very, very busy and was emotionally available if you asked, but it was always known that she was a very busy woman and had things to do from 10 a.m. until 6 p.m.

Mom has always been a little passive-aggressive, so reading her and receiving mixed messages as a child was very confusing. Trying to figure out how things worked in our household, or in the real world for that matter, was a challenge. I learned to not ask questions and after being told on numerous occasions, "Children are to be seen and not heard", I stayed outside, rode my bike, played in the dirt, and found bugs to entertain me. Like many kids that age, I had several delightful habits: I used to pick up gum from the concrete, until my good friend told me that was disgusting and I shouldn't do that, along with picking my nose. I learned so much from my neighbor, Susan, it only makes sense she served as a big sister.

My father worked from 9 a.m. to 9 p.m., never once told his children he loved them, and never gave them a hug while growing up. Everyone knew the entire town's people and their business; think The House Wives of Orange County meets The Brady Bunch. It was a good close-knit community to live my first sheltered years. *"We spend the 1st twelve months of our children's lives teaching them to walk and talk, and the next twelve years telling them to sit down and shut up." (Phyllis Diller)*

My family lost our silver spoon when I turned 12 and we went bankrupt. We went from fast, silver Corvettes, green Jaguars, swimming pools, all the latest material things, to selling everything and moving 60 miles away to Corpus Christi, TX. We sold our nice vehicles and got older cars that seemed to break down frequently. One of the cars looked just like the Ford Grand Torino from the old show "Starsky and Hutch." However, by that time, the show was old and out-dated, just like the car my mother drove. I went from being embarrassed of our fast, flashy cars to being even more embarrassed of our broken-muffler-exhaust-blowing-has-been car. At that point, my mother got a job.

We moved into an apartment. It was the decade of "busing" when the public school system wanted to make sure whites and blacks and Latinos all went to school together. I was bused to a junior high school that was in the middle of gang territory. Life became hard just trying to survive each day at school. Coming from a background that included nice clothes and a decent upbringing, I inadvertently walked around school with the Scarlet "R" on my forehead. I was labeled as a "Rich kid", even though I wasn't. So, as you can imagine, I was harassed and bullied daily.

The anxiety that children and teens develop over the fear of going to school each day is mind-blowing. I would get stomach aches and feel like I was going to throw-up as soon as Mom pulled into the carpool lane at school. I remember being pushed down the halls in 7th grade by very large black girls calling me "blondie" and "cracker". The mean girls would say things to me, "You think you're hot stuff, cracker, don't you?" and "You sure are cool, look at you." Then they would do things behind my back, while I continued walking, ignoring them, and just praying to make it to class safely.

I really did not know what they were talking about. I was just there because I was made to move from my comfortable small South Texas surrounding which had about 50 percent Hispanics, 40 percent whites, and 10 percent blacks. We all got along for the most part, no one at my previous school labeled the others by the color of our skin. The race label was new to me and I was confused.

Hot? What were they talking about? I did not think I was hot or ANYTHING. I was depressed due to moving from my hometown and my parent's stress of going bankrupt. I was trying to survive each day in the hell hole that was referred to as school. I was definitely a product of school bullying in the seventh grade.

I remember the only thing that saved me in 7th grade was track and running the mile. I befriended an older Hispanic girl who took me under her wing and taught me how to breathe during longer distances. She would say, "Two breaths in, two breaths out" and "Don't breath in your upper chest; draw your breaths deep down in your abdomen." I hated that school, but loved that gal; it's amazing what you can draw on a blank slate. I took in everything she had to say, and her advice was good.

I love the words from a child's mind. My daughter wrote an essay in the 5th grade. Here it is.

> "Do you know how you're going to live your life when you get older? You say you're going to do something, but when you get to that point, you change your mind to do something else. Going through the DARE program helps you know what bad stuff will do to you and makes you think. Bullying is when other people are mean to you, make fun of you, hurt you (physically or mentally), and a lot more stuff. For example when people punch, kick you, and call you names like wimp, weak, baby, etc., that is called bullying. If you are ever bullied or see someone being bullied it is best if you stand up for yourself or go and tell someone like your teacher, parents, or someone close. You might even want to try to talk to the person that is bullying other people. Sometimes the bully needs to get their anger out on someone else because they might be very angry or sad."

How ironic that in 5th grade my daughter "got the signs" of a bully. Unfortunately, by the 2nd grade she too had become a victim of bullying by a boy whose parents are very wealthy in town. The boy was a year older than my daughter, but would trip her and hit her on the head with his books on the bus. As a juvenile probation officer, I had a little talk with the boy and the bullying stopped with my daughter. However, the parents were mad that I talked with their son and never did anything about the boy's behavior, so I'm sure he went from bullying my daughter to someone else. It's just plain sad. The bully tends to have more mental issues than the victim. He or she needs help to stop.

My parents moved two more times while I was in junior high and each school was better than the first. I learned to not connect with people as it may be a short period of time until the next move. It wasn't that I was unfriendly, just guarded after my seventh grade experience of being pushed, hit in the back while walking down the hall, and going to class as if I was in a bubble and nothing had happened. I should have received an Academy Award for the most stoic 7th grader in school. I could carry a mesmerized stare better than anyone I knew. An issue of not trusting people followed for years.

Iron Nugget:

What labels have you worn before?

What does it feel like with that label?

3 Sex, Drugs, and Straight A's

"If you find yourself going through hell, keep going." (Walt Disney)

My family's final move occurred in the ninth grade. We moved to a smaller suburb of Corpus Christi where the high school was similar to the one in the small town I grew up in. It was a more affluent school though with a kind of redneck and surfer twist. My parents were starting to get back on their feet financially and the move was a good thing for our family. However, everyone seemed to know one another at the new school so I walked into a new school to stares and cackles.

I did not enroll until November of that year and school had already been in session for several months. Needless to say, when I arrived people noticed me. At first, as I was the new kid in town, I had admirers. Being that I had become reserved, I was a bit uncomfortable with all the attention. It seemed as if everyone knew me, but didn't know anyone of them.

I remember being asked out by a popular boy in December. Technically, the boy sent his *friend* to ask me to go to a party with them. The friend, John, was a class favorite, a blonde blue-eyed surfer, and was dating an 11th grader. We were in 9th grade and I had no idea that boy was so popular when I was first asked out. I recall the boy that wanted me to go out with him having sleep in his eyes during math class and looking slovenly dressed in a flannel shirt. Evidently he was "Surfer Dude Cool," but that was not my thing back then.

I was Prep! Izod and Polo were my thing, not flannel shirts and Converse (Chucks) shoes. I shyly responded that I had plans to go Christmas shopping with my mother that evening. "Were they kidding?" My mother would not have agreed to a date at that age! Sixteen, perhaps, just not as a freshman. I am so glad I did not venture down that road; I grew up way too fast as it was. Those kids used to go "joy riding in cars," cruising through Sonic, drag racing, bon-firing, and, of course, parking.

The theorist, Erik Erickson, categorizes a person's stages in life. One stage is called Autonomy vs. Shame. It basically says young children need time to explore their environment on their own without their parents being afraid they will make a mistake and try to control the child's surroundings.

As a child progresses with appropriate autonomy they enter elementary school. This stage is Initiative vs. Guilt. It gives some decision making to the child. A child needs to be able to make some decisions on their own, along with mistakes. Like "Would you like lunch now or a little later" or "What would you like a grilled cheese sandwich or a peanut butter sandwich?" One would be surprised how little choices present huge milestones for children. A child may develop guilt-dependency or a co-dependent personality if they don't develop healthy choices at an appropriate age. Over controlling parents cause more harm than good with the developing child. *"A person who doesn't make mistakes, doesn't make anything." (William Connor Magee)*

Then there's the Adolescent Stage when teenagers may go through testing limits and defying certain adult's rules. For the most part the teenager is just starting to break the dependent ties they have had on their parents for years. As if to say, "Hello, world, I've arrived. Look at me, ain't I grand?" Many children tend to have a grandiose view of their world. Fortunately, this is typically just a temporary stage. The teens are just establishing their place in the world.

All of us want a sense of importance and there is nothing wrong with transitioning from childhood to adulthood. It's finding a safe and healthy way that matters. A teen who fails in finding his or her identity may end up with role confusion. A characteristic of role confusion is a bully or one with a low self-esteem. A bully lacks an appropriate sense of self, so they pick on others or make others suffer for their own inadequacies or their inadequate view of themself.

When the book *Please, Stop Laughing At Me* by Jodee Blanco came into my path, I cherished her story as Jodee was bullied all through her school years. This poor child even moved schools to try and get away from the bullies. On one of her changes she writes:

> "I portrayed the role of the cool teenager rather than the real Jodee. Even though my new friends seemed sincere about liking me. I still had to act my way into social acceptance. When I was in a situation that made me uncomfortable, rather than choose to do what was right, I pretended our neighborhood was the stage, my new friends were fellow performers, and we were all in a theatrical production. I made it easier to do things I was ashamed of because I could pretend that it wasn't me who was responsible, but the fictional part I was playing. There were times when the kids were especially rough on Jason. I should have spoken up, but I didn't. Being in a clique felt too good. I didn't want to jeopardize that. But my neat little this is just a play, it isn't real life psychological trick wasn't working anymore."

This is an incredibly poignant book written by a woman who is successful and seems happy today, but faced significant challenges as a teen. Erickson talks about Identify vs. Role Confusion and this teen was having some issues with her identity and confused about what role she really wanted to play. *"A sad soul can kill you quicker than a germ."* (John Steinbeck)

Some victims with PTSD cope with the trauma by dissociating or "going away in their mind." The victim may remove themselves from the situation at hand. Jodee decided to become involved in life by acting in a false school play. She left her body and dissociated from her true feelings and ideas to survive the unhealthy and traumatic school environment. It was a survival tool for her. In a sense she started asking herself, "What's wrong with me? Why am I doing this?"

Time passed and I reconnected with an old inner city friend from Jr. High who moved out to our suburb. I realized a few months later, after reconnecting, that Liza had become very worldly. *Parents;* pay attention to who your child is hanging around. *Teenagers;* think twice when you enter a relationship that your gut tells you is not the best thing.

Liza and I wandered the neighborhood and went shopping. The problem was that neither of us really had money to shop. Liza introduced me to taking items from a store. Yes, that would otherwise be known as shoplifting; I just hate to use those words. It started with lip gloss and makeup. I knew later that year it had become a problem when I had worked my way up to a bathing suit. My goodness, what had I become? I was just starting to venture into my journey as a teenager. I would do the self-talk about why it was OK to do what I was doing, but deep down I had to face my choices. When you do something over and over, it becomes so hard to break the cycle.

Research shows it takes a certain amount of time for something to become a habit. I had gotten into the habit of getting things *for free*. I was going to have a hard time breaking it. Liza started smoking marijuana as introduced by her much older brother. We would be in her room when her brother would come in looking cool and say, "Hey, girls, I have a present for you." Then he would toss a joint, or two, on the bed. He reminded me of a used car salesman that liked to smooth-talk girls and try to be Joe Cool at the same time. He was out of high school and too creepy for me. Now at this time, I did not partake and just let Liza do her thing. Don't think for a moment this introduction does not have an impact on a teen. I should have just cut my ties from the beginning and run the other way.

Liza became more and more worldly. Sex, drugs, alcohol, and stealing. I remember Liza broke her leg one time while trying to jump off the roof of a car. She had done some Angel dust and thought she had wings. I wasn't around her during this incident, and I sure wouldn't have approved of who she was hanging with.

Angel dust, or PCP, was developed after WWI as an anesthetic. It's a white, crystalline powder which can be distributed illegally in pills, powder, liquid, or capsules. It affects the central nervous system and just one dose can have physical side effects for months. The drug causes euphoria, loss of inhibitions, anxiety, disorientation, restlessness, drowsiness, disorganized thinking, among other issues. One effect of the drug is weightlessness and paranoia; hence Liza's ability to fly with wings off the top of a car.

In the body, PCP raises the heart rate and blood pressure. High doses can cause the user to become violent with attempts of assault, self-mutilation, or even suicide. Coma, convulsions, and death can occur. (www.cmcsb.com/pcpangel.htm) While I wasn't the model student, I definitely wasn't about to experiment with hard drugs. It's amazing how middle school and high school sets the stage for standing your ground or succumbing to peer-pressure. I don't blame peer-pressure for my choices for stealing; no one held me down and forced to do these things. I just think I was a lonely, confused teen and did irresponsible things to self-medicate; to escape from my real world. Whatever it was, the one thing I was *not* was promiscuous. On that, I stood my ground.

The dictionary defines promiscuous as "characterized by a lack of discrimination, esp. in sexual liaisons." Liza fit that definition and I didn't want any part of that reputation. Sooner or later, I would get a reputation myself, just by being her friend. There is some truth to the saying, "Guilty by association."

Now, to back up, I was an honor roll student, varsity tennis player, loved to run, on the drill team, and sitting in church every Sunday morning. Boy, I had them fooled. Due to people I choose to associate with and the parties I went to, I found myself in a violent situation. This was the first "Ah-ha" moment I was given, but the signs had been there all along. *"Life is a tragedy when seen in close-up, but a comedy in long-shot." (Charlie Chaplin)*

The signs that had been in front of me along my journey were the unfavorable friends I hung around. I remember not feeling fulfilled with these troublesome friends—almost feeling like a film of dirt was embracing me. Like I could never wash off the film of dirt that followed me, the association with those who I knew would only bring me down in the world. Charlie Brown's Pig Pen comes to mind.

Some people always have issues and seem to invite us into their drama (Paulo Cohelo). They create a movie in their heads and seek to include us. Some are depressed, some are bored, some are frustrated, and some are just permanent victims who tend to bring in others. Be very cautious as these people end up including us in their dramatic play and secretly want us to be their victims. They are in misery and just want company in their drama. Generally, when we join their little drama, we end up losing a piece of ourselves. Like the crazy lady used to yell years ago, "STOP THE INSANITY!"

I broke my ties with Liza and started hanging out with a new bunch. Some were involved with the Geek Squad rather than the Agricultural Department. And the girls in the Geek Squad didn't have bad reputations. My other friends were all straight A students. I had been a straight-A student until my sophomore year. While I still was in the top 10 percent, I didn't spend a lot of time cracking the books. Two of my good friends never went out at all. One good friend lived in a home where her mother drank nightly until she fell asleep.

Ally had two younger sisters, one and two years younger. The middle sister, Lila, had long dark hair, was thin, wayward, and a rebel. The youngest sister, Leigh, was best friends with my younger sister. She was a tomboy and looked quite masculine back then. Each sister was totally different.

Ally was smart, quiet, and a great friend. She had reddish hair, a fuller figure—but not fat— and a lot of freckles. Poor thing, it was the era of sunbathing with baby oil and she would burn to a crisp, yet she lay out with us nonetheless. I was the leader of our pack and was worldlier due to my earlier experiences. We started drinking and going out. I came out of my shell and felt more comfortable in my environment. The middle-school years seemed so long ago.

My freshman year consisted of making decisions that would affect me for the rest of my life. We went to parties, while our other buddies on the Geek Squad stayed home. By the time the summer after freshman year came around, we were exposed to marijuana at many parties. Ally did not partake. I would occasionally smoke just to experiment. No one pressured me into partaking, but being in the presence was enticing. Out of sight, out of mind was certainly not the case!

By my sophomore year, I had large size C breasts, a 23-inch waist, and was athletic. I played on the Varsity tennis team, was in the drill team, and worked as a lifeguard. My birthday is in the early fall, so I got a car before most of my friends. Naturally, we cruised.

I started partying a lot my sophomore year, and became friends with a large group of athletes. I only dated football players or athletes. I grew up in a surfing-ag community, so surfers were the exception if you weren't an athlete. I started looking like a snob. My prep days were changing and my shell was starting to crack. A boy I didn't know all that well told me I would only go out with guys who had nice cars, "That's not true!" I replied. Looking back, this was true. I was becoming too worldly and materialistic for my own good. Image played a large part of my personality.

I wasn't easy. No sleeping around for this gal. Guys I went out with told me I was considered a tease. I was told I would make out then go no farther. The truth isn't always pretty. I was a bit loud and hyper, but did not feel I wanted to cross the sexual line. Somehow my hyper, "party-going nature" gave guys the wrong impression.

I remember the first boy I actually "dated" lying to his friends and telling them that he and I went "all the way". This boyfriend, Jay, had wavy blonde hair, a dark tan, and was a surfer.

He failed at his attempt to play football probably because he was a skinny, lanky kid. He had a crooked, unpleasant nose, yet I remember he used to make fun of my nose all the time. He told his friends to call me "the beak" because he said my nose looked like a bird's beak.

Jay's best friend was always rude and tried to embarrass me in front of others. I tended to give him "go to hell" looks. His friend, Mark, would laugh at my nose or make sexual comments to me. On one particular class day when the teacher walked off, Mark started describing how Jay and I "did it" to a group of kids. He yelled out and questioned me, "So tell us, Dana, what's it like?" I told him to shut up and stop making up lies that confused me with he and his girlfriend's bedroom rituals.

Comments like that radiate in other kids' minds, whether they are true or false. The sexual lies, that is. This would be called sexual harassment in today's terminology. I could have denied his rumors as long as I wanted, but some of those kids were going to believe the worst. That I *was* sexually promiscuous. It's just human nature to have visual images that appear in our minds whether they are true or not.

You only get one chance to make a first impression with people. If you show up to school on the first day tired and dressed like a bum, the teacher is going to make a visual image of you. Most likely geared toward the negative. Furthermore, if the new girl shows up at school with the rumor she's a tramp, people are most likely to believe it as true, regardless of if it's true or not.

Ironman Swim. Wisconsin

Iron Nugget:

When have you felt like people are laughing at you instead of with you?

How did you work through the pain of being judged or laughed at?

4   A Royal Pain in the Ass

Domestic violence is the leading cause of injury to women in the United States. (U.S. Surgeon General)

Sexual harassment is unwelcome sexual comments, advances, requests for sexual favors, or other verbal or physical conduct of a sexual nature. It generally results from someone who has power over another like a boss or teacher or coworker.

People who are sexually harassed may feel: angry, hurt, depressed, become easily distracted, unable to concentrate, feel trapped, suffer from physical ailments like stomach aches, headaches, or insomnia. Their self-esteem may begin to suffer with the lack of direct contact with others and less emphasis on their appearance. Like dressing down or gaining weight.

Most people can visualize physical sexual harassment, but examples of verbal harassment can be jokes, remarks, teasing, comments about one's body or sexual activities, or a request for sexual favors. The best way to handle these situations is to talk to someone about it, keep documentation on the times and dates of the harassment, tell the person to stop, find out about policies on sexual harassment at your school or work place, and finally seek assistance if it continues.

Turns out Jay was very similar to his bullying friend. What I did not know was that Jay's father had been abusing his mother and they were about to get a divorce. Jay had it all. He came from a wealthy family, they had a large home with a beautiful pool, a manicured lawn, tennis courts, and, of course, a trampoline.

I remember going over to swim one afternoon. His parents left to run some errands. Jay and I jumped on the trampoline and then he started tickling me incessantly. I told him to stop tickling me and he was such a sweet guy that he said, "I'm going to tickle you until you pee in your pants." What was I thinking dating a loser like this? We got in the pool after jumping on the trampoline and then playing some tennis where his goal was to "beat my pants off." Jay wasn't very good at tennis, so there was no beating my pants off.

In the pool Jay proceeded to tell me how the girl next door loved to come over and swim topless. She was our age, had been a cheerleader, got into drugs, dropped out of high school, and was touring the town with the Banditos bikers. Rumor was that she was a topless dancer. Age 16. Wow. What a great start in life.

I said, "Sure, I'll be like Angie and swim topless." Not even close. What was he thinking? It wasn't as if I was going to take my top off simply because his loser neighbor did. My boyfriend pulled on my string bikini that was double-tied until it started to come untied.

I yelled at him, "TIE IT BACK!" He laughed and swam away. I swam to the side of the pool and tied the suit myself. I got out upset and said, "I'm going home." I stormed out of the pool with an angry look on my face.   Jay convinced me to stay and said he was sorry. He did the "poor me" route and said that he just needed someone to be with as his parents had been arguing a lot and he didn't want to be alone. I will say this: Guys are very intelligent when they think with their second head at this age. We, females, buy the "poor me" story and feel like we should take care of them.

So I stayed. He asked me to come upstairs to his room to listen to some music he just bought. Once up there, he tried to get intimate, I pushed him away. Jay then got into his drawer and pulled out a large baggy of pills. Uppers, downers, etc. I asked him, "Why do you have those?" He said it made him think better; it cleared his mind. He offered, and I preached. I yelled, "Are you crazy, you could end up killing yourself and taking too many of those things." I took the baggy from him, walked over to the bathroom, and threw the pills in the toilet. Flushed them and watched those colorful little kaleidoscopes make their way down the pipe. It was a pretty sight in more than one way!

Jay actually looked relieved that someone cared about him. I was mad and not wanting a part of his behavior. As a truce, he offered me a drink of Jack and Coke as he went downstairs to make it. He brought the drink back upstairs and I took a sip, but I ultimately didn't want to drink with him in the middle of the day. I asked Jay if he was afraid his parents would find out he was drinking. He said they wouldn't even notice. I remember him going into his parent's room to get something. I decided this was a good time for me to leave, exited his room, and walked toward the steep staircase. Jay stopped me as I started to walk down the stairs.

I turned back to hear what Jay had to say. He asked if I trusted him. I told him, "I'm not sure." He said he wanted to earn my trust back and would I play a game with him. "Depends on what it is", I told him. He asked that I grab his hand and lean back. I said, "NO!" He was trying some sort of mind game. Somehow he grabbed my hand, and then gave a little push, and I went tumbling down the stairs. I remember being in so much pain when I landed on the tile floor at the bottom of the stairs, but not wanting to let on that he had hurt me.

My pride was a big downfall. (No pun intended!) He apologized. He jumped on me and started tickling me. Why? I have no idea, but I was in serious pain trying to get his insensitive ass off the top of me. He continued to wreak more havoc on me. Torture! As I drug myself out the door in a hurry, I headed to my car. Jay, the Royal Pain in the Ass, started spitting on me. Really. What an idiot. I yelled to him as I was limping to my car, "You're an asshole and need some therapy!"

Later, I asked what the hell Jay was doing and why he would act like a two-year old. Jay said he was mad because I had been getting a ride from "Mike." Mike was a neighbor up the road from me who was 6-foot, 4-inches and on the basketball team. My car had been in the shop and Mike had been giving me a ride home from school earlier that week.

What, all this abusive behavior because I was getting a ride home from a neighbor? I don't doubt the sexual tries were just for his gratification, but the tickling, pushing down the stairs, spitting and meanness because I needed a ride? This guy had some serious issues and was already becoming like his abusive father.

> Cut those ties! "Stop the insanity!" There was an article in the Los Angeles newspaper (AP) about how exposure to violence in children affects their DNA. The article goes on to say "children who are exposed to violence experience wear and tear to their DNA that is similar to that seen in aging" furthermore, "they face a heightened risk of mental and physical disorders as adults."

This guy was already an angry teen who thought releasing his anger on innocent victims would help his plight. The only thing his anger got him was a drug problem and lack of intimacy, as far as I'm concerned. Turns out I chipped my coccyx (tailbone) that day. I could barely drive my Nissan stick shift. I remember my mother asking me to run an errand. I told her that Jay was giving me a piggy back ride on the tennis courts and I fell and injured my back. I wasn't about to go into the whole sordid details of all that happened with Jay. She wouldn't trust my judgment of boyfriends and might become too protective. It's sad when a teen feels such lack of trust for anyone that they cannot talk about being physically abused. Communication is key.

So, I told Mom I was in pain. Mother said if I was in that much pain, I would have to give up my car for a while. I'm sorry, but I don't care what happened to you and how much pain you're in, tell a 16 year old to give up their car? No way. I ran the errand and continued to be in excruciating pain for at least a month. No wonder childbirth was a walk in the park for me!

It wasn't until six years later that I was in a minor—very minor car accident—which traumatized the chipped coccyx. The doctor said that as a result of the chip, I had grown a cyst in that area. The bump during the fender-bender traumatized the cyst. I had to have surgery.

Let me tell you, they don't sew you up back there. "The stitches would come out when you sit down", the doctor told me. I had three feet of gauze stuffed into the wound for a week. I passed out on several occasions standing up at home after the surgery. My first bath, I had to get my mother to help me in the tub. I couldn't even look at the incision. It's humiliating to be in your 20's and have your mother help you bathe. I couldn't move my legs to get in and out of the tub or the car. I was a teacher and had to take time off from work. It was completely frustrating. When I went back to have the gauze removed, I passed out when the doctor showed me the three feet that was stuffed inside my wound. No wonder my mobility was limited after the surgery.

The chipped coccyx continued to cause trauma years later. Something happened a few years after the surgery. I went to see a specialist. I was in another city at the time, San Antonio, teaching public school. My husband was a psychotherapist at a psych hospital and did not get off until after 5 p.m. I was having issues with my tailbone and drove myself directly after school to see the specialist.

What I didn't know was that the doctor was going to reopen my wound. He told me he was going to give me a local anesthetic and I wouldn't feel a thing. Still having no idea he was sticking me with a knife, I felt an uncomfortable prick, then just some pulling. Nothing major. He told me what was going on back there and what he did should relieve the problem. I went to stand up and passed out in his office.

After coming back to consciousness, the doctor let me know he had to reopen the wound "slightly" and the pain must have caused me to faint. He told me he would give me a pain pill. I informed him that I could not take Demerol, Darvicet or Codeine, as it makes me feel violently ill. Doc said this was not any of those and that the Vicadin would work just fine. Mind you, I was in downtown San Antonio and had a 45 minute drive at rush hour back to my apartment. I trusted him, took the Vicadin, sat in the lobby for a while, did some deep breathing as suggested, and drank a glass of water.

I was "somewhat fine" on the drive home, until thirty minutes into rush hour. I started to sweat profusely; my head started spinning. I thought I was going to puke and pass out at the same time. I pulled over into a parking lot, sat and prayed for God to get me home safely. I was literally five minutes from home and trying to make it in one piece and without getting sick.

God saw me home safely. I was miserable all night. It felt like I was going to pass out and throw up. I went to the toilet several times, but I can't recall if I ever threw up. Time passed and my wound got better, but to this day it has times it swells and causes me major discomfort. (At the time of press I'm currently a month away from another surgery on this area.) There were some rough years though, all because a dysfunctional teenager with emotional scars had to make sure someone else suffered alongside of him. (For those attorneys out there, is it too late to sue?)

Facts about domestic violence: Many batterers feel a need to control and tend to be looked at as possessive and demanding. Often the cycle continues as they are victims of domestic violence themselves. The batterer may have poor impulse control and a short fuse (problems with controlling their temper). They may suffer from depression and actually be co-dependent on others in the family.

The batterer may be narcissistic where everything revolves around him or her, an exaggerated ego and sense of extreme self-importance. Think of Charlie Sheen during his tiger-blood catastrophe where he was so full of himself on every news channel. Charlie's issue may have been due to a drug-induced manic state, but nonetheless, he acted narcissistic. Many batterers have a low self-esteem and are insecure, yet come off looking jealous and defensive.

Batterers may rationalize that violence is their way of dealing with pent-up feelings. However, no person should deal with their feelings by becoming violent toward themselves or others. Therapy is needed to break the domestic violence and teach victims to become survivors, not another statistic. We have to be able to love ourselves before we can attempt to love others. Sad, but true, as too many teens think that if they have a child they can love the child and make up for the love they never received. This irrational thought is so far from the truth, and I pray that teens in domestic violence situations will reach out for help and counseling.

The U.S. Department of Justice estimates that 95% of the victims of domestic violence are women. Out of emergency room visits it is said that 35% are a result of domestic violence, and to add fuel to the fire of those who abuse their partner, over 65% also physically and/or sexually abuse the children in the home. (The Federal Bureau of Investigation)

Iron Nugget:

Have you had an experience with domestic violence? Explain.

How did you deal with the violence, abuse, pain?

5 Generation LOST

"Love your crooked neighbor with all your crooked heart." (W.H. Auden)

With so many lost souls like the Columbine boys, the Colorado shooter, the TX A&M killer, and the Virginia Tech shooter we may wonder, "What the hell is going on with our young men?" Clinically speaking many of these cold-blooded killers have earned the right to be labeled sociopaths or as the lay person says, "a psychopath." Many of these young men started out clinically depressed and became so tangled in the depression web the sociopath label followed when society failed to notice the warning signs.

I'm not blaming any of us about what happened to those poor innocent souls caught in the fire of a madman. I'm just saying each troubled soul showed unusual signs of distress, and I'm about to give examples of a few troubled souls I've personally worked with who could have easily turned into a sociopath. Some say a sociopath is born, not made. Characteristics include a lack of empathy, a disregard for social norms, or the suffering of others. These are your rule breakers, your manipulative students, your generally contemplating kids, which mean they usually have a bit of intelligence associated with them. Look at the Colorado shooter; he had been in pre-med or nuclear physics classes. Not a stupid individual, I must say.

The Virginia Tech student wrote in his manifesto prior to killing others and himself, "Do you know what it feels to be spit on your face and to have trash shoved down your throat? You have vandalized my heart, raped my soul, and torched my conscience. You thought it was one pathetic boy's life you were extinguishing. Thanks to you, I die like Jesus Christ, to inspire generations of the weak and defenseless people." (www.wikipedia.com) (Seung-Hui Cho).

Seung-Hui Cho had been diagnosed with anxiety and major depressive disorder in middle school, and his writings in his later years were disturbing enough to receive a referral to the counselor. He ended up killing 32 innocent people and wounding another 17 before taking his own life.

As a juvenile probation officer and then as a counselor working with abused youth in a residential treatment center, I have had the privilege of working with a diverse group of teens. I must say I enjoyed every time-consuming moment of it as a probation officer. The job entitled long hours and being on call, but I felt that if I could change the direction that just one troubled youth was headed into a positive direction I had done my job. To point them in a productive direction, not coddle them.

Not everyone we meet will "be saved." However, by believing in our troubled youth and chipping away at the hard stone that encases their soul, we can, and do, make a difference. This is the true meaning of this book. If I can inspire just one lost soul to take on a dream to realize that our body, mind, and soul are entwined and need to be challenged together to become a better, whole person, I will have accomplished so much.

Ominous. I will refer to one of the teens I was lucky enough to work with by his rap name. This 16-year-old boy was from inner-city Minnesota, living on the streets with gang bangers before coming to Texas. His mother got pregnant at 16 and had him at 17 years old, but she was more interested in doing things so wealthy men would buy her nice cars and clothing than raising her son. Her "baby daddy" was out of the picture. When Ominous' mother told her son's father that she was pregnant, he ran off and denied that Ominous was his. The boy grew up being told he was a "bastard," as he told me on more than one occasion.

Ominous' mother would hook up with abusive men with regularity. Ominous remembers one dragging him out of the house where he stood watching his mother get beat up. Young Ominous tried to go after the "loser," but got himself nowhere. Ominous grew up physically but not psychologically. He grew to be 6-foot 3-inches and more than 200 pounds. No fat; all muscle.

This young rapper portrayed the attitude that "no one will ever f**k with me, again," I know because he told me, and it wasn't hard to read in his body language and face. I learned about Ominous even before I met him. The department I was working in was alerted by the school police officer. Within a week of being in town, Ominous had immediately started a fight with two known drug dealers. His image preceded him. I'll never forget my first encounter with Ominous. It was a court day and all the juveniles set to stand before the judge were in their green jumpsuits shackled and handcuffed as usual. I was only aware of the kids on my case load. The courtroom was full and each officer was dealing with several hearings that day.

One of the teens on my case load continued to re-offend, and I was having a conversation with him about recommending to the judge that he be sent off to boot camp. The next thing I know this huge, mean-looking teen chimed in, "Have faith, nothing is set in stone." I remember looking over at him with a look like, "And who the hell are you?" Ominous just continued giving this kid positive feedback.

I walked out of the courtroom that day with a puzzled look on my face. Here I am telling kids to believe in their future and have faith yet, ironically, I was scolding the other kid (who by the way needed scolding) and then this teen, large in presence and stature, chimes in like he is an adult or something. Who was this kid? It only took a minute or two to figure out this was the Minnesota gang kid that the officer had been warning us about.

When I first started working with Ominous, he ended up being assigned to my case load, his terminology and speech were all gang related. I'm not sure if this was just an image he personified or if it was from hanging around those gang bangers for so long. I remember having Ominous in and out of lock-up more than any other case. On one occasion he ran from six different police patrol units. However, each time he was on the run he'd end up turning himself into me without any incidence.

One particular time, he had been on the run for four weeks and I decided to start tracking where he had been. I would start putting the heat on the culprits who were harboring him. Ominous finally called me and said, "I hear you are looking for me, you seem to be getting better at it." I told him I wasn't getting better, but that I had enough of him being on the run and just now started looking for him. I replied, "I figured you'd screw-up sooner or later and get arrested before I had to go out and find you, but now it's been four weeks and you need to come on in or I'll start charging your buddies for harboring you. You don't want to get your buddies arrested for something you did, now do you?" I was sarcastic, I was serious. I would let the police squad know who had been harboring Ominous and they would circle by those homes numerous times a day.

Teens say they don't like to rat out friends, but they do like to know what's going on with their "homies". It's a "know-it-all" image. Juveniles like to talk. I like to talk and listen. It's amazing how much you can find out with friendly conversation. It's got to be annoying walking in or out of your house seeing police units drive by real slow and look over at you. Ominous turned himself in with the conditions that I arrive in the probation squad car without any "pigs," as he said. However, he knew I would have a co-worker with me and I wasn't stupid.

We arrived at the location he said he would be. He flicked his cigarette to the ground, walked up to me, asked, "How ya been?" with a smirk on his face, and put his hands behind his back to assume the position. During the time I worked with Ominous I saw him go from an angry, ready-to-fight-anyone teen to one that was more relaxed and a bit conscious of his actions. *"Happiness is not a state to arrive at, but a manner of traveling." (Margaret Lee Rumbeck)*

Along my journey with Ominous, he lived with his aunt or grandmother when he wasn't being kicked out of their homes for boozing it up, I found out how talented a writer this kid was. This teen was a genius with his words and loved to rap. Ominous' journey had not ended when the judge sent him off to boot camp. I tried to get him to self-commit to a drug and alcohol treatment center, which he refused, so with numerous offenses the alternative was to recommend boot camp for six months to a year.

It seemed Ominous rather enjoyed his drinking problem, and didn't think he had issues since he'd kicked his drug habit back in Minnesota. His goal in placement (bootcamp) was to work on his writings; however, when he returned it was a matter of time until he had idle hands, went back to getting drunk regularly and using cocaine. There appeared to be little lessons learned from his time away.

I've interviewed Ominous over Subway sandwiches, his favorite, for my book on numerous occasions to see if his life has gotten back on track. I'm sorry to say that it appears it hasn't. What I want to stress is the fact that I served as a "make-shift mama" to this boy. You can too, by getting involved with a lost soul out there. Hillary Clinton was right on one thing when she said, "It takes a village to raise a child."

Ominous knew I saw the extreme talent he possessed and that I believed in him; he also knew I wasn't going to put up with his behavior and I would arrest him if he broke the law or violated his probation. Just as a mother sends her child to his/her room for a timeout or puts them on restriction. No different, Ominous just got a timeout in a cold, sterile cell room. His time out and restriction were served at the same time, except his room had no windows with a steel toilet, steel sink, and a cement block to sleep on with a thin little pad under him. He would spend many days and nights on restriction.

The point I'm trying to make is that wayward youth can improve with someone who believes in them, but sets boundaries. I used to tell adult friends that I never yelled at a kid on my caseload even when I was arresting them on numerous occasions. Yelling doesn't do anything. If you are old enough to commit the crime, you are old enough to reap the consequences and serve the time. What is yelling or demeaning them going to solve? My goal is to be a part of their life so that one day the positive may transfer. Kids knew I would do whatever I could to plug them into the right activity or direction to help them with whatever issue they were facing. It's that belief in them that would start to get inside their soul. A little light would start to flicker.

A common mistake people make is thinking that these lost souls are confident. I believe that 95 percent of the at-risk youth I dealt with all had low self-esteem. Bullies are some of the biggest kids with a low self-esteem. Meeting the bully on their level is all I can do. I accept them and try to model approach behavior and let them know the difference in right and wrong through stories of people I've worked with or self-disclosure. It's amazing how it goes back to sharing and *it's all about the stories* in life.

Here is a letter from Ominous that was written in lock-up prior to being sent away for boot camp.

Dear Mrs. Cardwell,

First off, I would like to thank you for having faith in me and giving me several chances which I took for granted. I am greatly appreciative for everything you've done for me, especially going against yours and everyone else's better judgment. I know you want what's best for me. As I turned myself in I knew that I had used up all my lifelines, and I would have no choice but to get sent off.

Even though I do not want to go to a placement, I know that it is the only way that I will be able to change my life around. Almost everyone that has been involved with me has lost hope in me including family, friends, and people involved with the law. Yet you still keep trying to help me.

If I were to get sent to boot camp, it would not change my way of living nor thinking. The only thing it would do is make me physically fit and bring me that much closer to being 18 years old, ready to get off juvenile probation and hopefully not be on adult probation. TYC would also not be a place for me to change because once you get there and been through it, you're ready for prison.

Rehab is totally unnecessary because I'm not addicted to drugs which my past urination assessments have proven. Though liquor is a bit more of a problem, I don't see myself as addicted. I know I tend to get violent when I drink which is something I will work on with time. The truth is why I get so violent and angry when I drink is because all my stress and problems from the past pours out when intoxicated. I am not using it as an excuse; I am just filling you in.

The only place I can see myself truly making a change for the better is at Gary Job Corp. It sounds to be a laid-back surrounding. I can leave campus, I get to wear my own clothes after 3 p.m., I get more of an education, plus many other things. I already got my GED and prefer to further my education with a trade instead of being sent somewhere else. Realistically, I think Gary Job Corp. is the only thing that could possibly help me change my life.

I know I'm on the road to prison, and I also know I need to change my way of living. The only way a person can change is if he is willing and ready to change. I know it sounds crazy, but I am asking you to recommend that I be released on my next court date on one condition. I sign and go to Gary Job Corp. right after my birthday when I turn 17. I know the reality of me being released is slim-to-none. I am just hoping that you will have trust in me, and know that I will not ruin if given this chance to go to Gary Job Corp. All I want is to be released so I can celebrate my birthday. I wrote this letter to you to sum up my feelings and situation. I am ready to get an education and change.

Sincerely, Ominous

Man, what a waste of talent. After working with Ominous for a year, I had already tried to get him to go to Gary Job Corp or into the Army (he had issues passing the math portion of the Army ASVAB test). He chose not to do either.

Ominous was so immersed in his drunken conduct that he could only think straight when locked-up. Of course, he said he wanted to get on the right path. However, without drug and alcohol intervention and perhaps proper medication, I thought he would go straight back to living life drunk most afternoons through the evening, making bad decisions, and continue to commit crimes. He was his own worst enemy, no matter how hard he tried.

According to the Texas Commission on Alcoholism, 50 percent of all teens age 15 to 19 years old said they had been in one or more situations in the past month where alcohol was present. A survey was done with those who had been drinking alcohol in the past few months. Thirty-nine percent said they drank one to three drinks in one day, 29 percent said they drank four to eight drinks, and 14 percent admitted to drinking nine or more drinks in one day. When asked how many times the teens had driven a car when drunk they responded: Half the drunken kids are not driving drunk, but the other half are.

Seventy-five percent of the teens surveyed said they drank beer, 12 percent drank liquor, 9 percent drank wine, and 4 percent drank whatever they could get their hands on. Twenty-six percent of the teens surveyed admitted to drinking alcohol two or more days a week. The rest, 19 to 25 percent, drank once a week, or every two weeks, or less than once every two weeks pretty evenly.

So what can we do for those teens who all have limited executive skills, which mean their decision making skills alone can be limited and then throwing alcohol in the mix really suppresses proper decisions? Communication is the channel. We all have a moral and legal responsibility as the Texas Commission on Alcoholism points out. Many teens believe a can of beer is less intoxicating than the average drink of liquor. The TCA notes that a 12 ounce can of beer is the *same* as 1 ounce of liquor or a 5 oz. glass of wine.

I don't know too many teens that would only put one ounce in their "Gin and Juice" as Snoop Dog sang about. I'm sure the ratio of Gin to juice was more than one ounce to 8 ounces of juice. Taking a cold shower and drinking a lot of coffee are only myths to sobering up. And not everyone staggers or slurs their speech when drunk (Texas Commission on Alcoholism). The Texas Commission on Alcoholism recommends some general points on the topic: Honestly explore your own behavior when drinking and driving before you talk with teens. Be honest in exploring your feelings and in stating your own values and preferences. Encourage the same from your female or male teen. Be calm, firm, and consistent as I was with Ominous.

Recognize that teens are not able to control all the situations they find themselves in. Have a Plan A and Plan B to refer to in case of an uncontrollable situation. Most importantly, listen. Don't yell or judge. I used to tell teens I worked with over and over and over...like a broken record, *"It's not you I dislike; it's your behavior."*

My daughter and I recently had a conversation about how she learned to blow her nose. Part of what she said was on the right track, but most of it was way off. I don't remember all the details, but basically I told her when toddlers are learning to blow their nose they have no reference point to go by. Kind of like when I was pushing her out in labor and all doped up. The nurse said, "Push, push!" I just grunted and made a pucker face. I had never delivered a baby before, I didn't know what pushing felt like, plus I was enjoying all the drugs they gave me and feeling no pain at the moment. Finally the nurse said, "Act like you are going to the bathroom!" Perfect, a cultural reference point to go by. I guess it worked because she ended up popping out and is an early teen now. Point being, I had no reference point to go by at first.

I digress, back to blowing the nose. I told Cami that before she was able to blow her nose I stuck this suction thing up her nose and did it for her. As she had no reference to blowing her nose, all I could do was try numerous ways to try and communicate how to blow her nose. Over and over and over. I have to admit it does get frustrating teaching a toddler how to blow their nose or take a poop for that matter, but the fact is we have to be patient and try different ways to communicate the idea with them. We have to wait for the "Ah Ha" moment for them to get the idea. *"The most wasted day is without laughter."* (E.E Cummings)

It's no different with at-risk, ADHD, and some teens getting the message across of whatever it maybe you are trying to get across that they *JUST DON'T GET!* Think of your task like teaching a toddler to blow his nose or go potty. It's going to take a lot of patience, support, and direction in different ways for them to actually get it and have that "Ah-ha" moment! Whatever you are trying to accomplish always use humor. *"Before you criticize someone you should walk a mile in their shoes. That way when you criticize them you're a mile away and you have their shoes."* (Jack Handey)

The Bible says, "Encourage one another and build each other, as indeed you are doing." (1 Thessalonians 5:11) I truly believe God has given each one of us a unique talent. Mine happens to be the gift of gab and being able to talk with the most dirty, repulsive person, all the way to a woman who works for the Queen of England herself (true). I just feel comfortable encouraging people and learning their story.

Before I continue, I'd like to include some of Ominous' writings.

STRESS

Stress is my Anger
Stress is my Rage
Stress is the only reason I wrote on this page
Stress put me on edge, got me bout to explode
Stress be the main reason I ain't trusting these hoes
Stress got me by a string
Stress will eat me alive
Stress has candy coated everything smothered inside
Stress is knocking at my door
Stress wants me to answer
Stress is some kind of sickness, it's worse than cancer
Everything I do is stressful it's blocking my spirit
Stress got me ready to scream as I spit out these lyrics
Stress is marching non stop
Stress steps on my hope
Stress is cutting off my oxygen it works like a rope
Stress is the only feeling I've had this year
Stress got me hemmed up so close to tears
I speak the truth about stress

What I gain if I lie?
Stress got me giving up never looking to try
Stress
Stress
Will be the cause of my DEATH
STRESS
STRESS
Until there Ain't Nothing Left

How well said, and Ominous was only 16 when he wrote this.

I ran into Ominous before summer started. He was all tatted up from his face (with a music tear drop) to his neck and arms. I gave him a hard time asking, "What the hell is all that crap on your body?" He laughed as he gave me a hug and said, "Ya know, the chicks dig it!" I replied, "Yea right, not the ones you were looking to attract years ago!"

The previous time I had seen Ominous he only had a couple of tattoos, not his neck and a sleeve. The funny thing is, every time I run into him he always talks with such respect to me and gives me a hug. I felt like such a failure with this kid who is now in his early 20s. He had such talent and was so smart, street wise, not so much book smart. I tried so hard to point him in the right direction.

Unfortunately Ominous lived up to his rap name and did go back to using alcohol, drugs, and women and has been thrown through a car windshield with a major scar on his forehead from drinking and driving. He's been in and out of lock up as an adult. The last time I saw him, it looked like Ominous was using and might have been selling since he was unemployed but was leaving a nice restaurant with another old probation kid. The other kid was definitely in to using and selling drugs.

The other kid told me he needed to come see me for drug and alcohol counseling as Child Protective Services (CPS) had taken away his two babies due to his drug use. Man, this other kid was 21 and already had two kids in the CPS system. What's wrong with society that we have allowed these things to happen?

More of Ominous' writings:

Lockup

In and out of lockup, I guess my life won't change
No matter how hard I try I'm steady causing this pain
This type of criminal mentality is stuck in my brain
I can't even smile and look at my loved ones the same

My chances have hit the border
My visits have grown shorter
I used to want it all, now I don't even have a quarter

Pigs get to pick and choose everything that you do

When you're surrounded by these goons living just like you

You get labeled as a f**k up like it or not
F**k going back to lockup, I rather fight and get shot

Throwing handcuffs on our wrists leaving bruises for days
Jump in single file line, jumpsuits like we're slaves

All the lawyers and judge think we do it for kicks
Break the law committing crimes so they see us as pricks

See me spitting on my time as I eat up my stress
I think of lockup in a cell nothing more than a test

I can't tell you how deeply I agree with his statement that people see these kids as breaking the law for kicks. I think these kids are hurting extremely and as families and role models fail them, they turn to the only people that accept them—the rejects—and do as the other law breakers do. It's human nature to want to be accepted. If society as a whole rejects these kids, they will find people who accept them and follow those rules. Ominous was like the fraternity boy "Pinto" in the 1978 movie, Animal House: an angel on one shoulder and the devil on the other ordering two totally opposite demands. The Angel on one side saying, "Don't do it! Don't do it!" and the devil on the other, "Come on do it! **Do It!**"

Below is another complicated writing from Ominous. Note the irony:

Complication

I sit here all alone as I plead for **LIBERATION**
A daily routine which I do with no **OCCASION**
Staring down the barrel thinking twice on **REVELATION**
Swallowing the bullet will stop all the **COMPLICATION**
Sick of all the liars and punks of the **CONGREGATION**
A bullet or a prison could stop the **ABOMINATION**
Created by a pen as I spark my **IMAGINATION**
Ever since a youth I been hated by **EDUCATION**
I'm not 'posed to rap cuzz I'm stuck as a **CAUCASION**
Swimming in this dope there's no hope for this lost **NATION**
I'd rather give my life than be stuck in your **SEGREGATION**
Trying to O.D. as I eat all this **MEDICATION**
Stress please me like a man with his **MASTURBATION**
I'm spitting on the flag I'm filled with this **PROFANATION**

To live with these thoughts and feel so alone in the world has to just suck. Yes, he did see a counselor and psychiatrist at the local mental health office as required for some of the youth on probation. However, he chooses not to take medication or get the counseling needed. Whether it was a lack of connection with the office or a denial that he had anything wrong, I'm not sure, but it was offered and there were mandatory meetings when locked up. I just wish there would have been a connection with someone in the counseling field at the time to save some of his heartbreak or law breaking and point him in a better direction.

Ominous' writings when I first started working with him were full of hate and doom and then later they started to change for what seemed the better, here are two examples. The first is from the early days and the second is from a year after working with him.

1.   THE WORLD OF OMINOUS

I wanna create a world of my own, where the lifestyles doom
Where everybody dreams of murder as they stare at the moon

There'll be no peace plans
Just drama
No morning
Just night
There'll be no cleanliness or joy
Just conflicts and fights

Where everybody's a lunatic
Or as ruthless as me
There'll be no cops, judges, or lawyers
Just thugs of the streets

Where every woman's a prostitute
Or some kind of hoe
And every man is a criminal
Or something below

I'll be the ruler of the kingdom of my world which is dark
I'll watch my planet burn in flames as it crumbles apart

People will think of me as god, screaming OMINOUS loud
And no one around will test what OMINOUS is about

There'll be no love for the others
Just hate for the people
And everybody who is born
Will be raised to be evil

Where everybody's going to be angry
With no sense of pride
Or they going to be scared as s**t
Afraid to come outside

2.   What Am I?

What am I?

I'm a man with a voice. This voice is power. With this voice I could demolish my enemies. I could speak of hate and violence and watch my enemies twist and lurch knowing that my words are true. At first, when I speak of such hate and violence they may not listen, but eventually they will have no choice but to listen and acknowledge that I hold this power. My voice will pry at my enemies insides, striking out at every emotion, thought and characteristic causing pain and grief they never knew existed. With this power I will cause depression and humiliation. My enemies will understand of my voice and it power...

What am I?

I'm a man with a voice. This voice is inspiration. With this voice I could inspire the minds of many. I could speak of pride and hope and watch people's minds unravel with an endless list of possibilities. At first when I speak of such pride and hope they may not listen, but eventually they will see the truth and have no choice but to acknowledge my words of inspiration. My voice will spark the imagination of all that hear me, causing self-worth and a severe sense of pride they never knew existed. With this inspiration I will cause hope and hunger to achieve. People will understand my voice and its inspiration...

What am I?

I'm a man with a voice. This voice is peace. With this voice I could stop the thoughts of evil. I could speak of life and happiness and watch wars of all kinds diminish. At first when I speak of life and happiness they may not listen, but eventually they will hear my words and have no choice but to acknowledge the thought of peace. My voice will create an option other than carnage, causing joy and a world lived in harmony. I will cause love and trust. People will understand my voice and its peace.

What am I?

I'm a man with a voice. This voice is...

My plea to you who read this? Find that lost soul who seems to be hopeless and don't dessert it. 1 Thessalonians 5:15 says, "Be sure that no one pays back wrong for wrong but always try to be kind to each other and everyone else. Be joyful always, pray continually; give thanks in all circumstances for this is God's will for you in Christ Jesus."

I've seen so many bad teachers out there who either consciously or unconsciously destroy a child's soul. I've heard them say, "Little Johnny, he just does that to piss me off." I don't think kids do things in class to anger you in particular. Everyone has a different learning style and too many times the public school system expects children to fit in this neat little box. What are we thinking electing people like this to make the decisions? Our society doesn't fit in a neat little box. Why do you think we have so many alcoholics and drug abusers?

No one says, "I want to be a drug addict when I grow-up." However, we have many people self-medicating out of frustration or hopelessness. They couldn't or don't fit into that little box, so they make their own box and fit quite nicely inside there while under the influence. It's a way of saying, "I feel good now." Don't hate the rule breakers. Don't pay back one wrong with another.

On the opposite spectrum, there are many wonderful teachers out there who are encouraging their students and building them up. These are the teachers making a difference and actually saving lives. Keep up the good work. (Dr. McGlamery) And for the others? (You know who you are!) Shame on you! Find another occupation; the fast-food industry comes to mind. If you don't enjoy working with kids, then leave. You have our permission and encouragement.

Ominous cut an exceptional rap album at age 19 when he went back to Minnesota temporarily. The best talent I've ever seen in a young artist is his song, "Lonely" it's basically about the love he so longed for from his mother as a kid. The album is titled "Ominous, The Monster." Please, Google it and find a way to buy a copy. Get this talented artist's life back on track! You won't be disappointed.

I've had the privilege to work with many girls who lost their princess tiara by becoming pregnant at a young age or self-mutilating or getting hooked on drugs instead of phonics. And I think each one of these young ladies is screaming the same rap song Ominous sang of "No Body Loves Me." Their pain tends to look a little different than the angry male gangster.

The following is a rap from a teen gangster out of San Antonio intertwined with drug dealers. It has no title. This was written specifically for my book by a 14-year-old troubled boy and addressed to other teens who maybe living in the drug and gang world or just thinking about it.

Dreams of gettin' rich, Nightmares of stayin' broke

So I started hustling and slanging coke

Laugh now, die never, but life's not a joke

*So I collect my paper, I get my own, F**k a hater*

I stay the same, but get that change

I'm a sharp shooter, but aim out of range

I got the touch, but ain't got no flame

Blood drippin' down like sudden rain

Bullet in your head, stuck in your brain,

I'm in the game, but ain't playin'

Mother on her knees, crying and she keeps prayin'

So listen closer to what I'm sayin'

Think about it first before you grab the gun and start sprayin'

*Next thing you know someone's on the ground f**kin' layin'*

Now you're dodging laws, living in the streets

*Then you're behind bars, without f**kin' sheets*

Now you're dreams are about being free, wishing you did better

And Listen to me, if you're gonna live as a G

You gotta be smart and have time to think

Don't forget what you got and face the heat

But turn around before you get burned

But as the sayin' goes, Live, Laugh, and F**kin' Learn.

Eric and Pat, Ironmen

Iron Nugget:

Why do you think there is so much violence in society today?

How would you stop the violence?

What is your opinion on what is being shown on TV and video games, today?

6   Signs and "Ah-Ha" Moments

Some of the teens I taught in school had been removed from their homes for traumatic reasons. They may have been involved with crime, drugs, been victims of abuse or neglect, or were involved with gangs. A couple of the kids had witnessed a loved one being shot by another gang and at least one student had received a bullet, himself. This kid's comment to the class was how much it hurt and how he thought he was going to die at the time. Well... Yeah it hurts, and yes, you may die. He continued to talk that day about how in the movies it doesn't look like it would hurt that much. OK, now we are talking.

These kids have become so desensitized by all the violence that they witness on TV and their daily lives, they are not even aware of how stupid a statement like that is. Hell yes, it hurts. It hurts each time you think it is normal to go around brandishing a gun, hitting your girlfriend, raping your friend, and so on. Why do we find entertainment in that sort of garbage? It's sick when you think about it.

"Curly" was 17 and had been involved with a group of boys who gave drugs to girls and then took advantage of them. This boy had a pretty bad reputation around town with law enforcement, however when you spoke with him he was always polite and calm. When I arrested him he was even cooperative.

His case left me concerned because he was about to age out of the juvenile system and graduate to the big boys if he didn't change the path he was on. Most people in my department thought he was worthless. I had hope. I was successful in getting him admitted to a Job Corp program that would allow him to complete his G.E.D. and give him a trade, while housing and feeding him—all supported by government funds. This boy's mother really cared about him and tried, but the family had no father figure present, and the oldest boy was involved with the adult criminal system after graduating from of the juvenile system, himself.

On the day Curly was to leave for the Job Corp, his mother dropped him off at the bus. In a brilliant move, Curly ditched the bus, went to a friend's house, and promptly got drunk and stoned. Curly's friend who had been on the run from the law for quite some time, got the bright idea to rob a store. The friend had the gun and Curly was the driver of the get-away car. They were caught.

Curly became a graduate of the juvenile probation system that day and enrolled in the big boy system with hardened criminals in his cell at county. No private toilet, no private cell. Slammed into a holding tank with 20 to 30 guys and left there for no telling how long. The stench of urine in the county is enough to keep most people from committing a crime. There are stories of men throwing feces at the walls and windows in the county jails. Many repeated criminals in the county jail are mentally unstable.

I will share a conversation I used to have with more serious delinquents; boys and girls alike. Not everyone internalized my story. I saved it for the bottom dwellers, the mullets, the teens that thrived on crap. I would tell the teen, *"Everyone has an "Ah-ha" moment in their life. A wake-up call you could say. Your wake-up call could be your involvement with the law, getting so strung out that you puke and wake up in your own vomit, sitting on a cold steel toilet, being deloused and strip-searched as you were admitted here, being raped and abused or being the rapist and abuser and having to serve a long prison sentence for it. All I can hope is that your "Ah-ha" moment comes to you before it's too late."*

As a juvenile probation officer I had the inside advantage of being on the front line to help change a kid's delinquent direction. Some officers work the job as a power trip, I did it to protect society and help kids become productive adults. As a past teacher, coach, and present athlete I knew the importance that exercise can have on one's self-esteem and thought process. I started a program titled YAC: Youth Against Crime.

Youth Against Crime was a running program. Although the original format was to have a sponsorship of $3,000 to actually outfit these youth and form a team per say, the backup plan had to be put to use when companies refused to sponsor or give money for juvenile delinquents. Maybe I should have said the teens I worked with had physical handicaps. Then we might have received some monetary handouts.

YAC running program allowed for juveniles to earn community service hours by participating in a rigorous hour and a half workout. In that hour and a half, I learned more about each juvenile that participated, their home life, their habits (good and bad), and other pertinent information that I would not have learned in a one on one office visit. Each week, we discussed the basic rules of society that came up. Our topics ranged from drugs, to stealing, lying, how to treat the opposite sex, dealing with authority, etc. Our talks were an example of CBT—Cognitive Behavior Therapy. Allowing the juveniles to express their ideas with other kids their own age, I was able to step in and give ideas or suggestions in a non-threatening way. I'd ask them what they thought. I have learned by past mistakes with the toughest kids if you get these youth to want to change, rather than threatening them, you will surpass your goal.

My experience teaching in a high-trafficked gang area of Corpus Christi taught me this. While I did make strides with these kids, I was a new teacher and did not get to know my students as individuals. I was teacher, they were the class. When I moved to a small town and started working with teens from a residential youth home, I had no choice but to get to know each individual. They had behavior disorders and emotional disturbances from so much abuse in their life that you had to get to know what set each individual off and made them tick. Ninety percent of my population was on probation when I first taught in the alternative school setting.

To make a difference in these teens' lives, I had to get on their level. I had to get to know them, their life, why they had the view they had, etc. I was able to start chipping away at the bad stuff once I got to know them as individuals. People are not born criminals or delinquents. It's generally a learned behavior. Relating my experience as a victim, perhaps my perpetrator was a victim himself. Maybe his dad beat him or exposed him to porn, maybe he had anger issues that had not been dealt with? Maybe he was afraid of being abandoned, left alone, and not being loved or belonging? Who knows, but there's always something behind what makes us tick. Have you taken time to think about what makes you tick?

Many kids that are displaying bad behaviors have never been shown appropriate boundaries or limits. They actually want and need these boundaries. I can't tell you how many juveniles I've "timed-out" (sent to lock-up) actually thanked me later for the talk we had, the time away from drugs or stealing, the time they spent locked up or sent away to face the issues they were dealing with.

I am a big fan of the reality show star Dog the Bounty Hunter. He arrests the law breakers, but tries to hear their stories and give them some *hope*. Law breakers could have been stealing, drugs, assault, truancy, you name it, but when you are left in a cold quiet cell for 12 hours there's some soul searching to be done whether you want it or not. Years ago I had a female delinquent who I worked with who actually did make the connection chose to quit drugs and turn her life around. As with many delinquents, some shape up and ship off where others seem to be castaways on a doomed voyage who may forever stay lost on their journey through life. The castaways never seem to have an "Ah-ha moment." The female I'm referring to was involved in my YAC running program and grew in her experience with juvenile probation.

What follows is her letter to me prior to being released from probation:

> *"My name is X. I am on probation because I brought drugs to school. My, used to be, best friend told on me. I feel bad for what happened. It really messed me up and messed up my whole tenth grade year of school. I am ashamed of myself for letting that happen. I know I am better than that. I should not have never started smoking and everything else. I want to thank you Dana for being there for me as my probation officer and not Probation Officer Y. ha, ha Don't tell them I told you that. It's kinda sad but then good that I am getting off probation. You don't know how much I'll miss you. You help me a lot believe it or not. You are by far the most awesome person I know. You're funny and just really cool to talk to when like times get hard and what not. I feel like I can tell you any thing. Even if it gets me in trouble. You are the one person that has the control of me telling the truth all the time. I can never lie to you. And that's a super good thing. I hope you keep this. Well I have to go to bed. I'll extremely miss you, Dana!*
>
> *Love,*
>
> *X*

An update: Curly has a good job and has straightened up. I see him at the gym weekly. X was seeing me for counseling after being on probation as an adult. She now has a baby and wants to move on with her life. It's amazing how God puts the troubled soul back in our life. Don't ignore the signs, please! Each one of these troubled souls gave me permission to use their story to help other teens.

Iron Nugget:

Have you had an "Ah-Ha" moment? Explain.

Who or what has made an impact on your life and why?

7   The Ghost in My Closet

Most victims are assaulted by someone they know. (National Center for Victims of Crime)

After "stairway to hell boyfriend," I dated different boys. I was in my junior year of high school and was still partying and still not promiscuous. So, here I was at age 17. This particular senior football player, I happened to be a "little interested in" drove a really nice, fast sports car and had been "scoping" me out at the last few parties I went to.

It started at a town hall dance when he grabbed me and had me sit on his lap. He talked a good game, flirted with me and frankly, I enjoyed the attention. Mr. Football was a big man on campus and known as being cocky and arrogant. He earned respect by being loud and he could get violent at times. We girls tend to have our own games. We don't just fall for whoever asks us out. We have criteria to go by, generally speaking. Not that being athletic, arrogant, and driving a nice car is a good criterion to go by, as I learned later.

After a football game one night, he asked a friend and me to go to a party. I was staying at my friend Ally's home (whose mother would pass out after drinking). Each night was different. She could pass out early or late.   We opted for later that night and told Richard (aka. Mr. Football) to park just down the road and pick us up at 11 p.m. On this particular night, I was staying with Ally's sister, the dark-headed rebel. She was up for some mischief that night, as was I. Ally didn't want any part of what we were doing. In retrospect, I don't blame her!

My friend's mother passed out on time, just after the evening news. We stuffed our bed with pillows and clothes under the sheets. The next project was the challenge of getting the screen off Lila's window. That one was a booger to get off.   We spent probably fifteen minutes working on it. A little muscle, giggling, and a lot of "Shh, she's going to wake-up," and task accomplished. The screen finally came off. I doubt that it was in one piece, though. I think we left a hole in it from finally resorting to using a screw driver to pry it off.

We had already done our pre-party warm-up exercises, consisting of two rum and cokes, changing clothes at least three times, and spending time on hair and make-up. After using up a bottle of hairspray and assuring each other that we did not look fat in whatever we were wearing, we were on our way. Mind you, Lila and I were both a size three.   How could we ever look fat? The sad part is that most young teens feel this way even today. Granted there are a lot more overweight teens. It's the ones that are in shape that seem to obsess over their image and weight. Lack of self-esteem plays more problems in peer pressure than most adults realize.

We found our ride, waiting down the road.   The car lights were off, but when they saw us walking down the street there was a blink on, blink off signal of where they were. It was pitch dark as Richard and his friend took us to the party just a mile up the road. Lila and I were giggling and looking forward to having fun. We did not sneak out every weekend—this was one of the few times. The party was starting to die down, as it was around 11:30 p.m. and most party-goers had to leave due to curfew. The remainder of the kids were stoned, drunk, or both. There may have been one sober one left in the group, but it did not appear that way. This should have been my first "Ah-ha" sign.

My friend and I were handed drinks immediately as we walked in the door. We drank, we laughed, and we mingled. After we had a drink or two, Richard went upstairs where there was a pool table and gaming going on. The house was full of the haze of smoke and loud rock music boomed throughout. I followed Richard upstairs. I was talking to some guys at the pool table upstairs when Richard yelled down the hall, "Hey Dana, come over here!" where he was standing outside a bedroom. The house was large and the upstairs was huge. There were a lot of rooms upstairs. I walked down to where he was. He told me he wanted to talk, since we did not get much time to talk at school. I remember it was hard to hear, so he closed the door.

I didn't think anything of it at the time. Another "Ah-ha" sign missed. He sat on a chair, not the bed. He pulled me to his lap and talked about what seemed like normal conversation. After a while he kissed me. I didn't mind and kissed back. The kissing transferred to the bed. No clothes coming off, just making out. The line crossed after fifteen minutes or so, he started to pull my pants down. I told him, "No." He said, "Yes." I said, "No." He said, "Yes." Until, finally, he said he wasn't going to let me leave until my pants came off, and he pulled them off with me consistently trying to resist. Once "the act" started, all I remember is his heavy breathing, pain, and praying for him to finish already, get off me, and leave me the hell alone.

Once it was over, I ran to the bathroom which was in the same room. I saw a lot of blood once I was in the bathroom. I heard him yell, "You didn't tell me you were a virgin!" and ran out the bedroom door and then the house. I still remember thinking, "That's what it would have taken to keep you from raping me?" "NO!" obviously didn't work, even after numerous attempts. Many young victims don't really realize they're being raped until the act has started. The music was so loud at that party; I never yelled, and was basically in shock when "the act" actually started. I never thought I would lose my virginity violently that night when I set out with a girl friend to "have some fun."

With Richard's running through the house, he caused curiosity with the few partiers that were left. Some guys ran into the room to find out what the commotion was all about, as I was exiting the bathroom. The room looked like a crime scene. There was blood all over the bed, all over the carpet—everywhere. I guess with the forceful nature of the rape, I bled a lot more than a virgin normally would. The depression and PTSD that set in that night followed me for years.

The act of the rape was not as depressing as the stigmatism that occurred afterwards. No one at that party knew I was raped, they assumed I had sex during my period. There were about five guys who came into that room and one happened to be Jay, the guy that pushed me down the stairs. Jay was the only one that seemed to know what might have happened as we had dated previously. He knew I didn't sleep around, much less on my period!

Jay, the Royal Pain in the Ass, hugged me and told me it was going to be OK, after everyone was making comments behind my back. He talked with me and truly calmed my state of shock. I was in shock and did not talk after the incident. You would think the other boys would have known something was wrong, as I was hyper and talking non-stop. I was embarrassed and stared at the floor. I made eye contact with none of them. No one knew what really happened that night, just that there was a bad scene in guest room No. 5.

The following Monday I could not go to school because my stomach felt so vile. This was the start of a stomach ulcer; which could have started due to all the alcohol I had been drinking or just the psychosomatic problems due to my home life and the rape. Psychosomatic problems are usually physical ailments that start due to psychological stressors. It could be a teenager having a bad headache due to the stress of trying to get into college or just day-to-day stresses. Anything can cause psychosomatic issues: a break up with a boyfriend, being bullied, taking tests, preparing for a football game or perhaps, say, an Ironman. Conflict in the home with parents or siblings can lead to psychosomatic problems. Yelling, loud noises throughout the home. You get the picture.

I had to take prescription medication for several years after developing a nervous stomach. My mother did not know of the incident since it was not a topic of discussion in our house. In fact, no topic was up for discussion in our house. We just didn't talk. Oh, superficial stuff was talked about, but never feelings of frustration and despair. Life was supposed to see through rose-colored glasses. No one in the Shepard family had issues.

I was ashamed of sneaking out and blamed myself for a large part of the incident. Was I wrong for sneaking out and drinking? Yes. Was it OK or my fault for getting raped? NO. Not back then and not now. No teen asks to get raped. Unfortunately, my "Ah-Ha" moment didn't come until after it was too late.

What is Sexual Assault? For sexual activity to be all right, it must be consensual, which means that both parties have to want it to happen. Sexual assault is when any person forces you to participate in a sexual act when you don't want to. This includes touching or penetrating the vagina, anus or mouth of the victim, touching the penis of the victim, or forcing the victim to touch the attackers vagina, penis, or anus.

Touching can mean with a hand, finger, mouth, penis, or just about anything else including objects. It doesn't always take physical force to sexually assault a victim. Attackers can use threats or intimidation to make a victim feel afraid or unable to refuse them. It is also sexual assault if the victim is drunk, drugged, unconscious, too young (ages of consent differ from state to state) or mentally disabled.

Some statistics show one in three women or one in four women has been sexually assaulted at one time in their life. This accounts for 25 to 33 percent of the female population. Some statistics show one in six men are sexually assaulted.

Some say, "Well if there was no penetration by a penis, then there was no rape." This is a myth. While legal definitions of rape vary from state to state, the National Office of Victims of Crime state that rape constitutes penetration with a penis, finger, foreign object or unwanted touching of sexual body parts without penetration.

The rape actually wasn't the first sexual assault I had encountered in my life. The first time came with the first boy I actually kissed, I mean really kissed. Not just a peck. I was in the 8th grade and my friend and I used to walk up to the Jr. High I attended to "play tennis." We weren't really there to play tennis. Britt lived near the school and would walk over to flirt with us. From there it became a game of "will Britt see us" and let's make-out in the walk way. On one particular make out day, Britt grabbed my hand and stuck it down his pants as we were kissing.

I immediately grabbed my hand back, yelled at him, and walked home with my hand extended 3 feet away from the rest of my body. A person passing by would have thought I was reaching up to Heaven in praise or telling someone to "Stop, in the name of Love…"   My hand was as far away from the rest of my body as it could go and I was walking as fast as I could. I would have run, but that would have meant my disgusting, germ-filled hand would have to come near my body to propel me forward. I couldn't get home fast enough to wash the grossness off my hand! He had crossed the line by grabbing my hand and forcing me to do something I had no intention of doing. Sexual assault includes making someone touch your penis/vagina when they have not consented.

Back to the rape aftermath, I couldn't stay home two days in a row, so I had to return to high school and face the music. I walked in the back door of the school that morning and immediately heard people talking about me in whispers. One guy didn't even bother whispering. Fernando was always friendly to me and would occasionally ask me, "When are we going to go out?" I'd laugh but not reply. On this morning, I heard him say in front of his buddies, "And I thought you were a nice girl. You're just a tramp!" I think this hurt as much as the crime. Many years later, I can still hear his words and they sting like a bee each time.

Word spread like a wild fire. People started calling me, "Split", behind my back. What a horrible thing! I guess word around campus became that I had sex at a party as a virgin. That part was right, but the rape was never asked, mentioned, or brought up while in high school. I lost my closest friends, except for one. I didn't discuss what happened, ever, even with Lila as we walked home the night of the incident. She didn't really ask, if I recall.

I do public presentations on sexual assault intervention. With the presentations I show videos, Power Points slides, and do a Myth or Fact question time with the audience. One question goes like this: "Myth or Fact? When a victim knows her assailant she is more likely to report the rape to the police?"

"Myth! The fact is that the victim who knows her assailant is less likely to report due to self-blame, fear that her friends and family will blame her, and the fact that drugs and alcohol are more likely involved.

Another Myth or Fact: Rape is most often perpetrated by a stranger? Myth, a woman is statistically more likely to be raped by someone she knows. (National Office for Victims of Crime.) According to the National Institute on Alcohol Abuse, more than 696,000 students between ages 18-24 are assaulted by another student who has been drinking. Alcohol plays a huge role on sexual assault.

A report came out a few years back that noted 63 percent of high school seniors have had intercourse. Just think what the percentage might be presently. I attended an STD class by the Texas Department of Health as a juvenile probation officer that noted 1 in 3 teens that has had sex, has or has had an STD. Can you imagine how many teens you know maybe caring an STD? That's just alarming. Herpes, gonorrhea, chlamydia, AIDS, you name it. And even cancer. Associated Press came out with an article several years' back that stated 70 percent of oral cancer can be linked to HPV.

Let me explain the article. A doctor noted 10 years ago his average oral cancer patients were men over 60 who used tobacco and drank heavily. Today, his patients with oral cancer are the opposite. Dr. Nussenbaum an ear, nose, throat doctor at Washington University, estimated that 70 percent of his oral cancer patients have tumors on the back of their tongues and tonsils caused by the human papillomavirus-16, otherwise known as HPV. Most of the clients are between the ages of 40 to 50. Experts suggest that all of the men and women with the HPV form got it from oral sex.

Dr. Nussenbaum stated that 98 percent of cervical cancer is caused by HPV, and mainly the HPV-16. No one talks about how you can get mouth cancer. It's taboo or not discussed, yet middle-aged women are walking around with canker sores and suffering tremendous pain from tongue and tonsil tumors.

The article from St. Louis (AP) goes on to note that Dr. Harald zur Hausen, a German doctor and scientist, was awarded the Noble Prize for medicine for finding the human papilloma viruses that can cause cervical cancer, the second most common cancer among women. The Nobel assembly noted that Dr. zur Hausen went against current dogma in the 1970s when he discovered that certain types of HPV caused the cancer and that DNA of HPV could be found in tumors.

Think of the 1970s. Ahh... the freedom movement, during and just after Vietnam. World peace, do what feels groovy, "good." Love your neighbor, get a VW van, have lots of love sessions. You get the picture. Peace and love were everywhere. And now those women have grown up and are suffering the consequences. We have studies now to change the future epidemic, though.

The Internet suggests it wasn't until 2000 that John Hopkins Kimmel Cancer Center reported a link between HPV and specific throat cancers. Medical experts suspect the increase in HPV oral cancer stems from a shift in sexual behaviors about 40 years ago. Did I not just mention the love and peace era? Now, we don't have to be a genius to figure out that there was going to be some sort of issues arising from that much love going on. Immorality? Revelation 21:8 reads, "But the cowardly, the unbelieving, the vile, the murderers, the sexually immoral, those who practice magic, the idolaters, and all liars—their place will be in the fiery lake of burning sulfur." I'll leave the interpretation to you.

Cancer from the HPV virus often develops on the tonsils notes one website. Should we suggest all teens have a tonsillectomy? How about telling them that numerous sexual partners and oral sex partners is not the answer to live a long and productive life? How about actually talking about it and not just teaching abstinence in the schools? Seriously? Telling a kid, "Don't do it!" doesn't work. I know when I was younger if my mother said to wear the pretty blue outfit; I was picking the red one, just because. Simply telling a kid, "No," is not the answer. They are probably more likely to go the opposite direction. Teens need to develop their own identity and fight their own battles, but with your love and support. We don't send our soldiers to war and then say, "See you when you kill all the enemies and come back home!"

Talk to teens, discuss, explain, and let them make the ultimate decision because they are ultimately the one in control of their decisions and their bodies. They need to hear from you over and over, not like a broken record, but in a sing-song kind of way. Encourage them to join in on the song. It can be a duet!

The John Hopkins study compared healthy people to those with the HPV oral cancer and concluded that people with the HPV virus were 32 percent more likely to develop oral cancer than those without. People who had more than six oral sex partners were 8.6 times more likely to develop HPV linked cancer. So, now society comes out with Gardasil, a drug that helps protect against human papillomavirus. Is this the answer? What are the ramifications from this drug down the road? I remember birth control when it first came out. Studies show there were serious detrimental factors with the birth control of our mothers and grandmothers.

Is the solution, go get this injection and have all the sex you want? Hmmm... doesn't seem like the best answer. The choice is ultimately yours. Do you want to be promiscuous and take a shot for preventative reasons with not knowing the real side-effects later or live your life in a manner that warrants pride and an increase in self-esteem in the long run? Experts suggest that the HPV lies dormant for years, perhaps decades, before causing cancer. Should middle-aged women in their 40s and younger consider getting vaccinated with the Gardasil, also? Better yet, older women who were sexually active years ago?

Should we suggest the majority of the population get vaccinated from HPV? No expert knows how long the disease can sit dormant because there has been such little data on the disease. The fact that cannot be disputed by the National Cancer Institute determined recently that the rate of oral cancer caused by HPV has risen significantly since 1973.

Laura Beil, notes that when children shroud their behavior in secrecy, they lose open, caring connections to adults who can help them make thoughtful decisions. These connections are especially important in matters of sex, since the stakes are high and sex seems ubiquitous in the popular culture. She notes that today almost eight in ten prime time shows contain sexual content, with an average of nearly six sex-related scenes per hour. You don't think your child is impressed by this? They can sure bet they are.

Parents often underestimate their own importance and ignore the difficult topics. Brown's anti-teen-pregnancy campaign has found that kids, when asked about the most influential voices in their decisions to have sex, rate their parents influence higher than their peers or the media. Even when you preach, parents. They know you love them and you care.

Discussion over preaching is always more productive. No one likes a boss who comes in and tells you how you need to do every minute of your job. You can think for yourself and therefore take care of business, just with a little direction and intervention. Studies show 80 to 90 percent of teens talking with parents, openly, helps delay sex. My husband and I have been bantering for years. My husband is a psychotherapist, and from the beginning of our relationship knew about my experience. I told him that when we had kids I would scare the crap out of them from drinking, smoking, or having sex due to my experiences. It would be such an unpleasant talk that they wouldn't even want to go there.

He calmly told me that scaring our kids would not be the answer and or course, he was right. We only had one child, a beautiful girl, at that. When our little girl was 9 years old, I hadn't had the birds and bees talk, yet, but don't think Hannah Montana, High School Musical and all the tween shows didn't expose her. She was at a friend's house one week when she came home and asked, "Mom, what does it mean when it breaks?" Hm... Now she knows what happens if you break jewelry, eggs in a pan, dishes, etc. This must be more serious or sensitive. "Where was this going?" I was washing dishes and so not prepared for this talk. Think calm. Think what your husband has been telling you all these years.

"Breaks?" I asked her. "What breaks?" She goes on to say, "Well, Meg and I were watching Sisterhood of the Traveling Pants II, and this guy came out of the bathroom, saying it broke. Meg told me that it was something that kept a girl from getting pregnant." Think...Don't preach...Think. Don't preach. "Well", I said, "First of all, what rating was this show? Sounds like PG-13, and you are not 13. It says PG-13 for a reason." OK, I started off preaching, but I held back.

She said she didn't know what rating it was, but that they had checked it out and it wasn't bad. I told her, "It sounds like they were doing things that teens should not do at their age.

Something that you should wait to do until you're married." Preaching... preaching. I then addressed the question. "What they were referring to was probably a condom. Something a man puts on his "weeny," (yes, I used the word 'weeny') as a form of protection from disease and getting a girl pregnant."

Did I mention Meg has two older sisters? Don't think older siblings aren't exposing our kids to sex when they overhear older phone conversations and computer dialogue. I admit, I did not handle that situation anything like I would have hoped. Teens talk with someone, don't wait until you are leaving that party after being raped or pressured into something you haven't prepared yourself for. Parents talk to your kids.

Beverly Engel writes in her book, *The Right to Innocence. Healing the Trauma of Childhood Sexual Abuse,* "What are the specific benefits of recovery?" She lists these headlines related to the benefits: "higher self-esteem, improved relationships, improved sexuality, increased ability to express emotions, relief from physical symptoms, greater sense of control, heightened self-awareness, staying grounded in the present, developing healthier defenses, and greater peace of mind." I recommend this book to those who endured childhood sexual trauma whatever it was. This book could save your soul!

Most importantly, remember; don't try to analyze a personality disorder (anti-social). Just leave. It won't help and doesn't work trying to figure them out. You never will. Run Away. (Call the cops, first!)

Websites for assistance:

The National Center for Victims of Crime, www.ncvc.org

Sex Etc.- Sex Ed by Teens, for Teens, www.sexetc.org

Sexual Abuse Statistics , www.prevent-abuse-now.com

Help for Victims of Sexual Assault

www.ojp.usdoj.gov/ovc/help/rape.htm

Eric during his first Ironman, not so pretty!

Iron Nugget:

Do you have any ghosts in your closet? Explain.

How did you handle the situation? Is it better or worse now and how?

8 The Balancing ACT on the Trapeze

"Be yourself. Everyone else is taken." (Oscar Wilde)

As victims of whatever it may be, we need to find a balance to survive. We can't get wrapped up in how we think others want us to be. When Jodee Blanco chose to be true to herself and not become like those who bullied her, she had to face her issues and look at the direction she was taking. "Knowledge is learning something every day. Wisdom is letting go of something every day." (Zen Proverb)

The following passage is by Jodee Blanco, but it makes me think of the two Columbine teens, Eric Harris and Dylan Klebold, who spent years of being bullied and finally lashed out at society by killing so many innocent people. Jodee writes:

> *"I sink into my desk. Here we go again. So much for believing I could make a fresh start at Samuels. The hardest thing about being an outcast isn't the love you don't receive. It's the love you long to give that nobody wants. After a while, it backs up into your system like a stagnant water and turns toxic, poisoning your spirit. When this happens, you don't have many choices available. You can become a bitter loner who goes through life being pissed off at the world; you can fester with rage until one day you murder your classmates. Or you can find another outlet for your love, where it will be appreciated and maybe even returned."*

Wow, I love how Jodee explains the pain many teens experience every day. I remember my teen years as being the best *and* the worst years of my life. I didn't have it as hard as Jodee, but I, like many teens, had a lot of turmoil surrounding those years. Talk to someone, become athletic, work on those singing skills you have always wanted to develop, try out for a local play… just do something. Get up and stop thinking about the pain; it will pass, you will work through this. Choose to live. *"If at first you don't succeed, you're about average." (Marion Hamilton Alderson)*

Go for a jog or walk. It's amazing how the brain processes while you are moving. The endorphins kick in and you are able to think a little more clearly. The water, or your brain, becomes muddy when you sit and let stagnation take place. I'm so serious about this. Plan a daily 30 to 45 minute jog or walk. Write down what you are thinking prior to the exercise, then write down what you were thinking during the 30 to 45 minutes you were walking/jogging. It's just amazing and it's free.

The CDC website on *Understanding School Violence* states that a quarter of the schools reported gangs at their schools and a quarter of students in schools were offered or sold drugs on school property. More than 30 percent of students reported being bullied during the school year.

Can you see how bullying and drugs can play an intricate part? The CDC says that children who bully are more likely to get into fights, vandalize property, skip school, and drop out of school (www.cdc.gov/ violenceprevention). Another statistic shows that many bullied kids or those that are doing the bullying end up self-medicating with drugs or alcohol.

Eric Harris and Dylan Klebold showed signs of aggression on their website and issues of hatred toward society in general prior to the killings. Both were on probation due to being caught with tools and equipment that had been stolen. There were numerous signs of a distressed mental health with both teens prior to the tragic death of 12 students, 1 teacher, and the wounding of 21 others. Many boys, after being social outcasts, will show signs prior to "flipping out."

Why do people get so angry? All of us have the ability to feel the emotion of anger, it's how we process the emotion that counts. Some get angry over the loss of self-esteem, the loss of face, the threat of harm, the loss of valuables or possessions, the loss of a perceived role, and the loss of relationships. To deny that you get angry over these things leads to repressed feelings which could harm rather than help you as in the case of the teens who go on shooting sprees.

There is a common belief that more than 90 percent of the prison populations are men and 80 to 85 percent of those men grew up in fatherless homes, this can include the emotionally-absent father. Many of these boys are angry; angry that they have to figure life out by themselves and have inappropriate guidelines on what to do. They become angry and addicted.

Children NEED to feel needed. It is one of Maslow's hierarchies of needs. Children need food, water, clothing, and a place to stay and feel safe and not get the crap beat out of them. After the basic needs of food, shelter, and safety are provided, a child needs to feel love and a sense of belonging prior to meeting any self-esteem needs. When a child does not feel a sense of being a part of a family nor NEEDED they most likely will fall short when it comes to relationship issues, closeness, intimacy, and healthy sexuality. For families who have a father that lacks any emotional support and a mother who works most hours of the day, we see children who don't feel needed. These children may feel like they are a burden to the family. This plays a huge role on their emotional development or the lack thereof. A healthy emotional development requires attachment and bonds to others.

In my past career, I spent more time parenting the juveniles and their parents than my own child who suffered after my long work hours. My daughter had a father providing a healthy environment for her sense of belonging, but not necessarily a mother providing the much-needed love and support that a child craves from her "Mommy."

We cannot blame teens for feeling angry and unwanted. We adults, have failed them in so many ways. I'm not saying I have the answer as how a man and woman can get away with not working so many hours. I am saying society is falling short on raising our children these days. We plop them in front of the TV or a video game and expect that tool to raise our children. And we wonder why we have violent or highly-sexualized adolescents? Seriously? We gave them the OK; we set the standards for them. Adults need to take some ownership; it's not the teens' fault. It's the way we have programmed them. Garbage in, garbage out!

Supposedly, the D.A.R.E. program really has no correlation to keeping children off drugs. Yes, it's educational, but when an adolescent chooses to use drugs they don't have a light-bulb go off in their head and say, "Wow, maybe I shouldn't smoke this joint, because that officer that came to talk to me in the 5th grade said marijuana could affect my thinking and I could become dependent on it."

A new statistic out there reported that a child is less likely to abuse or become dependent on drugs related to their attachment with their parent or parents from age newborn to 3 years old! Isn't that amazing? We spend billions of dollars on drug education programs, yet one study showed the choice to use drugs really depends on a parent's attachment with their baby.

Again, Maslow was a smart cookie. He knew a child needed to be treated like a delicate flower. Give your baby bulb some water, potting soil with nutrition, keep it out of the hot summer sun and it will start to grow. Add some love and attention, and it is most likely to bloom into the most gorgeous flower ever.

On the other side, we recently hold the claim to fame of the home town hero, Johnny Manziel (aka. Johnny Heisman). My pastor recently said, "We want to be a part of something great." When Johnny made history as the first freshman to win the Heisman, Ray noted that everyone around town suddenly had some Johnny story. Kind of like the fish stories men tell. Ray noted, "To have an attachment or connection gives us a sense of something that is significant." It has meaning in our lives. He went on to report that we as a community "Have a bigger role that is even grander than the Heisman trophy." "God wants to use who you are." God wants to be a part of something significant. (And he needs to get ahold of Johnny football it seems!)

This is the whole reason I advocate finding who you are through a challenging athletic adventure. My husband and I recently had a drug addicted couple in counseling. When my husband asked, "So you two are here for couple's counseling, what is it you want to work on?" I can't recall the young man's response, but I vividly recall the woman's response. She said, "I want to find out who I *really* am." She wanted to know what she liked and didn't like, what she wanted to be, what made her tick.

This is so true of many of us. I was there. This is why being athletic and getting counseling is so important and helps us get un-stuck. *"Most people are about as happy as they make-up their minds to be." (Abe Lincoln)*

God won't give up on you, even when you have given up on yourself. Look at present day society. Half of the Americans out there have **given-up**! Having peace and faith certainly is not the status quo these days. Society lacks the passion to know they can complete an Ironman or compete in their life. Many are just waiting to die. Sitting there eating Blueberry muffins full of 34 grams of sugar and 540 mg of sodium. Fooling themselves that a muffin is a good product to give them what their body needs. NO! A processed muffin does not give a body what it needs and it's no different than eating a large candy bar!

These "dead" people choose to fool themselves by not reading what is in their food. Oh what a vicious web we weave. Media has warped our minds and now in the last quarter century media has warped *your body*. I admit to the cynicism I have armed myself with from the TV shows, movies, radio, and newspapers I consume; however, I haven't bought into the media's food advertisements. Those food companies that are advertised are not loyal to you; they are only loyal to the almighty dollar. How many advertisements do you see for organic cantaloupe, broccoli, kale? You don't! You only see food products advertised for things your body does not need. It's all brainwash and you, my friend, have become a victim! So, if you didn't think you had ever been a victim when you started my book... I've just proven you wrong!

Similar to drugs, it's well known that many kids crave high carbohydrate, high sugary foods, but what are we doing to our children when we allow them to eat high sugar cereals for breakfast or muffins or doughnuts? Would we give our child a "dime bag" of crack packaged in a pretty little box and say, "Here, go have breakfast?" I have recommended proper diet and exercise for years. The best diets are high in fiber, low in glycemic index (foods that slowly convert to sugar), and supply protein. NOT crack cocaine, alcohol, or meth for breakfast. Whole foods, not processed!

Spring et. al. (1982) studied the effects of high carbohydrate and high protein meals consumed by adults at breakfast. They found that although the participants felt calmer after eating a high carbohydrate breakfast like a pastry and coffee, they performed significantly lower on tests of selective attention after eating these meals compared to the adults who ate a protein meal (eggs, toast and coffee). These are life lessons folks. Garbage in, garbage out. Don't consume garbage and definitely don't stuff your kids with it, you will only damage them in the long run.

Wesnes et. al. (2003) compared the performance of children on computerized tests of attention and memory following a simple carbohydrate meal with high sugars and glucose drink, or no breakfast, or one with proper protein and complex carbohydrates (ex. an egg with whole wheat bread and orange juice or milk and oatmeal). Those with high simple carbohydrates, sugar breakfasts, and those with no breakfast showed significant declines in attention and memory. The ones with a balanced, complex carbohydrate and protein meal showed gains on tasks of spatial memory, auditory memory, and auditory attention.

On a side-note, adults with ADHD tend to have more issues with substance abuse, divorce, child abuse, family conflicts, unemployment, smoking, obesity or eating disorders, poor driving record, unplanned pregnancy, sexually transmitted diseases, psychiatric conditions, and sleep disorders.

Dr. Leslie Brown reports in her 2008 blog that exercise has a profound effect on ADHD and can modify behavior in the ADHD child, and may even promote brain growth. Exercise increases levels of neurotransmitters dopamine, serotonin, and norepinephrine. These neurotransmitters provide emotional stability, the ability to focus, mental alertness, and calmness (www.tenerife-training.net). Dr. Brown notes that a deficiency in neurotransmitters can cause depression, mood swings, irritability, anxiety, attention problems, stress, and sleep disturbances. Building a child's confidence through physical exertion and multi-sensory tutoring may prevent future decay of the body, mind, and spirit.

Many ADHD youth have issues with left and right. Directional confusion may take a number of forms from being uncertain of which is left and right to being unable to read a map accurately (Strydom, 2000). Yoga spends time challenging the left and right directional hemispheres of the brain. Yoga makes use of relaxation techniques which not only calms down the central nervous system, but also strengthens it.

Whatever our issue is, mine happens to be ADHD, there is a purpose for all of us. We have to find our way through the maze of our teens and twenties to figure out our purpose, our destiny. Hang in there, it will come. Good things come to those who....wait. Once you pass your twenties, be open to crossing that finish line and finding God's purpose for you in life.

Don't stop living, keep your eyes open. Persevere, persist. One foot in front of the other. This too shall pass. OK, enough of the clichés. You get the picture, you're not dead if you are reading this. You are **smart and amazing.**

A passage from the inspirational book, _Walking through Adversity_ by Rob Bryant a once-athletic active man who found himself paralyzed from the waist down in a split second at the prime of his life follows: On Rob's first meeting with his physical therapist he informed her that he was eager to get started as he wanted to learn to walk with braces in the near future.

Her reply: "Well, let's not get too far ahead of ourselves. The man walking with braces next to you is much younger than you are and he can move his legs, you can't. Maybe I'll let you try that in the future if I feel you can. But try to be realistic. You'll only be disappointed with unrealistic expectations."

Rob tried to explain to her that he had already decided he was going to walk someday, she replied, "I am your physical therapist, and I am in control here. I will say when you are ready. Now let's get back to business." (Bryant, 2001)

Too many times we forget the *power of positive thinking* with the child or our inner child. They can accomplish remarkable goals, but may need a different route to get there. We need to believe in them and support them. Rob Bryant? He went on to set a World Record for walking 24 miles on crutches and set a Guinness World Record for rowing 3,200 miles across America while raising money for charity. Rob points out, "At some point in our journey on this earth, each one of us will have to face adversity. It can either make us better, like fire tempers steel, or it can break us" (Bryant, 2001).

Iron Nugget:

How would you encourage people to be themselves and not give a flip about what others think?

When have you set an example to others for being true to yourself and not falling to peer pressure?

What is your opinion about how to stop bullying?

9   And They Call It Puppy Love...

"It is your attitude not your aptitude that determines your altitude." *(Zig Ziglar)*

If you have had hoops to jump through or obstacles in the road to get where you are today, you probably have positive memories to look back on, also. Not all of my teen days, which set the stage for my adult years, were traumatic. I had many budding relationships that "almost made it", but made me a stronger, wiser person for not making it.

Love can be like a drug. New love provides a warm, euphoric feeling. You get tingly all over when you are first in love with someone. You think of that person all day whatever you might be doing, the vivid image of their face pops up in your head. You become like a drug addict and need a fix. A love fix, to be around that person, smell them, touch them, and take their being in. You think of ways you might be able to leave work early, get out of class, or bring them coffee. You get the picture.

Think about love and those who have never experienced healthy love. The drug does become their love. They have felt isolation, anger, rejection and then this drug shows up one day. Wow! It feels good, it provides all those feelings that new love provides. (Why do you think we have so much divorce? Too many people want to find a new love to start over.) It makes them feel safe, wanted, and improves their self-esteem. They become that girl on TV or that masculine male they have been watching for years on the big screen. Yes, relationships come along, but not the real feeling of love. The drug makes them feel a false sense of security—a false sense of belonging.

I remember having three real "loves" (or so I thought) prior to meeting my wonderful husband. I dated a lot, but each guy turned out to fall off that pedestal in more than one way. I already mentioned I wasn't promiscuous so when I say I dated a lot it does not mean I slept around. Most boys I met ended up boring me, having too many issues like the guy who pushed me down the stairs, or just wanting to have a roll in the hay. I would soon tire of their games and stop returning their phone calls or just start dating someone else. But my first puppy love? Oh boy, I thought this was going to be a long courtship. Little did I know?

O'Neil came along when we both were 17. It was after my date rape experience, and I was not looking to get attached to anyone. O'Neil went to a different school, and I knew nothing of him until I laid eyes on him at a local dance. I was smitten from the start. He wasn't tall or well built, but he had this dark hair and gorgeous blue eyes. He was on the tennis team at his school like I was, so we had communality. When I met O'Neil, his friend had been hitting on my girlfriend, Amy.

O'Neil's buddy became extremely drunk to the point O'Neil had to load "drunken boy" in his car and tote the poor guy back home. "Drunken boy" was embarrassing himself by acting a fool and then throwing up everywhere. Ahh, the effects of too much alcohol are so attractive. This is what gets me, teens will drink to look cool, and then end up looking the fool and puking their guts up. Now that's real attractive having the eau de toilette cologne of puke all over you. Just what a date wants.

O'Neil asked for my number as he was shoving "drunken boy" in the car, I gave it to him never expecting a call. He did call and we spent many hours on the phone prior to our first date. I was even more smitten. Once O'Neil and I started dating, we spent time together every chance we could. This usually meant weekends because we lived almost an hour away from each other. I normally dated guys with cool, new cars, and O'Neil did not pass this test. But he did drive an old black Camaro, the cool part.

O'Neil was very laid-back as opposed to my hyper personality. We complimented each other like icing compliments warm cake just out of the oven. We oozed warm and gooey sweetness. OK, that's a lame example, but it's the only thing that really popped up, and it fit!

O'Neil's grandparents lived on a working ranch. When his grandparents would go out of town, O'Neil would feed the livestock and take care of needs around the house. I had such a fun time feeding cattle in the field, and getting sweaty and dirty with O'Neil. I was a teen who never got so dirty or had so much fun. I used to steal my brother's dirt bike and ride it all the time, but that wasn't in front of a boy. I was worried about looking presentable (or so I thought) in front of boys I liked. O'Neil and I were comfortable together. I didn't have to work at looking cool. I remember long kisses in his grandparents' kitchen, after coming in all filthy and sweaty from tending the livestock and getting some ice-cold water.

It was summer in Texas, I sweating like a pig and just wanting to jump in the water trough. O'Neil and I would be in the middle of the herd feeding the cows or washing our hands and just look at each other and start kissing. I was in love. After three months of living on Cloud 9, I was about to tell O'Neil what had happened to me earlier that year. My rape experience happened at the end of football season prior to Christmas, and I met O'Neil around spring break.

We were starting to get serious about conversation, and I remember asking him if he was a virgin. He immediately changed the subject and became distant. I wasn't sure how to handle this new rejection. Didn't I just ask a question? I was going to follow my question with my rape experience, because I had never told anyone. My friend who was with me the night of the rape knew something odd happened, but never asked and I was in such a state of shock I didn't say anything.

I had become very quiet and sank into depression after the incident, until I met O'Neil. I thought that the depression had lifted. Little did I know that asking O'Neil the virgin question would result in the end of our relationship? O'Neil became distant that night and then broke up with me on the phone a few days later. I felt like I was knocked in the head with a baseball. There were no previous signs of distress in our relationship, just me being curious about O'Neil's sexuality and wanting to disclose with someone I trusted about what happened to me on that horrible night.

Wow, I never realized you guys were so serious about that word. After my first real break-up, I cried for days. I was depressed again and in an attempt to feel better, I started partying that summer like crazy. Drinking boosted my confidence and made me the life of the party again, when I wasn't normally feeling like the life of the party. I counted the days until the weekend. When I could get drunk, loud, and hoop and holler like I had no cares in the world. If you can't tell, I was self-medicating to take the numbness away.

O'Neil? He ended up dating a younger floozy from my school. I came to the conclusion that O'Neil was a virgin when I asked him and was embarrassed. He had no reason to be embarrassed, as I was about to share something very sacred with him. I believe he hooked up with a piece of "white trash," because he wanted to become a part of the "club" all the other boys were joining at that time. My next love came the following year, my senior year around the end of football season. I had been going out with different boys—one was in college and would come home every so often. I really liked him, but it's hard to have a long-distant relationship when you are a senior in high school and there are so many available local guys. So, this football player I had known for four years came onto my radar. He was most valuable offense player from his sophomore year through his senior year. It wasn't until his senior year that he appeared to really become cute to me. He was the proverbial sweet guy, the perfect athlete. Everyone's friend: kind, considerate, strong, funny, and athletic.

Chuck had been dating a loose girl who was younger than us for a couple of years and had finally broken up with her. I never knew what he saw in her as she was lacking in social skills, class, and looks. I guess it was "the club" that brought him into that relationship. After two years of being in "the club," Chuck actually grew tired of his membership. To the point he later told me he fantasized of football touchdowns while doing the "club scene" with his old girlfriend. Man, that's a dedicated football player. He said he had to think of football plays and touchdowns to get turned on with her. She had a very strong appetite and was really into the "club scene."

Chuck and I became one of those senior couples who were always together. Younger classmates looked up to us as we appeared to be a healthy, athletic couple. And we were for a period of time. Chuck was ending his famous high school football career and had a few scholarships on the table. I let Chuck know that I was only going to Texas State University. No other place was open for me. He originally had several schools he was looking at with football scholarships and then the next thing I knew by spring, he decided to come with me to Texas State.

I was excited and scared at the same time. I loved being with him, but college is a big step and sometimes it's healthy not to spend every waking hour with your teen boyfriend. We had been attached at the hip since the end of football season; time apart could do us good. I always used to tell my girlfriends, "Absence makes the heart grow fonder", when they were having male problems.

Mother was looking forward to me becoming a part of the social clique and joining a sorority. I went through "rush" and had a decent time with the experience. Chuck was against sororities and fraternities, at the time, and gave me hell about joining. I was like a rag doll that season. My mother encouraging me, telling me about all the positives related to being in a sorority and then Chuck whining and being cynical about them. "You're gonna meet another guy, and you're gonna leave me. Those groups just use people and teach you how to drink and get laid."

I ended up listening to Chuck and dropping out of the whole rush process. I was depressed, again. I didn't get to meet any new friends. All the people who hung out together were in some sort of club. Not me. I was in a scuba diving class. Whoopee! Scuba was fun, and then

Chuck decided to join, too. Now I had my boyfriend with me in the only club I could meet new friends. Chuck was my "Siamese" twin, so no one cared to talk to me.

If you cannot tell, Chuck, the great guy he was, turned out to be co-dependent and sucked the air out of me. I needed someone who wouldn't cater to my every need. I came back to Corpus Christi that summer and again worked at the pool as a lifeguard. I tried to break off the relationship with Chuck, but he sent me a dozen roses weekly, bought me gold necklaces and a diamond ring, and then Sylvester came into my life.

I had always wanted a silver Persian cat. You know the furry white cat with slivers of silver in its fur. Beautiful. Sylvester was a little baby ball of cotton when I got him. Chuck put a note on my car that read, "Careful when you enter, don't let him out." "What out?" I thought. After getting in the car I heard the faintest meow coming from under my car seat. I looked under the seat and found the most adorable thing I had ever—I mean ever—seen. Now, how could I break up with Chuck after this token of love was given? I stayed with him and we became a family.

On one occasion I just couldn't take Chuck's smothering me anymore; family or not. Chuck had gone out of town to see his grandfather for the weekend and I attended a party at the pool. A younger lifeguard who was a senior in high school was always asking me for dating advice. At this particular party, Shane convinced me to show him how girls like to be kissed. Yes, I fell for it!

This kid was slick and naïve at the same time, with a body to kill for. He was tan and on a national gymnastics team. Shane trained at the gym so often; he didn't have time for a social life. As for the kissing lesson, I really fell for it and Shane was good at receiving instruction. Chuck decided to come back in town early because he just couldn't take being away (ya right) and caught me and this young, ripped lifeguard kissing. I felt like a cradle robber, but that kid was so hot it was hard to resist the help he was so desperately in need of. That's a lame excuse, don't buy it.

That instruction session was actually a good thing as it allowed me to tell Chuck I felt like he was always around me and I just needed some space to be me. I had been dating him for more than a year and a half now, and I wasn't ready to settle down. Chuck agreed that we would not spend so much time together. Chuck tried, he really did.

On one occasion, he left town again for the weekend. My parents were out of town, so I decided to have a party at the house. The music was loud and Chuck tried calling me over and over that night. He finally got a hold of me the next morning and asked where the hell I had been that night. I told him I had some friends over.

Chuck said he was in the ER because he cut his wrists getting something out of his trash can. Seriously? How does that happen? Turns out he later admitted to me he slit his wrists with his scuba knife when he experienced an extreme low point. Chuck called for help when he realized he didn't really want to die. Appears I wasn't the only one in the relationship depressed as a teen.

Chuck was the best, positive role model back then, but extremely co-dependent after he grew up without his father being present and his mother was just plain crazy. His mother hoarded and never cleaned house. I refused to go to her house after seeing it a couple of times when we first started dating.

Chuck was born to a teen mother who met another man and had two other children later. Being that Chuck's dad was not present, he was pretty much raised by his paternal grandparents. Chuck's grandparents were wonderful, but the lack of love in those early years really affected Chuck and his relationships. He was so afraid of losing those he loved that he ended up driving them away by clinging to them like Saran wrap.

After Chuck and I broke up, he joined what he previously said was despicable... a fraternity, otherwise known as "rent a friend." This is where Chuck met his next love: cocaine. Cocaine became a big part of Chuck's life. This is a guy, in high school and early college, who had never smoked a joint or cigarette. He would drink occasionally, but never any drugs, cigarettes, or anything harmful to his sacred, athletic body. So he jumped right in, didn't he?

Chuck loved my parents, and they loved him. My dad had more conversations with Chuck than he ever did with me. Chuck would come down from college periodically and stop by to see my parents. On one occasion I came home to see his car outside. It had been awhile, so I was not dreading the run in with Chuck. I was kind of exited to see him as he was getting on with his life and had a brand new red sports car. Cool, I loved fast cars! Chuck asked me to come outside with him to check out the new car that his grandfather just bought him. He motioned for me to get in the passenger side, which I did. He got in on his side. He asked me to close my door and then opened the glove box.

Chuck pulled out a small vial of cocaine and asked if I wanted to do a line. "No," I replied with 'tude—aaattttitttude. I did not want to do a line! I told him he shouldn't be doing that and could get arrested with coke in his car. He was not concerned and it was ironic how he had developed a new sense of confidence. At that moment, Chuck became like one of those idiots who seem invincible. "I won't get arrested. I won't develop a habit. I can handle it." And I knew at that point Chuck had found a new love.

That was the last I remember of Chuck, but he did call me a few years later to tell me he was happy and that when he met his new wife she helped him get off cocaine. He divorced his old love, cocaine, and was starting a family. I really hope Chuck received some counseling, because the co-dependency was not his fault. Nor is it yours.

"The only time a woman really succeeds at changing a man is when he is a baby." (Natalie Wood)

"A word to the wise ain't necessary, it's the stupid ones who need the advice." (Bill Cosby)

Iron Nugget:

Describe your first love?

How did it end?

Do you think people under 25 really are in love or is it just lust?

10   Father, Father Wherefore Art Thou?

"Were it offered to my choice, I should have no objection to a repetition of the same life from its beginning, only asking the advantages authors have in a second edition to correct some faults in the first." Benjamin Franklin

No story is complete without a dysfunctional family drama. So here's mine.

You got the intro when I mentioned my family looked functional on the outside, but living with a father who was not present physically or emotionally takes a toll on the developing child. Some children have attachment disorder issues which affect the development of relationships that child has with others around him or her.

I remember going on business runs with my father as early as 6 years old. The drive was one hour each way. We owned a restaurant and would drive to Corpus Christi to pick up boxes of chicken. There was never any talk in the car what so ever. It was almost like you were supposed to remain quiet in the vehicle like a trip to the library. Like the musty-smelling library trip, I started taking books with me, and although I was hyper I learned to read to pass the time and escape from my reality.

We sometimes have a love-hate relationship with the library as a child. It's intriguing going to the library, but there is a unique musty smell of all the old books and a sense of aloneness due to the quiet nature of the place. I always loved and hated my trips to the library, an oxymoron, like I love-hated the business trips with my father. The nature of being alone and the smell of Old Spice resonated on those business trips. As with many dysfunctional households, the memory of a smell or sound or the lack of sounds brings back memories. I hate being all alone as a result. It's almost like a punishment.

My sister, brother, and I were afraid of my father as he had a vicious temper. The "tiger blood" would really come out when he had been drinking more than usual. My dad came home to several beers every night, however, when he got together with friends he got drunk and meaner. Dad's day started late with a morning Dr. Pepper and ended with several beers being consumed in front of the TV. As a child, I never knew how many he consumed each night. All I remember of his beer at an early age is making numerous trips to the refrigerator to "get him another one."

At age 8, being curious and hyper, I would "pop a top" for him and take a sip with a grimace on my face. It was gross and made my face pucker like a lemon, but I liked lemons. Why was I fascinated by sipping the beer? *Probably because I secretly wanted my dad to pay as much attention to me as he did his love of beer.* **Children pay more attention to adults' actions than you think.** They may not be capable of verbalizing their thoughts at a young age, but your actions around young children can bite you in the ass when they get older, because that's when it comes back to haunt you.

On several occasions when I was in early elementary school my father would come home after drinking to my mother's exhaustion from dealing with three children under the age of 7. My brother and I were a little hyper and always fighting. My sister, the middle child, was a perfect angel. This is when we learned to hell with "Don't Mess With Texas," our household represented "Don't Mess With Dad".

Dad came home one night and just started hitting us as we were sleeping in our beds or pretending to be sleeping, as was the case many nights. I really don't remember all of that night, but I do remember being in what I thought was the safe bubble of my bed and then getting, excuse me, the shit slapped out of me on my head, back, butt, whatever he could hit. He was raging.

He then went into my brother's room after ransacking my sister and my safe zone and went after Kevin. I didn't get to see what happened exactly, but that was when my brother got a black eye and my mother said to my father, "Now what is he going to tell the people at school?" Evidently father took his belt off to hit Kevin and father's belt buckle hit Kevin in the eye.

We learned to tread water lightly around my father so as not to upset him. Living with extreme fluctuations of anger in households can cause stress on developing children. The emotional scars may lead to illness, anxiety, and anger as a child becomes a teen and adult. Many angry teens are carrying band aids of emotional outbursts to deal with their early trauma.

Statistics show families with dysfunction have a high rate of drug and alcohol use. People who develop unconscious ways to remove themselves from their surroundings often become victims of self-medication or self-destructive behaviors. Besides drug and alcohol abuse, eating disorders are common or obsessive-compulsive disorders with people from dysfunctional homes. There is a sense of control that the person from a dysfunctional household does not have.

Choosing to get drunk, high, not eat, binge and purge, or keep our house abnormally clean/dirty is all an example of how we can control our body or our environment. The person creates some sort of functional control in a dysfunctional environment, you might say. If you live with a "neat freak" that is driving you crazy take it easy on them, maybe there is an underlying issue you are not aware of.

On the opposite spectrum is the person who eats until they may break the scale, or those who hoard and have a house full of unwanted junk. My mother-in-law is a hoarder and although I know it stems from an abusive childhood and a very low socio-economic upbringing—they were very poor—I have a low tolerance for those who hoard. That's an issue I have to deal with, not her. While she needs to deal with her abuse issue, the hoarding doesn't bother her. We cannot change the behavior of others by controlling them. I just chose not to visit her in her environment, we meet elsewhere.

A simple way one can find wholeness is through the act of sharing our experiences and feelings. Often we may not see how we are hurting ourselves by the way we think. By sharing and talking with others we can sort through our dirty laundry and perhaps look at the situation in a cleaner manner. Sharing can release our inner burdens and release the feelings of shame, guilt, discouragement, fear, or anger you may be holding on to in your unconscious mind. I will get into the shame and guilt factor shortly, but first I must go back to my dysfunctional father.

In the 7th grade a nice-looking, popular Hispanic basketball player liked me. I liked him too, however, there was a group of large Latina girls who loved this athlete and would have no business with me in the picture. I received numerous threats in writing stuck in my locker about how if I didn't stop "messing" with Reggie; they were going to kick my ass when I walked home. First of all, there was no messing. I hadn't even kissed a boy by this time. OK, I'll confess, later he did walk me home one day and gave me a peck. My first kiss was just a sweet little peck.

On one particular day the threats were upped a notch and I was a little scared. I ended up telling my mother, who then told my father about the threats. My father was home early that day and drove me up to the school to talk with the principal. As we drove in silence, he started an angry conversation asking why the "Mexican" girls were after me. "What is this guy's name?" "You don't like a Mexican, do you?" "Of course, you don't." "Why would you even be interested in someone like that?"

And there it was, the elephant in the room, in no uncertain terms are you to like a "Mexican guy." To be friends with a Mexican girl was perfectly OK in my household, but to like the opposite sex of a different ethnicity. No Way Jose!!! I grew older and moved away from Corpus Christi. My father decided to leave my mother after his last affair and moved from Corpus Christi to the Hill Country where my husband and I resided. My husband and I were selling our home and my father decided to buy it to "help us out." He had us sell the house to him at the note pay-off rate and made us pay for all of *his* closing costs. Such a dear man.

I had a hint of excitement as I felt like I could use my father as support, physically. He never would be able to give emotional support without some counseling, but being present in body was something that was in the back of my mind when Cami was born. Perhaps he would have the relationship with my daughter that I never had with him. It was a possibility. However, after she was born Eric and I spent weeks in the hospital, while my father never once called us to see if we might need, say, an hour break to have adult time and get away from the depressing sterile hospital environment. Cami was in the hospital eight times prior to age 2 and a half. Each hospital stay lasted about a week at a time with my baby hooked up to IVs.

Our preacher Ray said, "Have you ever loved something so much you refused to relinquish control over it?" He went on to note that it's easy giving God the things we least care about, but it's hardest giving God the things we care about the most. I remember thinking years ago, "Not another cold sterile X-Ray room for my precious infant" when the doctor said, "It sounds like pneumonia, again." After the fight of keeping that poor sickly baby still long enough to snap the X-Ray, we inevitably would hear the words we were praying we wouldn't, "Its pneumonia, we need to admit her and we'll get the oxygen tent ready."

That wasn't the bad part. The bad part was the five nurses it took to find my poor, sick baby's veins to start the IV. She could hardly breathe as it was and then the torture would start. Nurse Number One would come in confidently. We would help hold poor Cami down, while she poked and prodded. Three pokes while poor baby cries trying to get air in those fragile wounded lungs. The first nurse would leave and return with Nurse Number Two.

Nurse Number Two would come in looking as confident as Number One, but the same scene would take place only this time the cries were more faint and less oxygen would be getting into those little, weak lungs. By the time the last nurse came in our baby would have little fight, little air, and the most awful whimper a child could muster. I would be one visit closer to a nervous breakdown.

It was somewhere after our fifth hospital stay that I realized it wasn't about me and my control over the situation. That no matter how hard I fought to keep her from getting sick, I wasn't in control. God was the true force. I could fight him all the day long, but in the end he knew what the outcome would be. I had to learn to sometimes just let the chips fall where they may. I couldn't line up all the toy soldiers in a neat little row and have my way with my life and Cami's like a game of chess. Yes, there was strategy in keeping her safe from snotty-nosed ill children, but the seasons would come and go and I couldn't control other factors like support from my father.

The situation got to the point that I became Momma Bear and had enough of my father's selfishness. I wrote him a letter that I felt in my mind was to open real discussion. It talked about the lack of support he gave me as a child, his lack of support for my child, and his bigotry. I told him that if he wanted me to be a neo-Nazi (yes, it was extreme) he should have sent me to private school like our spoiled, rich, obnoxious cousins. The letter was just to release anger that I had pent up for years and to attempt a real conversation with this man. I thought he would be different when he had a grandchild. I expected my father to be angry at first and then say something like, "Wow, you're real angry at me." We were both adults, weren't we?

That scenario didn't happen. He basically told me that since I was in high school I was the one who started being distant and not talking and that the situation was all me—my fault. My father, in his reply letter, said something about not talking to me in the future. I can't remember all the details because I threw his letter away. I was angry. That was more than *12 years* ago.

Needless to say, he was ending our relationship, not that there really was one to begin with. We were dealing with a very sick baby, and at that time, my husband, Eric, and I were just trying to survive... the day! There was very little planning ahead as we never knew when we would be back in the hospital. When I mentioned we visited the doctor weekly, I wasn't embellishing. We really were there weekly. Eric and I spent a lot of long hours waiting to see the doctor for our poor, little, beautiful and sick baby.

The visual I give people in counseling about needing help from a parent follows: *When a person is in the middle of a lake drowning there's just a thrashing commotion that takes place with a vivid look of distress on their face. Many times that person can't even yell out for help. They are just trying to keep their head above water. It's our job as parents or loved ones to recognize that look of distress and offer help. Throw the life preserver to them! Go to them! Don't wait for them to swim to shore or come to you. They can't!! They are drowning!!* (It helps being a lifeguard.)

My favorite author, Paulo Coehlo, posted on his Facebook recently, "Close some doors. Not because of pride, incapacity or arrogance, but simply because they no longer lead somewhere." I had been trying to have a real relationship with my father for years and the fact of the matter is, he obviously wasn't capable of having a real relationship. I'm OK, now. I can't change him.

Years ago, my father would not come home at night and was evidently having many marital affairs around our small south Texas town. One of them was his current wife. My father happened to be active in politics and the social community at that time and drove the only green Jaguar in town. One night my parents were at a social party and my mother said she needed to leave to let the babysitter who was watching us go. She got a ride with someone who was leaving the party at that moment.

The story goes that people saw my father's green Jag at the local Holiday Inn, which was down from the party, later that night. When my father didn't come home that night, he told my mother that M, otherwise known as BroomHilda, had thrown-up on herself at the party so he took her to Holiday Inn to wash her outfit. Hmmm, that sure does sound believable, right?

We were very young at this time so I don't remember my father not coming home on a regular basis. However, I do remember in the 6th grade he would stay out all night on numerous occasions. I would look out my window at 6 a.m. and see him pulling up in the driveway and walking the walk of shame back into the house. The fact is that I'm sure my mother stopped questioning him after years of infidelity. My father was so self-centered that on Christmas Eve at 6 p.m. he would drive me around town to find a store that was still open to go get my mother a present, while he waited in the car. He would only give me enough money to buy one gift. I always felt sorry for my mother at Christmas. Birthdays were similar, but at least the stores didn't close early on the eve of her birthday. Many times the store would be closed and we would drive down to the next store.

I was so hyper-active that I never looked past my world either. It didn't dawn on me that I could have prompted him a few days prior to Christmas. I was in elementary school and just dealing with my own issues. I really regret not being put on medication earlier. My life would have been a little more focused, but I probably wouldn't have found athletics to channel my activity through. So it's all good in my neighborhood!

Several years back, when my daughter was around 5 years old and my father still lived in our town, my sister's mother-in-law passed away suddenly. Carol, my sister's mother-in-law, died of a heart attack in front of my niece and nephew. It was tragic—those kids were so close to their paternal grandparents. Clint and Hailey's grandparents owned a ranch, and they would spend weekends with them on the tractors or weeks during the summer hanging-out. It was a special relationship as they didn't know my father and my mother lived hours away from her grandkids. When my father closed the door to a relationship with me and my child, he closed the door to his other two children, also. No one is sure why. When the funeral was planned my sister asked if I would call and let our father know.

My sister always had hopes of repairing the relationship with our father as she was the "hero" of the family. She is two years younger than me and one year older than my brother. Her personality is more of the helper, not the impulsive sometimes aggressive personality like my brother and I. She never showed anger growing up. I told her, of course, I would let him know. I called his house and BroomHilda answered. I asked if I could speak with my father. BroomHilda proceeded to tell me that I was a very angry person and I needed to look at that. First of all, I called with a normal tone and just told her who I was and that I would like to speak with my father. This was not a time to reconcile; it was a call for informative reasons. I replied, "I'm not calling to address issues with my father, just relay a message from my sister. Something has happened."

She proceeded to not let him on the phone; he may have not been there for all I know. I finally told her I wasn't sure if she was hearing me, that all I was calling for was to speak with my father to let him known his grandkids just witnessed their beloved grandmother die in front of them, suddenly, while eating cereal with the kids at breakfast. When BroomHilda continued to not listen or hear me, I ended up hanging up on her.

Somehow the message got to my father, but when she relayed the message she told my father that I had called very angry yelling at her that I needed to talk with him. There were more fabrications she added, but it's been more than seven years, and I try not to remember or dwell on the trauma related to my father and BroomHilda. How can someone be so cold? There was a death! A tragic death and she used her own agenda to compromise the situation at hand. Watch out for those people. Stay away from friends like this. They may have a personality disorder and there isn't really a medication prescribed for those issues. If they aren't willing to get therapy for their disorder, they may likely drag you into their daily drama.

Personality disorders need years of counseling to form a plan on how to deal with their histrionic, narcissist, borderline, etc., personalities. I learned years ago that many people with Borderline personalities come from abused homes. The abuse can be sexual, physical, or even emotional. It makes sense as these people are not processing thoughts and emotions in a logical manner. Their viewpoint is skewed from the years of abuse, and they may have a co-morbidity of depression, which medication will help.

Some psychologists report that we women want to date a man like our father. We have a huge attraction to this type of Marlboro Man because we secretly want to go back in time and make our childhood right. You know, a time when the man doesn't leave, where he is supportive, perfect looking, and a perfect role model. What 6 year old remembers an ugly dad?

The problem is, we didn't grow up with that perfect man and he was never fixed by our mothers back then, so we will never, ever fix that man if we try to marry him. You may find yourself attracted to the strong, mysterious type and think you are madly in love with him; you think he is the one that will finally complete you. Hold your guns, Orphan Annie! Our mothers couldn't fix him, and chances are there is a screw loose somewhere in their life.

Please, don't make the same mistake they did. Marry the John Wayne who is in touch with his feminine side, has had therapy, or brought up in a functional family. Spare yourself the grief. You deserve better. Who needs a controlling Marlboro Man, anyway? Don't be fooled by his big cowboy boots and the passion he lassoes you with. I can almost promise you will fall off that big stallion and onto your ass in the end.

Iron Nugget:

How would you rewrite your first life?

11   La Familia Is Loco in La Cabeza

"When we remember we are all mad, the mysteries disappear and life stands explained."
Mark Twain

So after my trips with my father and learning the unwritten rules of the household I had the pleasure of dealing with my schizotypal grandmother. What is that you ask? Schizotypal is a mild form of schizophrenia. Schizotypal people tend to be aloof, indifferent, have magical-type thinking, superstitious beliefs, and may use unusual words with peculiar ideas.

This is my diagnosis of my grandmother, although I don't have an affirmative on the true diagnosis (she is deceased now). It started with my stay with her in the first grade which I don't remember much of. We called her "Gambi," like Bambi the deer—except she was no sweet deer. My mother sent my friend Susan and me to stay the weekend with Gambi. I remember Gambi's house being all closed up. She stayed in her bed all day except to get up for a can of Pepsi that she wrapped with a paper towel and stuffed a piece of tissue in the opening.

She didn't want us to open the door or look out the windows. She recited passages of the Bible to you if you went into her room to ask her something and would write down Bible passages all day. I think she assumed the end was near. She had paper lying around her bed with passages everywhere. She posted them up on the backboard of her bed and other places. I don't remember her cooking for us, but on this one and only stay, I got sick.

Looking back, it was probably food poisoning due to the lack of cleaning she did. Anyway, I tried to make it to the bathroom to get sick, but threw-up everywhere in the living room. Gambi heard the commotion and came out of her thrown, I mean bed. She started yelling at me immediately and told me that I meant to throw up all over the living room and could clean my vomit up myself. Seriously? It was the end of my first grade, and I remember feeling so sick and weak and just wanting my Mommy. As noted, my mother was a very busy, social woman, but when you were sick she definitely put her activities aside and made sure you were cared for in a loving manner. I could barely move and was being yelled at and told to clean my vomit up. I felt like I was in a chapter from Cinderella.

Susan, my friend who was with me, was a couple of years older than I and like my big sister. This day sealed the deal; I loved and admired her from this day more than any. Susan told me not to worry that she would clean the vomit for me. She got me a cold rag to put on my head and nursed me back to health until my mother would come back in town to pick us up. Ironically, Susan's mother was a nurse. I probably was dehydrated, too. I remember feeling like I was going to die. I was so young, I don't remember all the details just that Gambi had odds ways of thinking, was aloof, and out of the ordinary from other people. My mother did not make us stay at Gambi's house after that, especially since I threw a fit if it was mentioned.

Gambi was used as a last resort if mother couldn't find anyone to stay with us while my parents went out of town. The next time we were subjected to Gambi's terror was when I was in the 5th grade. My parents were out of the state and they left Gambi to watch us at our house. I remember Gambi surprising us and actually taking my brother, sister, and myself to the movies one Sunday.

We went to an early evening movie and returned after dark. As we pulled up to the back of the house, Gambi said, "Why is that outside light on?" in her dry serious tone. I told her we must have turned it on when we left. She inevitably aroused herself from a dormant mama bear sleep and began to go on a tirade about how that outside light was most certainly not on and the light inside *was* left on (it was pitch dark inside the house at the time). Gambi became a paranoid character and went off on a story about how burglars must be in the house and that I needed to go inside to see if anyone was in there.

My grandmother's talk scared the total piss out of me, and I, as the parentified-child, told her rationally over and over that there was no one in our house and one of us just forgot if we turned the lights on or off prior to leaving. She continued in an irate manner and insisted I go inside to see if anything was stolen or if anyone was in there. Now looking back in retrospect one might think, "Who in hell has a conversation with a 5th grader about going in a dark home alone that may have an intruder in it?"

First of all, deep down I knew no one was in the house. Second of all, I was a kid and deeply afraid of the Boogey Man, ghosts, Bloody Mary in the dark bathroom mirror, aliens, Lizzy Borden, and on and on and on. Now my grandmother tells me the boogey man may be presently in my house and to go in there alone? I've heard of facing your fears, but this was ridiculous and dangerous if you think about it. I hadn't even gone to my first haunted Halloween house and this felt like a Halloween ordeal! Of course, crazy woman, Gambi, refused to go in herself and sent me. I think I dragged my brother in there with me who was all of 3-feet tall and in the second grade. Wow, an 80-pound girl and a 40-pound boy weighed much less than one Boogey Man.

As Gambi was mean and 'loco in la cabeza" there was no way we could have stood up to her. I would almost rather have the Boogey Man watch me for the weekend than that crazy woman! I proceeded up the path to our home which was a good 40 feet away. I opened the door, turned a few lights on, and looked very slowly and methodically around the house. It appeared no one was in there or had been there for that matter so my brother and I ran back to the vehicle where my grandmother and sister waited. Gambi immediately told me to get the car and that we were going to stay at a motel because she *knew* someone had been there. She just knew it! I was terrified.

My sister and I still remember the sleazy, roach motel she took us to. There was a couple making, loud, passionate cheap-motel love next to us. The bed was banging while the lady was yelling all night. I was afraid to get under the covers and touch anything in the place it was dirty, gross, and disgusting! To top it off, Gambi never got us up the next morning to attend school. We actually missed school. Now how was I going to explain this to my teacher the next day? No one would believe my story except for my own mother who knew how crazy her mother really was.

Mother didn't make us see Gambi often after the last incident; she went to see her loco mother by herself. I remember having to go see Gambi on Mother's Day the year I was 15.

Gambi had blown-up her 2nd or 3rd microwave by putting the wrong products in it and we were taking her another microwave.

Her place was filthy. The sinks were grown over with mold and mildew and the toilet was a science experiment. She was in bed with Bible writings surrounding her just like they were 10 years ago. Gambi had moved many times and was in a different rental, different place, same scene. Armageddon obviously had not arrived, but she was prepared in her mind. I could barely understand her as she spoke through the few teeth she had. I asked my mother why Gambi was talking that way when we left. My mother informed me that she was taking so much Valium it gave her a heavy tongue and slurred speech. It wasn't until years later that I realized addiction runs in our family. My grandmother ended up living a very long and lonely life with very few visitors.

"Seven days without laughter makes one week." (Mort Walker)

Iron Nugget:

Is your family normal or crazy?

What do you like about your family?

What do you dislike about your family?

What do you like about yourself?

What do you dislike about yourself?

12   Las Mujeres (The Women)

"A woman is like a tea bag. She only knows her strength when put in hot water." (Nancy Reagan)

Fast forward to today. It's been more than five years that a close relative has been taking pain pills. This relative has had three hip replacements and has not exercised for years. Her muscles have most likely atrophied, and she continues to carry extra weight on her medium-build frame. When your muscles atrophy they basically waste away from lack of use. Think of the old saying, "if you don't use it, you lose it." It is so sad to watch her as she forgets things over and over or repeats stories within a matter of 10 minutes.

As a drug and alcohol counselor, I have been so concerned about my relative. I've tried to talk to her about healthy choices years ago, but she gets very passive-aggressive when you breech serious subjects about her health. This relative has a nervous laugh and may laugh after every sentence. The sentence might go like this..."Oh, my poor friend had to be admitted to the hospital the other day...laugh, laugh, laugh." It bothers me. It's not necessary. Why laugh when you feel sad? Do you know someone who talks and laughs when subjects aren't even funny?

Another part of my relative's drug dysfunction is that she will tell you she will be somewhere and then either doesn't arrive, shows up hours late or even a day later. As of last weekend, she told Cami she was leaving at 11 a.m. to head up to Houston. When my niece, Haley, later called to check on this relative's drive, she said she would be leaving at 3 p.m. The awaiting family members still hadn't heard from her by 5 p.m. so my nephew, Clint, called her to make sure she wasn't going to miss his high school graduation. She said she would not miss his graduation the next morning and would leave by 7 p.m. to make the long five-hour drive from her hometown.

My sister was livid and asked me if she should confront our relative's behavior. This was typical of her, but Clint, my nephew, desperately wanted her there to see him walk across the stage and receive his diploma. I didn't want my sister to anger our relative and have her not come. I just asked my sister to leave it for now and we could deal with it at another time, her son's graduation was the priority and we weren't going to spoil it by addressing our relative's childish behavior.

Clint's graduation was at 9 a.m. in Reliant Stadium which meant we had to leave my sister's home in the Woodlands area at 7:30 a.m. to arrive on time and find a seat. Our relative knew about this months in advance and chose to leave at night prior to waking up at 6:15 a.m.? She's older and driving on the road at night is not her strength. Let's just say I don't drive with her in the daylight and sure as hell wouldn't be on the road with her after dark. The fact that she obviously has no concept of time, forgets information consistently, and drives too slow on the highway scares the whole family. When my sister and I heard the fact that she was headed up to Houston at 8 p.m., we immediately said a prayer to ourselves for her safety.

My daughter is in middle school, and is the queen of texting. She is always on the phone, so it's no coincidence that my daughter calls this relative frequently to check on her when we have plans for a get together. Cami started checking on our relative about 8:45 p.m and learned that she was just past the Longhorn Store, which is only 45 minutes outside of home town. We were upset and afraid.

Have you ever had a premonition? It's like we knew ahead of time. My daughter called several times later around 10 p.m. and got no answer on several attempts. Finally, just after 10:30 p.m., my daughter got an answer on our relative's phone; Cami immediately looked at us with a worried look and passed the phone to my sister. Cami said to me, "She sounded really weird and asked to speak to Aunt G." My sister got on the phone with an, "Oh no, are you OK? Where are you?" From there she started talking with someone else and writing down a phone number.

Our relative was rear ended while driving in the fast lane. Her car was totaled and she sustained lacerations to her calf and issues to her neck. Her arms were already all black and blue by the time of the phone call, the seatbelt hurt her left shoulder, but saved her life. She was being taken by ambulance to the local hospital. My sister and I had had a couple of glasses of wine that evening and did not feel safe to drive. So the duty was left to my brother-in-law.

Craig is a coach, and the poor guy had just finished his last day of school for the summer and was woken-up with the news. He received the job of driving two hours to pick up our relative once she was released from the ER, which meant a two hour return trip—four hours total! I felt bad having him drive all alone to pick up *our* relative, so I said I would go with him. We arrived while they were waiting on CAT scans. The process took forever. Nothing moves fast in an ER, even when it's in the middle of nowhere and there are no patients! I was livid that this even happened. We arrived at the rural hospital at 1 a.m., left at 3 a.m., and returned to my sister's home at 5 a.m.

Our alarm clocks were set for 6:15am to attend Clint's graduation. Needless to say I ended up missing my nephew's graduation. I drove six hours to see this event and even left on Thursday to be there all day Friday to support Clint. The morning of the graduation I had the worst migraine and sore throat from being up all night and walking around a frozen ER. I couldn't even see straight, I stayed in bed all morning.

Ironically, my relative never had remorse about her behavior. She made excuses as usual and blamed the accident on the person who rear-ended her. Granted the person was speeding, but how fast was she going and why the hell would a 60-something-year-old woman leave at 8 p.m. at night to make a long road trip alone? I don't even make long trips at night. Nothing good happens on the road past 10 p.m. It's an unwritten rule!

Drug addiction, whether it's prescribed or a street drug, has lies involved. For those of you associated with someone who is addicted you will most likely always find...denial. The person is generally in denial of the fact that they are responsible for their own behavior. You may hear, it's usually someone else's fault that they feel the way they do or make the choices they make. It could be a boss' fault for working them too hard or not appreciating them, a husband or wife's fault for not treating them the way they think they should be treated, a parent's fault for being too strict or too mean, or whatever reason. Hopefully you get the picture. Just know, it is never our fault that a person becomes addicted. Never.

My relative slept most of the late afternoon on Saturday after the graduation and was so drugged on Sunday when I was leaving that she couldn't open her eyes fully to say good-bye to my daughter and me. Five days after the accident, she was discussing the graduation and that she wished we would have taken a group photo at Clint's graduation. I could tell my relative had no idea I was not present at the graduation ceremony. I reminded her that I didn't attend the graduation. At least three times she proceeded to tell me that I *was* there. She finally stopped and made excuses that she was still in a state of shock that day and was in a fog from the lack of sleep.

I agree she was in shock, in a fog, and had a lack of sleep. I also know that as soon as the car hit her and a Good Samaritan stopped by to help her she had the stranger get her purse in the banged-up vehicle. Before the ambulance arrived, she told my brother in law, that she was able to take a hydrocodone and muscle relaxant. My theory is that she was doubling up on the medication more than her normal four to six hour span.

I worry that she will die of a heart-attack, in a car accident, or from a stroke. Her blood pressure is high and was at 192 over something at one point while in the ER; it went down to 184, and finally 164 at the time of discharge. I'm sure pain pills, muscle relaxants, anti-depressants, cholesterol meds, and hypertension meds should not all be combined at the rate she combines them. I suspect she doesn't have just one doctor prescribing her meds. It appears the left foot doesn't know what the right foot is doing. Too many times families make excuses for addiction because the abuser has been "prescribed" the medication.

About addiction: Addiction is treatable. Common research now shows that substance abuse is increasingly accompanied by co-occurring mental and physical health conditions. Many require simultaneous treatment such as depression or bipolar along with an addiction. Individual or group counseling is the most practiced treatment for substance abusers. Family therapy, if available, is generally advised to restore healthy family dynamics.

An abuser must learn to tolerate negative emotions like anxiety, sadness, shame, anger, and yes, pain without resorting to self-medicating by becoming drunk or high. Many treatment programs or group counseling sessions address courses in life skills while one is in recovery. George Carlin made a remarkable comment years ago, he said, "Just because you got the monkey off your back doesn't mean the circus left town."

Here are some signs of when to talk with a loved one about addiction:

When someone displays a high level of risk and dangerous behaviors like driving while under the influence or becoming physically abusive or self abuse.

When someone shows signs of physical deterioration.

When there is a pre-occupation with taking or getting the drug.

When legal, family, or money problems come into play surrounding the drug.

When someone develops a tolerance and must take more of the drug or add a mix of drugs into their equation.

When there is a deterioration of relationships (boyfriend, girlfriend, spouse, family, and friends)

When someone shows signs of withdrawal and refuses to stop using due to avoiding the discomfort of withdrawal.

When someone is in denial. "I don't have a problem!"

Painkillers or narcotics like oxycodone, hydrocodone, morphine, codeine all lower one's perception of pain; however, they can be extremely addictive. A hazard includes the need for increasing amounts of the drug, even if they have been prescribed. Overdose may lead to coma, convulsions, respiratory arrest, or even death (Texas Department of State Health Services Offender Education). Many addicts I've personally seen have a serious issue with lack of proper nutrition. Help is available through the Center for Substance Abuse Treatment's National Helpline at 1-800-662-HELP.

My relationship with my close relative tends to be superficial. There was some time in my childhood where I received the message—we don't talk about important subjects. We laugh and pretend things are funny even when we are talking about serious subjects. Oh sure, we talk a lot about those around us, but not deep-down Paulo Coehelo stuff. We keep to Diary of a Wimpy Kid talk. Just kids-on-the-playground kind of stuff.

I don't have all the answers in this area as it is hard to help those who don't want help when dealing with a loved one with major issues. I am praying and learning as many of you are. I take it step by step.

When my daughter was born, I knew I would talk to Cami about important subjects. About sex, drugs, rock 'n' roll, religion, puberty, boobs, menstruation and all the good stuff a kid either wants to hear or is morbidly embarrassed about. My daughter is a little of both, she enjoys talking about some deep in depth subjects, but other times she is just plain scared that I'm going to bring the subjects up when her friends are over.

The barrier I have broken with my daughter is "moms are involved with their daughters" and "moms can occasionally be cool." I must point out that the only time I'm cool is on birthdays when we play pranks on the neighborhood kids. When we go to school events I am told not to talk, as I talk way too loud and fast. That's an age thing. My daughter as a teen is at "that stage." We have conversations were she voices a lot of her opinion, but when I give my opinion, she might say something like, "You always disagree with me." Of course, I don't ALWAYS disagree with her, but there are times when she is handling difficulties with friends that I think might have a different avenue. I just give her a "what if this is really what is happening?" Too many of us look at things the way we see them—one-sided.

The point is that I have told her over and over…"Sweetie, I'm not disagreeing with you. We are just having a discussion and I might be seeing the situation differently than you, so I'm just giving you my opinion. It doesn't mean that either one of our opinions is right or wrong, it just means that people learn differently and have a different way of looking at things. Chances are your friend or friends look at things a little differently, also."

This has taken at least a year to get across, but PART THE HEAVENS… I think she is finally getting it. She just came back from a trip with a friend and was able to solve difficult situations on her own from thinking that the other girls may just be looking at things differently. "We have to agree to disagree at times." It doesn't mean I don't support her, it just means we have different views or opinions on certain matters. Adults, forthright communication may involve a few healthy dis-agreements. This doesn't mean we have to yell and scream and stomp our feet at our children, this means we need to listen to EVERYTHING they are feeling and have to say. Then we can try to piece together what is really going on or being said.

Granted, as adults, we are going to hear, "You never hear me" or "you never listen." That's just the children saying they feel they aren't being fully heard. Personally, as a hyperactive parent, I had to wait until she finished the whole story which could go on forever in my opinion before I replied or gave an example. This was aggravating at times, but it was so important in developing my teen's relationship with me and with other women. There are subjects she just doesn't want to talk about with my husband.

More Facts about prescription drug abuse as reported by www.drugfreeworld.org:

"Normally, when a person remembers something, the mind is very fast and information comes quickly. Drugs blur memory, causing blank spots. Drugs can make a person feel slow and cause them to have failures in life."

"Abuse of prescription drugs has become a more serious problem than most street drugs. Painkillers, tranquilizers, antidepressants, sleeping pills, and stimulants appear safe due to being prescribed by doctors, but they can be just as addictive and potent as heroin or cocaine sold on the street."

"Painkillers, depressants, and antidepressants are responsible for more overdose deaths in the U.S. than cocaine, heroin, meth, and amphetamines combined."

Request a booklet or facts from Foundation for a Drug-Free World at: www.drugfreeworld.org.

Choose an Ironman, not drugs. Ironman: the best high, ever.

Iron Nugget:

What is your opinion on the vast supply of narcotics prescribed?

Do you know anyone addicted to pain pills? Explain the situation

13 Mi Gusto El Mexicano

"In each human heart are a tiger, a pig, an ass and a nightingale. Diversity of character is due to their unequal activity." Ambrose Bierce

It wasn't until I was in college that I breeched my father's unwritten contract. I was a lifeguard from 15 to 23 years of age and worked my way up the swimming ladder as a lesson coordinator for the City of Corpus Christi Aquatics Department with an office in City Hall at age 21.

It was a dream job to work in the aquatics department all year long. We had one particular pool that was a heated pool which stayed open all year. There were a few of us employed full-time, year round. At age 20, I met a lifeguard/manager at one of the city pools during one of the many parties we lifeguards had in the summer. There would be a different party each week. Such fun. Frank and I became friends first, and then started dating a few months after we met.

I started dating Frank who was a tall, handsome Hispanic guy with hazel eyes. Frank's father was from Mexico and had very blue eyes. He had three brothers. One was very light skinned with blue eyes, another had an olive skin tone like Frank but with brown eyes, then there was the youngest brother who had really dark skin with dark hair and eyes.

It was amazing how different these four brothers looked and they all had the same father. The brother with light skin and blue eyes married a white gal with similar hair and coloring to mine, and the little boy had very light skin with blue eyes. I find it interesting how mixed-racial children generally are very attractive. Halle Berry, who has mixed ethnicity, is one of the most beautiful women in Hollywood.

After my parents found out about my relationship with Frank, my father became very cold to me. I was back and forth in college so I didn't think too much about it. Until I had to move back home; I couldn't afford living on my own anymore. My father would walk past me like I wasn't there. I spent many hours when I was at home locked-up in my room to avoid him. One summer, when my brother and sister where home from Texas Tech college, I decided to make some macaroni for us. My father came over to the stove and told me to turn the water to the noodles down because it was going to boil over. I was at the stove and starting to stir the dish. Evidently I said something that was not to his liking and he told me to get out of his house, that he had enough of me, and then when I started commenting back to him, he raised his hand to hit me.

I had enough too, of being afraid of that man and told him to go ahead, "I'm tired of being afraid of you. Hit me. I really don't care. Slap the s**t out of me. Feel better. Go ahead." My brother and sister ran into the room due to the commotion and my brother actually grabbed my father's hand as it was up in the air aimed at me. Kevin told my father he was not going to hit me, and then yelled at me to leave, "Now!" That was the first time I saw my brother become the parentified-child, I must say.

I remember driving my car so fast it almost didn't handle the first curve I rounded. I also remember thinking that maybe I would just drive so fast I would run into a telephone pole. Now, this was not a scared thought, this was a maybe-I-can-solve-some-problems-by-hurting-myself-so-bad-I-won't-be-aware-of-my-surroundings thought. I was crying so hard I couldn't think straight, and I had no idea where to go.

My high school buddies were all off to college and most of my college buddies were not girls that I would just drop in at their house. Some were married and some lived at home. Texas A&M Corpus Christi, at the time, was a hometown college. They have dorms now and apartments on campus where many students from out of town live, but the majority of the students back then lived in the Corpus Christi vicinity. I had lived in an apartment across town, previously, but didn't receive school funding for it. The only place I felt I could turn to was my boyfriend's home, but he was away. Two brothers were still at home and the other brother didn't live there anymore.

I showed up at Frank's home crying. His mother was so dear to me, let me in, and said I could stay there as long as I needed. She kicked the one brother out of his room and told me to take some time and relax. I cried, rested, and then came downstairs for dinner. I think my mother called later to tell me she was going to have a talk with my father about his behavior.

After my mother had the talk, she called me to tell me she gave my father a choice: work things out with me or else. I actually felt support from my mother at that moment. My mother spent her days making sure the family appeared happy and calm, so much of the time she would laugh and smile and not bring up serious topics around the home. We didn't discuss feelings or issues in our household, which can be so confusing for an adolescent. Mom asked me to come back home the next day, and we would have a group "pow-wow."

Let's talk about statistics. When I was studying for my LPC exam—Licensed Professional Counselor exam—I remember the death rates for adults are in this order, from one to three, heart-attacks, cancer, and stroke. Other external factors of death for adults include: tobacco, inappropriate diet (junk food, fast food, etc.) along with lack of exercise, and alcohol. The top three reasons for death with adolescents ages 15-24 include: alcohol related incidents, homicide (41 percent of black males in the inner cities fall prey to this statistic), and then suicide. I've read other statistics where they place suicide as the second leading cause of death with similar ages. Regardless, it's tragic. People should not become a statistic.

The results show that three times as many girls attempt suicide and three times as many males actually complete the act. It's when many young people don't think straight that suicide becomes an option. Some of these teens think they have issues that cannot be helped. We have so many roads and so many obstacles in our path as teens, there were many times as a teen that I just wanted to abandon the road that I was on, but didn't know how. I couldn't even see straight as I was anemic, had impulse issues, and was dealing with hypoglycemia on a daily basis. Throw an obstacle in my path and really watch me turn circles —like a gerbil on a wheel in its cage.

To top off the statistic factor a new theory by Joiner notes that those who actually complete suicide have three things in common they are a "thwarted belonging" feeling alone, "perceived burdensomeness", and the "capability for suicide". Joiner notes that the top four candidates for completing suicide are: doctors, prostitutes, bulimics, and.......athletes. I'm not surprised as many endurance, collegiate, and professional athletes are cursed with the Type A gene, perfectionistic.

The frontal lobe, which handles executive skills like calculated planning, decision making, and sequencing, is not fully developed until 22 to 24 years of age. Young adults who suffer from ADHD may not show the frontal lobe fully developed until much later.

I was a young adult with ADHD, and I can say when this crisis arose I *did* think about suicide for a split *second*. I drove that car like a bat out of hell secretly hoping I wouldn't wake up and have to deal with the fact that my father may never love or approve of me, period. I finally realized it just wasn't going to happen in this life time. You may be surprised to find adolescents have used their vehicle to end turmoil in their life and it's never reported.

Suicide is never an option and talking with someone can help us see through the fog. Just talking with Frank's mother and knowing I had a place to live calmed my heart palpitations considerably. I felt accepted and loved there. Out of place, but welcomed. I never acted on that fleeting impulse, but the thought did flash through my mind when I was being threatened by my father and told to leave my home. If you are under the age of 18 and feel you live in such a dysfunctional home where you are not safe, talk with your school counselor or call a suicide hotline (1-800-273-8255). Go to the website: www.suicidehotlines.com to get some valuable information.

There is a solution to suicide. It's amazing all the things I have been able to see, feel, and think since that day when the thought of suicide actually crossed my mind. That day I wondered if it would be easier to make my problems just go away seems like a dream. I am confident to say that working through my problems and facing them led me to be a much wiser and stronger person. I learned so much about other people by going through that crisis. That sometimes our parents are not the people we would like them to be, but there are other options in this big world. The door to trusting others opened ever so slightly on that day when Frank's mother welcomed me into her home, *unconditionally*.

I grew up with my mother saying over and over, "You're friends won't always be there for you, but your family will." Such a lie. I believed her all those years, and when this happened I thought, "My God, my father has thrown me out, now there is no one out there for me." Not true. A note to impress upon to the reader is that **love should always be unconditional**. Even if your kid likes a Mexican, alien, someone of the same sex, you should always love them. There *is* a yellow brick road out there somewhere. As with Dorothy's journey to the Wizard of Oz, we **must be** prepared for a few distractions along that road. Don't let the Wicked Witch's forest lead you astray. The saying "this too shall pass" is so true. The pain of life does not last forever and we become stronger by working through issues and processing.

I believe God gives us challenges just to see how we will handle them and then makes us stronger by working through them with his guidance. Don't hear me wrong: God does not cause our loved ones to get cancer or die in a car accident. These are all misdoings of our society. It could be a bad diet or genes that cause cancer or reckless driving that causes an accident, but by allowing us to be in control of our own lives God gives us the strength to work through hard times.

There was a percentage a couple of years ago that showed there is a lifetime incidence of major depressive disorder in 20 percent of women and 12 percent of men (www.emedicine.medscape.com). If you are a woman, you may have a time in your life when you are going to face this disability. I spent many years with ADHD and Post Traumatic Stress Disorder and not being medicated which took a toll on my life as I was self-medicating.

A client who dealt with years of trauma told me recently after many years of therapy, "Today, I am having feelings. Little feelings that let me feel alive, and worthy to join the human race. I am no longer isolated and invisible! Feelings feel so great!"

At age 27, I finally sought help from a doctor with anti-depressants to help the pain that I dealt with for so many years. Granted, it took me a good three years to actually find the medication that worked for me and then another five years until I was given a high blood pressure medication that helped my ADHD. I do not have high blood pressure; however, this medication was a miracle for my hyperactive, impulsive, and angry personality. I tried to come off the anti-depressant on several occasions, but didn't feel balanced. I'd rather take meds and have a normal life than the alternative.

For those with ADHD and anger issues, beware of the prescription stimulants out there. Some have been known to add to anger outbursts rather than lessen them. Consult a doctor who regularly deals with ADHD, depression, and anger pharmacology. I ended up going to therapy in my late 20s, to assist the medication. Therapy does not have to be long term. I did short-term therapy and saw remarkable results. Therapy helps one find out who they are, why they think the way they do, and may reframe some misjudged calculations. It's like enlisting a travel agent to help you go where you want to go.

About my boyfriend, Frank, he received a liver transplant and was in Dallas when I went through the suicidal ideations. When I met Frank he couldn't drink alcohol as he was in a major car accident and sustained internal organ damage. After we were dating for a year, we found out he had developed Hep C after a blood transfusion. He was in need of a new liver. Both of Frank's parents worked. Frank moved to Dallas to wait for the transplant. He had no one to go with him and he was experiencing 104 degree fevers regularly with hot and cold sweats. There were even a couple of times when I saw his eyes roll back in his head. Frank's mother and I would take turns wiping down his body with cold towels and then applying alcohol all over to bring down the fever when they sprung up without warning.

I volunteered to move to Dallas in September of that year as my college semester just started and I was able to withdraw without penalty. It's not a coincidence that my father treated me even worse when I got back from Dallas. He was probably furious that I would drop out of college and move to Dallas to be with a "Mexican." I felt moving to Dallas to be with Frank was the right thing to do. It was. Frank and I met so many nice people at the Baylor medical apartments rented to those awaiting transplants. Unfortunately, around half of those people would not survive the transplant process. Many would last weeks or even months, but infections would destroy the new organ or the anti-rejection medication would not work and the body would reject the organ within a year.

I remember another young couple we befriended. They were so cute. The boy (we were all in our early 20s) had been a body builder and was literally wasting away before and after the transplant. (A thought that occurred to me is, I wonder if he contracted Hep C from sharing IV needles while juicing?) His body incurred an infection and he passed on. Frank, himself, had been up for a college football scholarship his junior year in high school, but broke his shoulder during the same game the scouts were there and ended his chances of playing college football, needless to say he was a good sized boy. Not by the time we moved to Dallas, he was yellow with jaundice and looked like an old, feeble man.

It's hard to watch someone go through life threatening issues. I got a wonderful job working for a company that did focus groups for Fortune 500 companies. Our offices were right by the Dallas Galleria and many days we had catered lunches when the "big wig" executives were in town. I gained seven pounds from eating such delightful lunches. During the day, I kept my other Florence Nightingale life secret, but during the evening I would go through the motions of providing whatever support or nurse aide I could for Frank.

There was a nurse on duty during the day at the apartments. Most days Frank spent across the street at the hospital in group therapy sessions or having blood work done prior to the transplant. We each stayed busy during the day waiting... for someone to die.

I pretended I lived in Dallas full-time and was a marketing student interested in learning the focus group field. Part of this was true, my undergrad is in marketing. I did learn a lot at the company. They just didn't know I was only going to be there for a short time. Frank finally received his transplant on December 4 that year, after moving to Dallas in early September. Three long months waiting, meeting people, watching them heal, and watching them die. Frank was in his early 20s and received his liver from a white middle-aged male after he was in a motorcycle accident.

I nursed Frank through the holidays and informed him I would be going back to school in January. I remember Frank's transplant opening, the incision. He was cut from the top of his sternum to his pubic area. The medical field doesn't sew you up; they apply large staples to the area. Frank would have yellow, slimy stuff oozing from his front side, and I would have to reapply bandages frequently. Luckily, he was under the hospital's care for a period of time prior to moving back to the apartment with me. I would spend days at work acting like I had a social life, evenings at the hospital, and then walk home alone to the apartment late at night.

Baylor Hospital is located in downtown Dallas. The area back then was the dumps with low income housing and drug deals happening everywhere. Downtown Dallas has since been revitalized and is a nicer area. However, it was very scary walking home alone in the dark and sleeping alone back then. Perhaps this is when my anxiety at night started?

Anxiety at night is something I have to deal with periodically, and it's not fun. I feel my heart beating like it's going to pop out of my body and start thinking that I'm having a heart-attack. Anxiety or panic attacks are a serious issue for some people and they can present themselves at the oddest times. Prior to or during a woman's period, during stress, during times of feeling tired, etc. Recent research shows the number one therapy tool for those stricken with anxiety is talking it out. Yes, talking. Not necessarily a pill. Another study shows talk therapy and exercise are the number one tool, not a pill. *"The art of medicine consists of keeping the patient amused, while nature heals the disease." (Voltaire)*

I continued to see Frank for about a year after he returned in April to Corpus Christi. I dated Frank a total of four years. This must have been stewing for years with my father; no wonder he treated me the way he did when I returned home. I was dating Frank while I was living under my father's roof. How dare I? My relationship with Frank was never meant to end in marriage. Frank was very set in his ways and refused to go to church with me, except the Christmas after his transplant. As mentioned his transplant was December 4. I was attending the Methodist Church just around the block from the hospital and I pleaded for Frank to go with me to the Christmas Eve service.

With permission from the transplant team and a surgical mask, Frank actually agreed to go. I hoped it would result in future church outings, but it didn't. I just could not see myself marrying a person who wasn't a Christian. He never said he wasn't a Christian, but he had an agnostic outlook on life. An agnostic does not live life loving the Lord. They have a laissez faire attitude "there maybe a God, there may not be a God" is usually the agnostic approach to life. There was very little spiritual emphasis surrounding Frank.

I wondered if he thought God had done this to him. It was when Frank was so close to death after the transplant that there appeared to be a hope of light, but it turned out to be a flicker and the candle finally went out. I tried numerous times once Frank returned to Corpus Christi to get him to attend church with me, but no success.

After meeting with my friends for lunch and discussing the issue, one of my friends said something, "You know, Dana, there's a time when you gotta s**t or get off the pot." Wow, well said. Jeanne was right. I was sitting in the bathroom reading self-help magazines for way too long in this relationship. It was hard, but I finally removed that obstacle from my journey. After the break up, there were times I would come home and Frank would be waiting for me on my porch or he would show up on my new apartment doorstep asking for the microwave he gave me two Christmases ago. I believe God put that obstacle in my path for a reason, but he also opened my eyes in so many ways.

Life was not as much about me after that relationship. I learned to put others before me. Not all others, I was still hyperactive and impulsive and when I wanted something I wanted it, which had a "me" emphasis to it. Overall, I learned to value each fleeting moment, to treat others how I wished to be treated, and don't ever take for granted that they will always be here.

I have recommended a book to friends and clients for years. The book came to me at a pivotal time in my life while I was vacationing off the coast of Mexico just outside of Belize. There was a shelf of books at the condo we were staying in. I decided to pick a smaller book to read while we were there. The book is by Paulo Coehelo who is from Brazil. The book is "The Alchemist." You have to be in an open state of mind to receive this wonderful gift—it was life changing for me. "The Alchemist" taught me to pay attention to the signs in our lives. The universe is smaller than you think.

Too many times we, with our human nature, try to take full control of our lives. The book teaches us that sometimes we just need to pay attention to the signs and maybe there is a different direction we need to consider. Maybe those obstacles in our path are there for a reason and instead of running over or through them, we need to take a different route and find what else is out there.

I was so pleased that I finally put someone else first in my life during Frank's trials and tribulations. The last I heard, he had a second transplant years ago, and I really am not sure if he is still alive. God Bless you, Frank, wherever you are, and I hope you finally gave your life to Christ. In the drug and alcohol field there is a saying that one needs a healthy detachment from the addict. If someone you know continues to bring catastrophe into your life due to their addiction, remove yourself from the situation and find a healthy detachment. Do not let the addict continue to tangle you up in their affairs of addiction. Sometimes this means going to stay with a loved one or moving out.

Just like dysfunctional relationships, I knew I had to find a healthy detachment from Frank. I could no longer feel guilty that he needed me to recover. He was at a place where he could stand on his own two feet, and our values were not the same. I was not into introjection, which is taking on someone else's belief systems or values because it is easier to think the way they think rather than create tension in the relationship. You would be surprised how many adolescents become prejudiced and introjection rules their way of life due to a parent's belief system.

Iron Nugget:

Do you think you should follow your parents rules? How about their ideals?

14   The Anger Within

"Laughter is God's soothing touch on a fevered world." (Kenneth Hildebrand)

I know growing up with an angry father, I felt angry—very angry. I was hyperactive and impulsive, so when I was feeling angry I lashed out and became aggressive. Usually my little brother was the target of my anger. He, too, was angry and it worked quite well for both of us. Unhealthy family issues still linger.

Kevin's control issues affect his relationship with his family. He showed up to visit at our house, recently, with some underlying issues we were not aware. My husband, brother, daughter, and I went out on the back porch to visit while dinner was grilling. Over a glass of wine, the conversation switched to my father. My brother asked if I had forgiven my father. I told him I had. He asked again, "No, have you really forgiven him?" I told him *again*, I felt I had. "I don't hate him; it's more sympathy at this point. How miserable it has to be to not talk to your three kids, how sad Father's Day and Christmas must be. I don't feel hate toward the man. Some anger and a lot of hurt, but not hate."

The Bible says to honor your mother and father. I try to abide by that, but it's such a fine line with my father. When I wrote the letter to him years ago it was out of frustration and lack of communication. I was trying to exercise my rights as an adult and open real communication with my father, not to dishonor him and never speak to him again. My brother went into a 30-minute conversation about how a year or so ago he looked my father up. Kevin asked my father if he could take him to breakfast, as Kevin was in town for business. My brother travels all over the state of Texas for business and lives in the Dallas area. My father lives just outside of San Antonio now.

My father agreed to meet Kevin and there was a superficial conversation that took place. My father didn't offer much, but Kevin evidently felt like he did his part by contacting my father and "forgiving" him. Eric and I listened to my brother, while my daughter messed around on her computer like most early teens do. Cami acted like she wasn't listening, but her radar ears were on. She was taking in the conversation.

Kevin continued to not hear me when he asked me several times if I had forgiven our father. Kevin apparently didn't think I had, because I had not called my father to meet with him and take him to breakfast as the he had. When I decided to go into a story of my own about childhood, my brother became angry with me. How do you feel when you let those close to you speak their mind and then they don't want to hear any of your thoughts?

I was confused. I let him share his story for more than 30 minutes, which was important to him. It was my turn to give my opinion, wasn't it? The words "agree to disagree" came to my mind. I was going to get to the moral of the story, but I didn't get a chance with my brother's frustration. I told Kevin, "This conversation obviously is not going anywhere," and walked inside to prepare the salad for dinner. I gave up. I have learned to hold my tongue when another family member may be looking for an argument. It is so easy for me to participate in their drama; I choose to not be a part of it these days. Nothing good ever came from me getting sucked into it!

Years ago, my brother and I would sit around solving our family problems over several bottles of wine. It was a family bonding or a family bitch session. I don't do this anymore as I have worked through my issues regarding the anger I had toward my father. No matter how many times I told my brother that I don't hold this animosity toward my father anymore, my brother wouldn't hear it.

Sometimes we get to a certain point in our life that we just let go of the anger within. We feel good, so we don't dwell on the issues that made us angry anymore. We become bigger than the problems. The problems don't define us. This is why I advocate running a marathon, becoming an Ironman, it will transform you._ *"You don't stop laughing because you grow old. You grow old because you stop laughing." (Michael Pritchard)*

The next thing I knew, my brother walked in after me and told me that he was leaving. I looked shocked. "Why?" Because I didn't handle the father issue the way you did? This is a perfect example of our family growing up with a lack of communication. Love is unconditional, and we should love each other through differences and all. Don't mistake this with the abusive, drug addicted person—we need to have a healthy detachment with these folks and love them from a far. However, the family member who acts or thinks a little differently than you should be loved and accepted for their opinions.

Communication needs to involve trust that each person is an individual and may have different views or opinions. My brother said to me earlier in the conversation that we grew up in the same house and things were not as bad as I portrayed them. He mentioned "It couldn't have been, I lived the same life and in the same house!" For those of you with puckered butt cheeks, lighten up, don't take life so seriously. Just chill!

This is the issue with dysfunctional families. There is usually a lack of real communication in these families and each member interprets issues differently. I am female and three and a half years older than my brother. Even though we lived in the same household, our experiences were so different. When I was in seventh grade going through puberty, he was in third grade.

Our parents were going through bankruptcy issues at this time and my brother was clueless. He didn't see the stress and turmoil in our household like I did. Not discussing childhood issues with family members may lead to anger as we age. We need to discuss past issues in a respectful manner. If you have differences with your siblings or family, take the time to respect their thoughts and feelings. You haven't walked in their shoes even if you grew up in the same house. My brother's shoe size has always been, and will always be, different than mine, plus I'd like to see him walk in *my two inch heels* for just 15 minutes!

My sister was in town a week or two after my brother stormed out. I asked her opinion, "Was there communication in our house and was I just too ADHD to notice?" Did our father communicate with her or express emotions with her? She agreed we had no communication with our father. The fact is my childhood views are mine, not my brother's. Just like your interpretation of your childhood belongs to you, not your siblings.

I was going to tell my brother that in my story I was the parentified-child growing up. A parentified-child is one who, as a child, assumes the role of a parent. Up until my brother was in the 5th grade, he slept on the floor in my room or in the room my sister and I shared. Assuming a parent role, I would prepare a chart and check off during the day if my brother had done well. "Well, you are about to get three checks for the day, and not going to be able to sleep in my room if you continue this path." He would shape up and follow my directions, usually, if he continued I'd tell him, "So sorry, you can't sleep in here tonight." I was assuming the role as parent, over-bearing parent, but parent nonetheless.

I was a little "OCD" (obsessive compulsive). I liked order and consistency because being hyper and living in a household full of disorder lead to instability in my life. I found I could make up my own world of security and made sure my siblings were included. I was the leader of my little wolf pack. The other part of my story to my brother that night was to include Cami's illness and the lack of support or concern my father displayed when our baby girl was critically ill. We even had a few touch-and-go moments. My father lived in town less than 10 miles away. I would spend days in a bubble oxygen tent with Cami. If you haven't spent 24 hours a day, over a week in the hospital with a sick loved one... you don't know what you've been missing. It was stressful and depressing. The nurses came in every hour all hours of the night.

The first part of releasing the anger came when I was changing my poor, weak baby's diaper. I had enough of living in and out of the hospital and was tired of fighting for her life. I looked up at God and yelled the worst obscene words to our Father above. After yelling at Him, I told Him I wouldn't try to control the situation anymore. That if He wanted Cami back, if she was meant to be here for a short time, I would respect His wishes. When I stopped trying to be in control......... things started to change. Miraculously.

When Cami was 5 years old, I took her to see a nutritionist, Jack Fairchild. He was another miracle for my daughter. Although she had numerous tests...cystic fibrosis, celiac, radioactive nuclear emptying of the stomach (torture), she did not test positive for celiac. Celiac is the condition where the body rejects gluten products, which, by the way, are in most of our breads, pastas, chips, etc. Jack looked at her results and noted that a lot of what the visual results looked like was a lack of tolerance for gluten.

After our appointment, we left Jack's office with some health-related products to add to Cami's routine and vowed to take her off of gluten for a period of time to see if improvement occurred. I started to feel the anger from within almost leave my body at that moment—like stepping away from traditional Western medicine was the right thing to do at that time. I say Jack was a miracle because within a matter of two months our daughter showed a HUGE improvement in asthma and stomach-related issues. One of the early tests concluded that our child had delayed emptying of the stomach—food would spill over into her lungs causing pneumonia.

Before the radio-active test on my child, our baby failed to thrive for a while. Isn't that comforting knowing the medical profession is shoving radioactive "stuff" down your child to figure out what is wrong with them? What's wrong with that picture? We found out Cami always felt full due to the food in her stomach, which was actually just sitting there and rotting. No wonder she ate like a bird and always cried.

With the lack of support from my father, I spent many days in a funk and angry. Instead of reacting to my sick baby or stressed husband, I would refrain from an angry outburst with silence by leaving the scene to go for a run. I can't tell you how this recipe improved my life, my baby's life, and my husband's life. I learned that silence is golden, and running can improve an outlook on even the most frustrating issues. "Hold your tongue and go for a run," I say.

My pastor, Ray, a young, well-spoken man, talked about forgiveness on Sunday. He said that what makes Christians different is that we forgive. I have forgiven my father, but when I tried so many times to have a relationship with him, he didn't participate. All I can do at this point is hope that someday he will return to his family like the lost sheep returned to its father. Ironic that the father is lost.

My daughter, Cami, wrote on her paper during this sermon, "Love is a way in life, find a way to live within it." Ray went on to say that there are relationships that do get torn apart by the pain of sin. My thought was that our lives and world are surrounded by sin. We don't live in an oxygen bubble like I did with Cami her first few years. Ray went on to preach, Jesus said, "How can I forgive you if you don't forgive one another?" Ray noted, "Sometimes you can forgive someone and let go, but you may never enter a relationship with that person again." I'm OK if my father never enters a relationship with me and my family. It's his choice.

People say things and later regret it, we shouldn't make a person walk the plank and leave them in shark-infested waters just for saying something flippant. That's just life. We live and learn, and like Cami said, "Love is a way in life." This includes getting over being angry at someone. My daughter followed up that sermon with "God is loving, love with him." Smart kid.

For years, the feeling of guilt, shame, and anger followed me by not having a relationship with my father, but it takes two to make a relationship work. I admit, years ago, I was angry and writing to my father, "If you continue your life the way you do, you will end up an old and very lonely man" was not the best choice of words, but his rebuttal letter said it all. *He chose* to close the door. Two wrongs obviously don't make one right. It's been more than 12 years and no one wins in this situation. In regard to my feelings of shame and guilt, Ray pointed out in church that God does not tell us to be a doormat. It is not OK for people to walk all over us.

There is a lesson learned in knowing the difference between assertiveness and aggressiveness. I used to be aggressive like my father, but when I had a child of my own something transformed inside me. The feeling of true unconditional love and patience arose. I learned that taking care of my needs and my daughter's needs included being assertive with people, not aggressive. *"By being assertive, I get things done."* "By being aggressive, I get doors slammed in my face!" And that sometimes hurts. Look the two terms up and think about it.

As my father and brother age with their cloak of anger, they should be aware that those with strong religious beliefs founded in faith will always lead a better life in an aging environment. If they are able to focus on the positive, they will be able to play down the negative. Aging is a frame of mind, if they take change in stride it will open up opportunities for them; however, if they look at change as a disruption, it will present trouble in their angry lives. Exercise will enhance one's health and benefit the aging angry person. Most important my father and brother might want to remember, "*People die the way they leave parties*". (Taken from Jim Speer's supervision group as reported by Eric Cardwell)

My sister tried to start a relationship with our father a couple of years back, but he continued to drop the ball. In fact when my nephew graduated from high school this summer, Gretchen looked up our father and asked him to Clint's graduation. My father said that it was his 16th anniversary and he had plans. He had not seen his grandson in more than 12 years, let's see, that would be prior to first grade and had plans for a 16th anniversary? I tried to be supportive for my sister, but it was hard, real hard. I wanted to tell her our father was a selfish asshole. Instead I just raised my eyebrows and smiled. I chose to take the high road on that situation.

Although no one actually makes us angry, we choose to get angry ourselves, there are some people we may know who tend to be very good at "getting our goat." Let's look at a few personality disorders to better understand the situation.

A *Borderline* friend might look like this:

> Hilda showed up at the party tipsy and continued to drink throughout the night. She laughed and flirted with the men at the party. Two of the men received an invite of deep affection from her. Several times during the party she disappeared for more than half an hour with a different man. After an angry exchange with one of the men, because he took too long to get her a drink, she locked herself in the bathroom and attempted to swallow a bottle of medicine in the host's cabinet. Her friends pleaded with her to go home, but she was afraid to be alone and stayed. (Taken from Dr. John Suler's Abnormal Psychology worksheet, no date)

Hmm... I wonder if years ago at a party a borderline threw up on her clothes, pleaded that she didn't want to be alone, and convinced a party-goer with a green Jaguar to take her to Holiday Inn where she could clean up and show him some of her deep affection while washing her clothes?

Let's look at a *Histrionic* friend:

> Tinkerbelle danced into the party immediately becoming the center of attention by sweeping her arms around and having a gallows laugh. She boasted about her new career as a marketing director in a local Fortune 500. During a whispered conversation one of her friend's asked her about the rumors that her marriage was having problems. In an angry fit Tinkerbelle denied any issues with her marriage and said it was "as wonderful and charming as ever." After the issue died down, while drinking her second glass of wine, Tinkerbelle fainted and had to be taken home. (Taken from Dr. J. Suler)

I won't go into a *Narcissistic* person because Charlie Sheen and Lindsay Lohan give really good examples of this type of personality. As a disclaimer, I am not saying these two people are Narcissistic; they just give some examples of what that type might look like. My father could fit into the narcissistic traits. I'm not claiming that he is, just that he has some of the characteristics.

A *Passive-Aggressive* person "*indirectly expresses anger by being forgetful and stubborn, procrastinates, cannot admit to feeling angry, and can be habitually late*". Think of the person who gets your goat by being sarcastic frequently and then asks, "What's wrong with *you*?" Yeah, right, with me? (Dr. J. Suler)

Many occasions I reacted aggressively and impulsively instead of thinking situations through. I needed someone to talk to and to communicate with in order to learn how to function. Children are no different; they need communication to figure out how society's wheel revolves.

Often childhood depression can look different than what it looks like in adults. With children it could be masked by hyperactivity, aggression, or absence from school. There is no single cause of depression. You could be raised in the best family and become depressed. Some factors related to depression can be a genetic component, loss of a parent, stress factors at school or work, divorce, or even physical illness. Numerous components can contribute to depression.

Some signs of depression could include: decline in school grades, withdrawing from friends and/or family, drug or alcohol use to self-medicate, breaking the law, over sleeping or lack of sleeping, overeating or lack of eating, angry outbursts, and conflict in relationships. Don't blame the depressed person—no one wants to feel like crap. By acting out in inappropriate ways, the depressed person is trying to cope with the unwanted feelings. This is why talking about it in a healthy manner helps the depressed person. Therapy and medication are a true miracle for many depressed people.

In counseling when we see an angry person who lashes out at their friends, family, co-workers we ask the person to practice expressing their feelings using "I" messages. Many times the angry person says, "*You* always do this, *you* always do that, yada, yada, yada." We tell the person to turn it around where the other person is more likely to listen. An example would be, "I'm angry right now, I can't talk to you, give me an hour to think." It's amazing what taking time to think through a situation can do for a person. Don't talk when you are extremely angry. Take time to collect your thoughts, remove yourself from the situation, and deal with it later. What medal are you going to win by dealing with it right then? None, you're most likely to lose.

Therapy can provide a place to safely express angry feelings; can identify the underlying sources of anger, can resolve old anger, and it can provide a safe environment for a person to practice expressing their anger in an effective manner.   Working in a residential treatment center with very angry youth, I tell them, "We all get angry at some time or another, but it's how we handle and express the anger that counts. Beating someone up or lashing out at others is never the answer." Many times children need physical outlets to release anger. Finding a healthy way to release anger is the key.

The roller coaster ride doesn't last forever, but I guarantee when it's over you will reflect and say, "Wow, that was one *crazy* ride." I'm so glad I didn't jump out of the seat while we were spinning 70 mph. For those of you who like amusement rides you can understand that we can't talk about the fun, scary, crazy, ride until it's over. You have to complete the whole thrill before you can reflect and tell stories about your unique ride. Take a dare, live a challenge, get out of your stuck place and get moving!

Proverbs 15:1. "A gentle answer quiets anger, but a harsh one stirs it up." I hope this is some food for your soul to think about as you venture through this crazy, hectic, angry world.

 "In times like these, it is helpful to remember that there have always been times like these." Paul Harvey

Iron Nugget:

Describe your issue with anger? Do you show anger or hold it in? Why?

15   The Taj Mahal

"The goal as a company is to have customer service that is not just the best but legendary."
Sam Walton, Founder of Wal-Mart.

Here's how my athletic journey started. I've always been a mediocre athlete. When I ran track in junior high my arches were always falling and getting locked up in cramps—so badly that the coach had to tape my arches. I would generally place 3rd in my 1 mile division, but I was never the Numero Uno, top dog.

When I played varsity tennis in high school I ended up choking at every—I mean every— tournament I played in. My brain would start over thinking my shots and the ball would end up going out of bounds. I had a mean backhand and serve and would tear up the courts during weekly practices, but come tournament day I played it safe and looked like a dork on the courts. Hesitating which way to go, lumbering around like I was a big ape without any speed at all. It was humiliating; I'd walk off the courts with another loss!

When college came around, I had to participate in events we would sponsor for the Corpus Christi Park and Recreation Aquatics Department. The CC Park and Rec hosted several duathlons throughout the year. The event always had a 5 Kilometer (5K) run in it with a mile or half mile swim. A racer would do the swim part first then get out, put their shorts and shoes on and run the 5K. One race you swam a half mile, ran the 5K, and then swam another half mile. It was hosted in a pool, all of us who worked there were lifeguards. If anyone had safety issues during the second swim there was always a certified lifeguard around who knew CPR and first aid.

I hated the 5K race at first. Really hated them. I loved to swim, but hated the run part. In fact, the first event we hosted, a co-worker who was a bulky, football-player type said, "Hey, let's cut this corner" when we were on the 5K part." Now the part we cut off wasn't really much, but we did it nonetheless. I did mention the hate associated with running? What I discovered is I really enjoyed running with someone. It was interesting talking and telling stories. I ended up starting to actually like the run part once a co-worker, who was an older bad ass triathlete, taught me how to breathe when I ran.

And did I score? Yep, I took home so many first place plaques and trophies it was embarrassing. I had them displayed on my bookshelf in my apartment, and everyone who entered thought I was "the bomb." It wasn't until I told them I took first place in my age division, because I was the only 20-to-25-year-old female who raced in those particular races, which I noticed the bomb failed to ignite.

We all had a good laugh. More than one friend told me, "Well, you did it and that's the amazing part. I wouldn't tell people no one was in your age group." They had a point, I did it. Obviously other collegiate friends weren't "hanging" back then, so it somehow did boost my confidence and athleticism. Those little reminders on my shelf started my path down the road to becoming an Ironman. Who knew? I sure didn't.

I learned a life-long lesson while working at the Park and Rec. My direct supervisor, Mr. Jim Kelsey, was Assistant Director of Aquatics for the city and was an old timer to the Aquatics

Department. He was in his late 60s and had coached so many swim teams in "the day" that he was respected city wide.

The rest of us just knew him as kind Mr. Kelsey who carried a pair of readers and a separate pair of distance glasses with him everywhere he went. He would always end up leaving a pair of readers at one of the pools and when I made a stop, I would pick up his left-behind glasses for him. He must have owned at least five pairs of each set.

We all loved Mr. Kelsey, but he refused to learn how to use a computer and would keep all stats on yellow pads. Not only did he leave his glasses everywhere, but he might leave one of his trusty yellow notepads behind and both were very important. He reminded us of the absent-minded professor. During the fall program, I was required to help run the one pool that stayed open year round and was heated in the city—Collier Pool. I would lifeguard for the lap swimmers. As a supervisor, part of me just did the lifeguard duties in robot form, I came, I worked, and I left. How many lap swimmers actually need to be saved? Really?

I thought of the presentations I was going to do that week...my mind was everywhere but there. My major was marketing, and I had implemented a marketing program for the city pools where I went to all of the local schools and gave water safety presentations. I became famous around town to the local kids. "Hey, guys, there she is! She must have Gus and Goldie with her!!" Gus and Goldie were life-sized animated mascots who represented the city's aquatic department.

The year I implemented the local presentations the city went from losing 10 percent per year in swim lesson participants to 25 percent. My title was swim lesson coordinator, and my job revolved around the swim lesson program: marketing it, improving it, supervising water safety instructors, etc. My mind was constantly on my marketing program, even when I was working at the pool watching a handful of people swim their daily laps. That part was boring. Watching people swim back and forth is not very entertaining.

I guess Mr. Kelsey noticed my lack of enthusiasm at the pool one day when he arrived, and he had a little talk with me. Kelsey went on to say how "we" wanted people who worked at Collier to make the year-round lap swimmers feel like they were arriving at the Taj Mahal or the local country club. He suggested we extend our hand in a handshake to the lap swimmers, say "Hello," and ask them how they are doing. I took instruction well and started doing what he said. This is the part where I see today that 90 percent of managers in the U.S. fall short, real short, on their jobs regarding teaching customer service to employees. I got to know these people! Just by saying "hello," first and extending a hand they went from walking in with a blank look on their face to a smile and conversation. They had more pep in their walk and my own self-esteem and outlook improved. I made them feel important which somehow bounced back on me and made me feel good. KARMA!

Mr. Kelsey was a genius in that Mr. Magoo exterior. He knew what the meaning of life was. To treat others like they are at the country club or the Taj Mahal and it will domino. Not only will that person pass on the feeling, but it will bounce back on the giver to make them feel good too. The Japanese company, Uniqlo, is a similar genius. The product? Nothing special, basic clothing, but it's the customer service and attention to detail that is getting this company propelled to the world market. Not only does the owner know how to make people feel good, but he has a purpose, a goal. The company's aim is to be the world's largest specialty-store, private-label apparel by 2020! Most of you haven't even seen the product, but I make a prediction that you will in the next five years. With drive, passion, a good outlook, and a goal, you can complete an Ironman or even become a world leader. What are you waiting for?

And boy did Kelsey have wisdom. Two of the remarkable relationships I made were with Don Winkley and Tom Hetzel. Don can be found on the web as a member of Transe Gaule an ultra running group who runs across France yearly, the Big Bend 50 miler ultra, and as the 2011 winner of King of the Road 500k race on www.runitfoot.com. Yes, that is a 314 mile race if you did the math which he won in 2011 that starts in Missouri and ends in TN, it only took him 5 days and 14 hours. I used to watch Don run in the pool for hours training for his ultra runs. I was in awe of this guy.

The other man, Tom Hetzel, became a friend. Tom died in October 2011 and was inducted years ago in the Swimmer's Hall of Fame. Tom was a retired New York City police officer and criminal justice professor at Del Mar college in Corpus Christi. I would join Tom at Masters swim practice with pizza and beer a couple of times, but they were the 30s-40s-50s set. I was in my 20s hyper and care-free.

Tom was a legend in Corpus Christi for his 8 crossings of the English Channel. He was one of Diana Nyad's coaches in the day and inducted in the National Marathon Swimming Hall of Fame in 1980. He set 3 new records years ago. Tom would swim laps for hours at the pool and he and I had many long philosophical talks, which I thoroughly enjoyed his NY and Irish accent. He can be found on www.openwaterpedia.com. Tom used to ask me out to the movies occasionally, but I declined due to our age difference. I couldn't figure out if he wanted to go on a date or just hang as friends. Regardless, I kept it professional just to be on the safe side. I enjoyed our friendship and didn't want to muddy the waters.

Iron Nugget: What do you do when you are….

Stressed, angry, sad, confused? Try going for a run with friends or alone. It helps.

16   Primal Instincts

"It is not the strongest of the species that survives, nor the most intelligent, but the one most responsive to change." Charles Darwin

I used to workout at the YMCA off Ocean Drive and jog three miles along the sea wall almost every day when I lived in Corpus.   Corpus Christi may be warm and humid, but the wind's always blowing, like Chicago, just hotter. The wind makes the temperature feel a little cooler.   I loved Ocean Drive so much that I got a run-down apartment on the shore during my first teaching job. It was 70's psychedelic with shag carpet and linoleum floors. The place was old and falling down, but I was living amongst million-dollar homes and able to ride my bike up and down Ocean Drive on the weekends. I had a car and didn't know mountable bike racks existed back then, so I usually rode my bike from where I lived. It was my dream to be able to ride up and down Ocean Drive at my leisure.

Many Saturdays I would wake up with my little "peaky boo" view I had of the ocean, drink my coffee on the front porch trying to see past the other decrepit apartments in front of me, then get on my bike and just ride up and down Ocean Drive No worries; life was good. I had a job, a car, a falling down place to live, and Ocean Drive! I started getting courageous after a while and ventured up Ocean Drive through town to my parents' home about eight miles away. It was a 16-mile round trip, which is nothing these days, but when you are on a Wal-Mart can't-go-any-faster bike and going through dangerous traffic, things can get a little haired. Little did I know the danger was lurking just around my parents' home?

Those of us who ride bikes are always aware of cars, which can create danger. Being young and ready to conquer the world, we don't always think of the other dangers around us. It must have been summer as I remember it being really hot and I had probably slowed down from my 10 mph pace to 5 mph (that's really slow by the way). I was concentrating on just getting to my parents' home to drink a cold glass of water. I cruised along the neighborhood just three blocks from my destination. A black mustang started tagging along side of me. I thought "I'm not in your way, just go ahead and pass me." After he stayed right next to me for a few minutes, I finally looked over at him to give him a "go somewhere" look. Man, oh man!

This guy, in a mechanic's shirt—button down short sleeved white with blue or grey pin strips and an embroidered name tag on the opposite side (I couldn't see the name)—was looking over at me with his pants pulled down and a large member of his family hanging out in salute form. Yep, full attention, being massaged while he looked over at me.

I was in total shock and at first gave a funny "Eeeeuuwww that's disgusting" look along with an afraid look and then... the primal impulsive instinct in me took off. I yelled obscene words at him and started chasing his car like I was gonna drag him out of it and slap the "you know what" out of him. As he floored the car, I was looking quite the crazy woman with my arm up in the air trying to get his license plate number, yelling, and doing my own salute with my powerful middle finger. I got all of his numbers except for one. When I realized he was out of view and gone, I back tracked to my parents' house and called the police immediately to report him with the license numbers I had. The Corpus Christi police said they would dispatch an officer to the area and call me if they found him.

I never got a call. Darn, I was looking forward to showing him who was the boss. I had visions of slapping him, if needed! After my rape experience, I became one of those women with the attitude, "I ain't gonna take s**t from no man." It really was not a healthy attitude, and it wasn't until I met my wonderful husband that things started to change for me.

I met my husband my first year of teaching in the ghetto. I had a face full of sandwich in my mouth when he came to tell me about his counseling services during my lunch break. He was making house, uh... school calls. Little did I know my ex-sister in law put him up to meeting me? A blind referral you could say. The rest is history.

My husband had quite a lot to put up with in the first few years of our relationship, but he's a trooper and made it through the roller coaster ride. As for my living arrangements, the shag carpet and linoleum grew old really fast, and I only lived on Ocean Drive for a short time, but the memories will last forever. When we first married, Eric and I moved to San Antonio. We liked visiting San Antonio more than we did living there, so we moved an hour down the road to the Hill Country. I thought the Hill Country would be a perfect place to start my athletic pursuits with the Guadalupe River running through the town. The problem is there was nowhere to jog alongside the river expect for a little bitty area. I became depressed and then finally put my big girl panties on and decided to get active, again.

For those of you who are not active at the moment, I know it's hard to start a routine, but once you give it a chance and stick with it, amazing results will follow. I didn't really have any friends the first year in the Hill Country, and when I decided to get active it was amazing how many friends I met. My husband was a state-ranked tennis player and became involved with a big tennis group here. I used to laugh and say all those rich people only let us in their clique because Eric was such a good player and provided a challenge to them. Regardless, we became involved with tennis, tournaments, and parties.

Life became interesting again when I started playing doubles with Rachel. My husband played singles and doubles, and Stan was his doubles partner. Stan, and his wife Rachel (my doubles partner) had money and an unusual relationship. Rachel would not take Stan's last name—not even hyphenate it.

Stan had an airplane. Eric and Stan would fly all over Texas playing in tennis tournaments and eventually became ranked No. 2 in their division. Eric also was ranked in the top five for singles. Many weekends Eric would play tennis tournaments and get sick from becoming dehydrated on the courts, not drinking enough liquid, and getting overheated. This type of athleticism would lead to another venture down the road.

One weekend, Stan was in an airplane crash that I knew had divine intervention. Stan told us how the propeller just came off of his plane and his plane started going down, the wings clipped a telephone pole, rolled, and then headed for a concrete embankment. Stan said he knew he was a "goner" when he saw that he was going to crash into all the concrete directly in front of him, when all of a sudden the nose of the plane pointed up and missed the head-on crash. The plane came to a rest with the nose up and over the embankment. I told Stan he might want to start attending church with his wife as God just saved him for some reason or another.

Stan said, "No, it just means that I'm like a cat and have eight more lives left." I was shocked and immediately blurted out, "I think I'll move away from you now, cause I know lightning is about to strike right here where you are sitting for saying that." I was shocked that this guy didn't think God had some divine intervention here. As Stan is a very smart and interesting man, he's just a little odd like his wife. We never had real conversations. Things were not really copasetic in that relationship. Where was the excitement and fun? I was looking for a fun and athletic outlet.

So I started hanging out more with a different, eclectic group of tennis players. We started out really challenging ourselves in the tennis arena, and then it turned into a Wednesday night drinking bash. It was weird, I was in church on Sunday, and even active in teaching a children's learning program, but getting drunk and playing crazy tennis once a week.

I say crazy tennis as some of the women had been married for quite some time and were going through the cougar period. Some of the men were my age and were in their late 20s or early 30s while most of the women were in their early 40s and just looking to stay fit and have some fun, if you get my point. One of my friends started flirting with a guy who adored women. This guy had been in a relationship, but was known around town as a ladies man. My friend obviously was developing a crush on this guy and I thought it was just a fling that would pass.

Many Wednesdays consisted of tennis and a lot of alcohol. On one night of drinking, my friend asked if I would join her and Mr. Ladies Man in a threesome. I was not into threesomes nor the Ladies Man for that matter, so I declined and backed away from tennis at that moment. Besides, it took at least two people to get a tennis match going, and I was ready to do something that didn't depend on others. I needed a break to be by myself—to just BE.

After my tennis career died down, I decided to start running again. I entered so many 5K races that I contemplated getting a second job to support my entry fees. As a lone runner, I'm really slow and ADHD. I start looking at the scenery and forget I need to focus on my pace. By participating in 5Ks on the weekend, I actually did a little speed work. Who wants to come in last? So I'd try to pass people in front of me. I started with the 70-year-old grandma that obviously ran a lot.

Those early running days were humiliating. You would think I had never gotten up off the couch before, but I continued to find the 5K races challenging and increased my endurance and decreased my time. On trips to the store I started picking up running magazines to get pointers on running form, along with health-related information. Besides running magazines, I started reading Prevention and looked forward to my nightly bath soaks in Epsom salts and reading. I was getting healthier by the day and my extra weight was starting to come off.

When you start any workout program you must remember, recovery is a very important part of your training. Don't, for one minute, forget that sleep, nutrition, and proper hydration is not as important as the exercise itself. It is and the lack of it on my journey played a big part in my successes or failures. Training is a breakdown of your muscles to later build them up. An athlete must take time to rebuild these muscles through sleep and a healthy diet.

I needed a bigger challenge, so I worked up to the Capital of Texas 10K in Austin and did this event for a few years with my weekly 5Ks. Exercise became my drug, and I needed more—it was a primal instinct. The only thing that made sense was to run a half marathon. My husband and I started training for our first half marathon in 2002. The San Antonio half marathon, now called the Rock'n'Roll Marathon and half marathon. The half marathon was challenging, but a piece of cake. I had a challenge before me… the long-distance events!

Years ago, during my duatlhon days, while working for the CC Park and Recreation, I came up with a dream list. There were only two things on the life accomplishment list, and one was running a marathon. I heard stories of those who complete a marathon crapping or peeing all over themselves, so I thought "Man that must be a hard-core race." I had fear and an excitement of maybe, just maybe, someday actually doing a marathon, but I obviously didn't want to be one who had poop dripping down my leg as I came across the finish line with thousands of people cheering for me. Not a visual image I wanted to think about. In fact, it was downright scary. The 26.2 miles must be so hard on the body that the extreme athletes don't even realize they just pooped in their pants. Why would anyone subject themselves to that sort of crap?

Viva La San Antonio! Running the SA marathon. The Alamo is in the back.

Dana, Kevin, and Janelle at the Dallas 9-mile Hot Chocolate Race.

Iron Nugget:

What challenge do you need to wake you up?

Is your life like static cling or exciting? Explain.

What does your weekend look like? What do you do?

17   You Are What You Eat

Endurance athletes may benefit from branched chain-amino acid supplements, which may provide another fuel source to sustain activity. (American Dietetic Association)

Your first long run, like a half marathon, tends to be a practice run. You just do a "hit or miss" plan and then learn from the mistakes and decide to improve on your next event. I did this after my first half marathon. I wasn't even sure if I could run 13.1 miles without stopping, so there wasn't much of a plan. Let's talk about nutrition which is crucial—I mean, so crucial—to any long-distance athlete.

First, an athlete must focus on quality of their food when training. You can't eat carbs like pizza and spaghetti all the time with no fruit and vegetables. If you need to shed a few pounds to get yourself in gear, I have a wonderful short-term program you can utilize for six weeks to get you on your way. This plan has to be credited to my buddy, Jose Flores, who owns True Fit Training, and is from Venezuela.

If you aren't concerned about pounds coming off then you need to add plenty of fruits and veggies to your plan. Focus on at least one fruit and one veggie with each meal, and then use a fruit or veggie as a mid-morning snack and a late-evening snack. Your snacks can be packaged to go with you to school or work. A good snack example: celery or carrot sticks with portable peanut butter disposables, an apple, pear, banana, clementine's (they don't have seeds), almonds, peanuts, etc. These items need to be consumed on a regular basis to start fueling the body. It's like a person quitting smoking, the effects of quitting are not seen right away, it's going to take a while for all that smoke damage to repair itself.

The same thing with athletes—a good nutrition plan takes a while to show benefits in the body. You need at least a good three months under your belt for these nutrients to improve your performance. Like a pregnant woman who is eating for two, you are eating for an event, for your body to be this fine oiled machine to be able to perform the way you'd like. The Tin Man on the "Wizard of Oz" didn't function well without oil, and you don't either.

I'm not saying don't eat birthday cake or the occasional pancake for breakfast, but add the fruits and veggies when you do consume these products. Just know if you eat cake and pancakes daily, it will hinder your performance no matter what you do. I'm not talking about athletics; I'm just talking about life in general. There's not a coincidence that 65 percent of the American population is overweight. We consume way too many nutrient-dense foods daily. We stop at fast food chains for lunch, sit-down restaurants for dinner, and drink sugary beverages all day. And on that note, if God didn't make it, it wasn't intended for you to consume.

Too many of our food products these days contain GMOs, which are "a genetically-modified organism whose genetic material has been altered." (www.wikepedia.com) Please, check out the website www.takepart.com/foodinc, which advocates for your food safety. A recent article talked about the proof related to GMOs causing tumors, organ damage, and premature death in rats. The documentary "**FOOD, INC.**" is one that every smart American should view. If you consider yourself one of the many idiots in society, by all means, keep doing as you're doing.

This muscle-head at the gym the other day was bragging to one of his buddy's about how to lift weights and workout, "properly." How you can get the most benefit isolating the muscle doing the preacher curl while sitting and not standing as it puts pressure on the shoulder joints. OK, fair enough. However, dude had this large pot belly that repulsed me when I saw him lift his arms up. Then muscle-head tells his buddy how Fast Food Joint Number 77 has a sale on some sort of crappy burger, he orders two by the way, but "stays away from the fries." Seriously? You're actually giving advice, muscle-head, about working out and you eat and look like that? Yes, you have big arms, strong legs, and defined calves, but have you taken a good look in the mirror? You sir, are part of the 65 percent obese even though you have muscles! You are what you eat!

Pay attention to your running log, as many people think because they are exercising more they can consume more calories (eat more). These people end up gaining weight while training for long-distance races, not losing it. Fuel up accordingly. Don't add an extra burden on yourself by becoming frustrated and gaining weight! It is so important that you drink plenty of fluids. Try drinking a glass of water prior to training, drink during training, and then a glass of water within an hour after training. If you have had a long run or bike ride consume some chocolate milk, the protein and sugar are great for muscle recovery.

You may not feel thirsty, but more athletes suffer during training or after by becoming dehydrated and not knowing it. There is such a thing as drinking too much water, so don't just drink 64 ounces at a time in several different settings. I will discuss hyponotremia a little later as it's a horrible experience. Consume a lot of low-glycemic foods. A glycemic index isn't a diet per say, but a way of eating for optimal health. As an athlete with hypoglycemia, I have to really pay attention to what I consume. Too much high GI foods and I'm crashing and burning later on.

Pick low-to-moderate GI foods which are wholesome and healthy. Foods with a high GI cause the pancreas to secrete too much insulin. Excess insulin will cause your body to store fat and prevent it from burning fat. It can lead to high cholesterol (the bad type) and diabetes when consumed in excess. (www.panam.edu)

Here are some Low GI foods: Beans, Cheese, Cherries, Chickpeas, Egg Plant, Eggs Cauliflower, Grapefruit, Lentils, Green Veggies, Meats, Nuts, Olives, Onions, Peaches, Peppers, Peanut Butter, Plums, Radishes, Soy, Beans Peas, Sugar-free yogurt, Barley, Tomatoes, Rye Bread.

Moderate GI foods: Bran cereal, Grapes, Pita Bread, Vermicelli , Apples, Angel hair pasta, Brown rice, Buckwheat, Kiwi, Pears, New potatoes, boiled, Shredded Wheat, Grains, Sweet Potatoes, Yellow Squash.

High GI foods: Processed breads, Sugary juices, Corn products, Liquor, Muselix, Cream of wheat, Pineapple, Pasta, Crackers, Pretzels, Chips, Ice cream. *Anything with sugar, glucose, fructose, white flour, white rice.*

Now you are supplied with your arsenal to go out and become a super hero. You can have rock-hard abs and kill the long-distance race with the right artillery. If you feel you need to carb load, remember, because I learned the hard way, that you need to carb load three to five days out of a race. Not the night before.

The night before will leave you full of poop and not able to crap on race morning. As my friend Bella says, "Thank you Lord for giving me my morning blessing!" Everyone needs a morning blessing prior to a race, even a 5K. Eat correctly the night before and you will have that blessing in the morning. Bella's a blessing herself—no, not in that way. She is this 4-foot, 10-inch powerhouse full of energy and a heart of gold. The Energizer Bunny on Red Bull and Pop Rocks!

I usually eat salmon or fish the night before a race with broccoli or salad. When you are out of town prior to long distance races you can always find a restaurant that serves fish and salads or veggies. Don't feel you have to eat meat, vegan diets rock! Substitute meat with other protein like tofu.

Are you severely overweight and need to drop a few pounds prior to thinking about doing a long-distance race? For the price of this book you are getting a lot more. A new body could be lurking around the bend. I learned about this diet, which I modified, from Jose Flores, certified personal trainer and avid Ironman athlete. Although I'm a personal trainer, I have hired Jose Flores on numerous occasions to get me to race definition. When I first hired Jose in 2005, I was 12 pounds over my normal weight and could not lose the fat from the weight I gained with my daughter. When I was pregnant with my daughter, I thought I could literally eat for two. The mistake I made was adding all the processed sugary crap.

My daughter popped out at 6.2 pounds, while my backside and stomach popped out at 68 pounds! I kid you not. It wasn't until two weeks prior to my daughter's birth that my doc said, "Ummm, Dana, you might want to start watching your weight now." I wanted to slap him. During my pregnancy, I had been asking all along if I was gaining too much weight. Doc never said I was until two weeks prior to that bowling ball dropping. Little did I know the bowling ball wasn't heavy at all, it was my rear end.

People who knew me socially had no idea I was pregnant. They just thought I was gaining some serious weight. My rear really did stick out more than my stomach. I looked like a rap star's girlfriend with blonde hair and bad skin. Pregnancy did not look good on me. AT ALL!! I was moody all the time, my skin developed acne and a lot of dark spots on my face, and I had a body that never ended. Not in a good way, mind you!

Five years after Cami was born, the dreaded 10 to 13 pounds were still there in my rear and thighs. I am blessed, as I never developed stretch marks on my stomach because it really didn't expand much. It's the upper thighs and butt that could regain the elasticity and lose the stretch marks. Besides working out, which I was doing a lot of, Jose put me on a diet. That's a bad four letter word to me, so I tell my clients, "It's a way of eating." First, the C.Y.A. disclaimers, if you are under medical care always consult your doctor prior to adding a workout regimen and a new way of eating.

A New Way of Eating:

Breakfast: 2 eggs or egg whites, a piece of high fiber toast, whole grain bran cereal w/ skim milk

OR Oatmeal w/ high fiber and less than 10g sugar, piece of fruit, skim milk.

Lunch: Peanut butter sandwich w/ high fiber bread (no jelly or only sugar free jelly), apple/pear, low fat yogurt w/ less than 10g sugar, water or skim milk

OR tuna fish sandwich w/ hi fi bread, apple/pear, string cheese, water or skim milk

Vegetarians can have a wholesome grilled cheese sandwich with a protein shake and an apple/pear. I love the spicy vegan cheese and Ezekiel sprouted bread.

Dinner: Skinless chicken, broccoli, salad w/ red pepper, sunflower seeds, onions, strawberries.

OR a piece of fish w/ peas, beans and/or a salad. (Broccoli and peas can be interchanged).

(If you want to opt out of a meat you can substitute black beans or pinto or kidney beans, but no refried beans which have lard that sticks to your ass. A black bean veggie burger without the bread will suffice, also)

Snacks: Almonds, string cheese (1), celery with peanut butter, jello's sugar free pudding w/ skim milk (1/2 cup not the whole box).

Sounds easy, doesn't it? Here's the challenge: This is what you eat for five to six weeks. Yep, that's the plan, the same stuff daily. It's amazing though! It really works. I was down to my pre-pregnancy size and weight in 6 weeks and I did it on a healthy protein diet, not the one where you eliminate all your fruits. This one really does work and if you like a glass of wine with friends like I do. I allowed myself one glass of wine once a week when celebrating with friends.

Like I tell clients, quite sniveling, it's only for six weeks. You can do this for such a short time. Once the weight is down, you will realize what your body needs and craves. It's getting the processed crap out of your system that takes time. Do the full 6 weeks and look at your new sexy curves. Just think, it only cost you the price of this book. That's far cheaper than hiring me or Jose as your trainer for an hour.

After your six weeks of eating the same stuff, you can add some variety back into your diet, but you want to focus on your moderate-to-low GI foods. If you have a sweet tooth, buy some of those small pieces of dark chocolate with a high cocoa ratio. I eat a pre-wrapped small square a few nights a week to go with my one glass of wine. Relax, you are working out. You need to enjoy, just don't over-indulge.

Be careful on listening to advertisements about all these miracle supplements. I used to take too many supplements and suffered as a result. These days, I wake up in the morning with a full glass of water and an Emergen-C packet. Next, the morning coffee, then a protein shake with a banana or some oatmeal or eggs and toast. As of press, I'm experimenting with the Primal way of eating and loving it. Look up Mark Sisson's Primal Diet. Cavemen are sexy!

Get plenty of sleep to keep yourself at an appropriate weight and fit as an athlete. Many who sleep less than seven hours a night generally suffer. It is important to aim for seven to eight hours of sleep on a consistent basis to look and feel sexy. If you don't want your sexy back, by all means, stay out all night and look like 65 percent of the rest of the Americans. While I'm on a roll, it just amazes me all the people who drink diet drinks and look like a fat cow. Can't you tell that diet soda is doing absolutely nothing to keep the junk out of your trunk?

Look up the side effects of aspartame and you might find the following: memory loss, migraines, reproductive disorders, mental confusion, joint pain, bloating, nervous system disorders, hair loss, food cravings, and the almighty weight gain. People, this is a million-dollar industry. It pays off your politicians, lobbyists, etc. Don't think it has your best interest at heart. It's all about the American dream—making money. Other soft drinks contain phenylalanine which has side effects of depression and paranoia.

Consume things God made, not synthetic (man-made) products. Look up the benefits of coffee and it's made by God. I'm not talking about the Grande mocha latte either which is equivalent to eating two candy bars in one sitting. Who does that? Who drives up and says, "Yes, I'd like to order two Snicker bars?" They don't, but that's how many calories you are consuming in your sugary latte.

But me, at my age? I'd rather look like a woman from Paris than Paris, Texas. No offense, but there are a hell of a lot more sexy women in Paris, France than in Paris, Texas. We have beautiful, sexy women here in Texas, but we also have a lot of cattle. Texas is not known for its supply of beef for no reason at all.

Figure 2 Janelle and me - 2nd place in the Cancun Half-Ironman relay. I turned 40 on this day!

My morning program for the last few years consists of a smoothie with half a banana, flax seed, chia seed, spirulina, liquid egg whites, low fat milk, and amino acid protein powder. Amino acids are essential for athletes, as they are the building blocks of protein. They serve a role in metabolism, hormone regulation, muscle repair, O2 movement through the body, immune support, cardio vascular health, mood elevator, and sooo much more. *Livestrong.com notes, "If you don't eat enough protein, your muscles will degrade and grow weaker, and your training won't progress. The American Dietetic Association says that endurance athletes may benefit from branched chain-amino acid supplements, which may provide another fuel source to sustain activity."* I wouldn't be able to do what I do at my age if it weren't for my smoothies!

Iron Nugget:

Describe what you ate all day yesterday and the day before?

What do you normally eat and drink on the weekend?

Do you think you eat what many would call a healthy diet?

18   DOING A 5K COULD SAVE A LIFE!

If you want to stick with 5Ks, stay in shape, and meet local people, this is a great goal. You can meet so many local people when you do a 5K. It is such a social experience. There are so many different types of people who show up to run 5Ks. I wrote a journal entry last spring talking about our local diversity.

Here is the entry:

> The weekend started off early, very early for a non-morning person. What started out to be three girls headed out to "chick-ya", turned out to be just two. The other "chick-ya" girl ended up being on call for the weekend. For the non-athlete let me define the term "chicking ya"—it is when a chick passes a male in a race. That is called "being chicked." As athletes, we like to "chick-ya." My girlfriends are much faster at "chicking-ya" than I am, but none the less, I too, take great pride in "chicking-ya" during a race.
>
> The first race I did for the weekend was on Saturday. The UTSA 5K Diploma Dash had a record turnout. It was quite cold and many of us were bundled up. I started off the race feeling strong with visions of taking Ichabod Crane's wife over. She was very tall and lanky. One quarter into the race, I thought, "Surely I can overcome this tall, lanky runner. She has no form and is staggering all over the place." NOT! I couldn't catch Ms. Crane. She had no form, but a good pace. I ended up with a time of 26:11. One to two minutes slower than my normal time, but oh well. A friend with me did win 3rd place in her age division with a time of 22:46. She did a great job for such a big race.
>
> Day two of the weekend consisted of an afternoon race. The Harper 5K sees a lot of local runners out and about looking to have fun and take home some hardware (a medal). There's the local man in his late seventies, Ed, who loves to look at the ladies. He has run more races than he probably can even count. Ed was at the UTSA 5K race the day prior. Then there is local favorite, Rob, who is in his 70s and also competes in triathlons. Rob loves life and runs regularly down Holdsworth Drive with his trusty golden retriever. The local favorite, Tara, showed-up with her husband, ex-mayor, Todd on her arm and their youngsters to boot. Tara won her age division, as usual.
>
> Janelle was the race director, and amazingly won the overall women's division. I think Janelle runs the Harper course daily just to make the rest of us look bad on race day. Memory is a remarkable woman who has overcome years of obesity to shed the extra layers and become a true competitor. Memory can't

outrun me, yet, but she sure as hell can out bike me. Memory has lost more than 100 pounds and sparkles with a twinkle in her eye. She is the example of a positive athlete and doesn't focus on what she can't do but what she can do. More of us should strive to be like Memory. She decided to become a personal trainer to help others who are obese and feeling isolated. Look her up on Facebook, Living the Transformed Life.

Real Estate mogul, Steven D, was there. He passed me and we ran neck-and-neck for quite a while until all those P90X workouts came to his advantage and he just kept going on past me. Good job, Steven. His lovely wife was behind us taking advantage of girl talk on the race course. As an athlete, we notice those in our direct competitive path and those who just show-up to have fun. I try to do both, but have a hard time not trying to chick people like Steven. Oh well, no chick'n Steve during that race.

The McKinney run group outside of Dallas is a wonderful example of a running group who has a fun, social running club. A running high could change the path at-risk kids are on; we should have more running groups in cities.

Kathleen , Robert Earl's wife, is improving in her 5K race time. I tend to be faster than her at the moment, but she is gaining on me. It's only a matter of time until she leaves me in the dust, too. She ran with the local Barista from Starbucks. Andy, Mr. Barista, did very well and placed for his first competitive run. Andy has long hair with a never-ending smile on his face and doesn't really look the athletic type.

Terry is an old hippy. He wears Hawaiian beads around his neck, a pony tail, and rides an old bike. Terry told me he wanted to enter the race, but had not trained. He said he showed up to "check it out." I hope he trades his steel toed boots for running shoes before he races. Go, Terry!

Melissa and James own the local Mattress World and have an adorable 5-month-old baby girl, Macy. This Iron chick just loves a man running with a baby stroller. James is such a doll that he let his lovely wife, Melissa, run while he ran the whole 5K with a baby in a stroller. God blesses a devoted father and husband. James even won 2nd place in his age division. Go men with baby strollers. To top it off, Melissa placed in her age division, too. The family looked like true royalty with their beautiful baby and medals around their neck. Go team Mattress World!

Then there was my twin, Kathy. A friend, Peter, last year went up to Kathy and asked about her recent bike ride and how Ironman training was going. Funny thing? Kathy does ride bikes, but she was confused about the Ironman part. She looked at Peter with a question in her eye and then Peter made eye contact. Uh-oh! He realized it was not me. I'll take the compliment, though. My twin smoked me this year. I despise people who get faster, while I seem to get slower each year.

Peter is an avid cyclist and retired to the Hill Country from Houston to take advantage of our beautiful view of the stars, not kidding, you should see his observatory. He lives with his lovely wife, Tess, who ceases to age! Tess' skin looks like a baby's butt, and her blue eyes accentuate her smooth skin. I'm not so lucky, myself.

The True Fit groupies were with Jose Flores who rocked the men's division with his fast kick and little smirk as he ran up in the front with the hardcore teenagers. Jose always has this little grin on his face like he just stole cookies from the Girl Scouts. Jose had smoke blowing out of his britches this year. His groupies change each year. I love seeing them each year as Jose inspires new people to the field of health and awareness.

Team Schmerbeck of Garrett Insurance took home hardware this year. Stephen placed in his division, while daughter Jordan ran with me until the 1.5 mile marker. Jordan had a hard kick. Brothers, Caleb and Joshua were in front of the pack somewhere. That Schmerbeck family has some athletic capabilities. Mom Carrie used to race, but she sticks to jewelry these days and is good at doing the Silpada thing.

The race day turned out to be gorgeous. On the way home, in the middle of the road, was another gorgeous sight. It was a beautiful Golden Cheek Warbler bird. I barely missed the injured song bird with my car, and immediately stopped. As I got out, an 18-wheeler was speeding down Harper Road. The massive truck missed the bird and I ran into the road to save the helpless little creature. I scooped him up in my hands. He still showed signs of life. I drove him a couple of miles away from the road to release him to safety. Fly, little thing, fly. You never know when doing a 5K could save a life, do you?

Iron Nugget:

How many 5Ks have you competed in?

Why or why not?

Have you competed in more than a 5K?

How many races do you think you can do a year?

19   Enduro Who?

"To give anything less than your best is to sacrifice the gift." (Steve Prefontaine)

A year ago when one of my friends called me an athlete, I corrected her saying, "I'm by no means an athlete. Have you looked at my race times?" She quickly pointed out all my accomplishments and all the races I have done. Unfortunately, I didn't take ownership of the title athlete. This was so wrong; I earned that *athlete* title years ago when I worked for the park and recreation doing 5Ks and duathlons. You too can become an athlete. You don't have to become an Iron Chick to join the *Athlete Club*. There are many different clubs to be a part of, just pick the right one that fits for you. Stay on the couch all day and you don't earn the title.

Let me tell you how the Athlete Club scene works. I'm going to start the road to Ironman off now when in 2009 I didn't even know I was going to become an elite member of the Athletic Club.

Let's go back to my story at the beginning of this book.... Where I left off with my ride to Ironman.

Why do I compete through horrible temperatures and push my body through excruciating pain? Because I can. Because I don't take for granted one hellish moment that other people can't do what I do, don't have the legs to propel them forward or the disease-free body like I have. Hell yes, I have problems. Hypoglycemia, ADHD, PTSD, and hypothyroidism. I take an anti-depressant, diuretic which helps my ADHD, and Synthryoid. I know what it's like to feel sluggish and not want to push through the pain! I know what it's like to be pushed down a flight of stairs, work through the pain of surgery, extra weight, lack of trust, and life's cruelties. But I also know that this pain will go away and I will be stronger and smarter after I work through it.

So with my first Ironman 70.3, it wasn't until mile nine that I felt like a ton of bricks slammed me against a wall. Hence, hitting the wall term comes to play. I started getting dizzy, and I asked out loud, "I think I'm getting dizzy?" Seriously, like Pat or someone is going to say, "Ya, you're dizzy." Pat said it was probably the heat and to get some of the wet sponges the event volunteers where throwing at us.

The problem? Many of those sponges were dropped on the ground and being re-used and were full of germs, plus the cold water wasn't so cold anymore as it was in the mid-90s out. However when you feel faint, you take whatever. I remember stuffing those sponges in my bra, the front and back, and inside my ball cap. This helped for two minutes. My dizzy spells continued and I finally took some salt pills that one of the aid stations had available, but this was at mile 11. Again, too late to help... I'd be about done when the salt pills started working. I felt like the Little Red Engine!

I had to sit at the aid station for a few minutes to contemplate whether or not I could make it the two miles to the finish line. Oh, so close, yet oh-so far away, from the finish line that is.

It's amazing how when the body is in distress just walking a few feet can be a major goal, right then I was at a major dilemma. Keep my course and fight my body's distress, or throw in the towel and give up that dream of completing my first Half Ironman. That's why I'm here to help. To learn from my mistakes, become a half Iron Chick or earn that tattoo and do a full Ironman, but whatever you do, heed my advice, and don't make the same mistakes!

When I sorted through the fog in my head, I realized it would take longer for a vehicle to come pick me up than it would to complete the last two miles to make the 70.3 miles that day. Pat was taking some nutrition for his debilitating cramps, as we headed up this MONSTER hill. It's cruel how race directors can put such a big thing, the mountain of a hill, at the end of a long race. I think they like to sit up in their director's chairs and just laugh at all of us at the end of a race. I told Pat I had to pee and was going to stop off behind some trees.

If you are going to be an endurance athlete, get used to peeing in public behind bushes, trees, cars, dumpsters, fire hydrants, pretty much anything that provides a little camouflage. I've peed behind all the above. After I balanced myself to pee and tried to keep upward bound without passing out, I proceeded up the hill. What a sight.

I came up to Pat on the ground flopping around like a penguin who couldn't get up off a slippery floor and some guy standing over him trying to help him out in some way or another. To this day, I will never forget the despair on Pat's face as he looked up at me and said, "Dana, what do I do? Both my calves just locked-up and started spasming, I can't even stand or get up! Can you try to massage them or something?" Pat pleaded.

As a personal trainer and sports massage therapist, yes, I knew how to massage cramps out, but he was obviously having an issue with lack of sodium, potassium, or magnesium and massaging those puppies was not going to be the answer. But, the good friend I am, I bent down with what very little—I mean very little—energy I had to massage his dirty, sweaty calves. I'm a "germ-a-phobic" so touching someone else's dirty sweaty body meant I really cared for you, especially if you were a friend's hubby and not my own.

The poor guy was in so much despair I couldn't have left his ass, but the guy standing there trying to give some sort of help looked at me as if to say, "Great! This is my ticket out of here, I'm off again." Big guy stopping to offer help went on up the hill like a sloth with one foot in front of the other. He wasn't doing much better than we were. The Chicago Marathon was taking place that same day with temperatures "only" in the 80s, but the heat was so bad a marathon contestant died due to heat stroke. We heard numerous ambulances called out, but I don't think anyone died, just ambulance trips to the hospital related to the heat.

I was trying desperately to help Pat's calves, but by bending down I was about to pass out. During my dizzy spells, Pat kept telling me to "Keep your head up, Dana, don't look down, and look up at the horizon." I did this, which helped some, but by bending down and massaging his calves I started to see the little colored dots that one sees prior to passing out. They weren't colorful rainbows with happy endings; these were blue, pink, purple dots causing a distortion to my vision. At this moment, some of you are thinking "Damn, and you think I want to do a Half Iron or Full Ironman race? No!"

There are solutions to our misery, and I'll get there. I told Pat, "I'm about to pass out, I need to stand up." Pat said he thought the massage did help and he continued to do what I was doing, trigger point to his calves, as I returned to upright position. Within a minute or two, Pat tried to stand up, and I helped him. He could stand on one leg and the other was still locked up, but he was able to gimp along up the hill with me in zombie form. This is the part of the race where misery loves company! If I had not had Pat with me to help focus without passing out, I would have been out of that race much earlier. What I mean by out is out of the race and passed-out on the ground. It's amazing what someone being there does for your physical endurance when the body and mind wants to shut down.

As Pat and I continued up the Monster hill and rounded the top of the hill, we saw a sight we needed in more than one way. Up in front of us were two runners, a male and female, and it appeared the female had a pair of white angel wings. I seriously thought I was having an apparition and something bad was about to happen, or good for that matter. I asked Pat, "Pat, is that what I think it is in front of us? Is it an Angel or girl with white Angel wings? Seriously?" Pat confirmed my sighting and we couldn't but help our mental trip to hell by laughing. Here we were, feeling like we were in the bowels of Hades, and an Angel appears. When I say God works in mysterious ways, this was a true example!

We were in such bad shape, and here is this perky little blonde girl having a blast, or so it appeared, running with Angel wings. I don't think this girl will ever, I mean ever, know how much she helped us. I felt a surge of spiritual renewal just by seeing her presence and her glorious spirit. I think we ended up passing Angel girl and her guy friend, but I'm not sure because somewhere out there less than I mile to go, my mind stopped focusing, and I couldn't even think straight.

My hypoglycemia and serious low blood sugar was making it hard to even remember who I was with. Pat recognized my distress because I probably was not making sense at all and just rambling on. I remember to this day Pat trying to tell me a story about his wife Sheri and I was thinking, "Sheri, who is Sheri? I think, "I'm supposed to know who Sheri is, but I don't. Is that his wife?" I gave new meaning to "dazed and confused."

Hypoglycemia refers to excessively low blood glucose levels. Triggers may include eating later than usual or eating less than required by the insulin regimen, getting too much physical activity for the amount of food consumed, or taking too much insulin (Texas Health Steps website). "Hypoglycemia is dangerous because the brain relies almost entirely on glucose from the bloodstream for its energy. As blood glucose drops, cognitive function becomes progressively impaired. Other organs such as the heart may also be affected to a lesser degree. Symptoms include: light-headedness, sweating, trembling, palpitations, headache, dizziness, double vision, confusion, irritability, drowsiness, and hunger." (www.txhealthsteps.com)

To combat my hypoglycemia I eat bananas. I love them. I add one to my morning protein shake with chia seeds, flax seeds, spirulina, and natural whey protein mix. Bananas contain at least three natural sugars: sucrose, fructose, and glucose. Combined with fiber you have a balanced boost of energy in the morning to get you off to a good start. Bananas have proven to sustain many endurance athletes during long training hours or races and have been my best friend, recently.

When I say I was bad off back then, I mean it. There are solutions people. Don't wait until you are this bad to think of the solutions. It's funny how I remember, to this day, what I was thinking, but couldn't focus. This is the first time I realized how using proper nutrition can make or break a race. Pat and I came around a corner that had mile marker 13! The Heaven's parted and our hearts started singing, "Halleluiah!" There was a photographer there taking pictures and I made him take a picture of Pat and me by the marker.

I had never been so happy to finish a race. When you look at that picture it shows how dehydrated I was and how my bones are sticking out of my clavicle. As I came across the finish line, I rushed to the medical tent and told the medics I was dizzy and about to pass out. They immediately set me down on a stretcher next to others in the medical tent and piled bags of ice under and on top of me then gave me a liquid power boost of a heavy Gatorade mix. I asked if I could get IVs as there were some by me with IVs and I thought I was going to die. I knew I needed them!

Figure 3 Austin 70.3 Ironman before Endurolytes

The EMT politely told me due to the heat they used most of their IVs and didn't have enough. They were saving the few IVs left for those already passed out, etc., so they wanted me to drink this liquid first and see how I was doing in 15 to 30 minutes. I remember looking up at the sky because I was on the very edge of the medical tent. The place was full with cots and people looking like they just came out of battle. As I looked up to the sky, I just stared out in a daze. I felt like part of my body was there and the other was up in the clouds somewhere. I didn't even react to the ice placed all over my body. That's just messed up! When you are lying on top of, and under, pounds of ice and you don't even feel it?

The EMT told me they had so many people with heat exhaustion that day it was hard to stabilize them and ambulances were running back and forth to the hospital. They didn't realize they would need so many IVs and had run the place bare of supplies. The reason they were bare by the time I got there is due to our times. Pat and I weren't exactly on the fast side with our walk on the 13.1-mile run. Yes, it's called a run, but some of us can only walk when we get off the bike. Cramps, blood sugar, and other catastrophes get in the way. Little did we know that my hubby was having a catastrophe of his own?

I was suffering from heat exhaustion and low blood sugar, while Pat's issue was a lack of sodium and salt supplies. He didn't need to be iced down, he just needed his cramps to go away, which did once he drank plenty of Gatorade and ate a meal. Eric was still out on the course, and we started to get worried once I was out of the medical tent 30 to 45 minutes later. I was weak, but not feeling faint anymore. Pat and I waited by the finish line, hoping and praying Eric would be around the corner at any time.

My husband is not a strong swimmer, but he can rock the bike and do a decent run if he needs to, so it didn't make sense that he was so far behind us. "He must be in need of medical help," I thought. Eric came around the finish line and I immediately started yelling, "Medics, medics!!" Eric and Pat remember me looking like a hysterical woman, but I was concerned that Eric was in bad shape and my ADHD self just reacted, prior to thinking.

Eric said something like, "I'm OK, just tired" but with me looking like a lunatic the EMT staff ran to my hubby and walked him over to the medical tent. They told him to assume the position on the cot and proceeded to place ice bags on him. They must have not thought he looked as bad, because I remember I received a lot more ice bags all over my body than he did. Maybe they just ran out of ice like they ran out of IVs?

Turns out Eric had a bike malfunction and not medical issues. Eric said he was on the bike ride and it felt like it was not moving. He would pedal and pedal and was not going anywhere. He said he contributed it to the large hills in the area and his lack of energy, until one of the SAG wagons came up next to him and said, "Dude, your spoke is broken! Pull over, you're not going anywhere."

Eric's mental status must have been suffering a little because that's like riding with your brakes locked. Something is holding you back immensely. Eric pulled over and the SAG wagon staff looked over his bike. They told him it was shot and actually lent him a bike or replaced something like a wheel on his bike. I don't remember the full details because I was so out of it when he told the story. I only retained part of the story.

Regardless, Eric said he sat on the side of the road for at least 30 minutes while the guys were taking care of his mechanical issues. He said that he had been feeling faint due to all the expended energy, but he was able to drink and eat nutrition while sitting there and actually started regaining strength and feeling better.

Alright, time to talk strategy. My first mistake was not fueling up early on with a good, full breakfast. I should have had a couple of hard boiled eggs, a piece of fruit, and probably a piece of toast. This would have been a great start. You can still have your morning cup of Joe, but just make sure you have been hydrating a week out prior to the race. A good start would have been a week out having two cups of water prior to each meal (16 ounces) and then some water late morning, late afternoon, and late evening. This would have hydrated me before my race.

The next issue to address would be proper nutrition along the race. I was using my gels, but when my brain got foggy on the run, I couldn't remember when I had used a gel and when I hadn't, plus you can't make a 70.3-mile race on gels alone. Think about it, doing 70 miles and no lunch? It doesn't work. I should have cut up a peanut butter sandwich in little squares, placed it in a baggie and consumed this periodically on the bike. A piece of fruit like a banana somewhere on the bike would have helped, too.

If you take the time to actually stop at one of the aid stations, they usually have fruit available and some will even pass bananas to the competitors. Your first Half Iron is a learning experience, so don't plan on a PR, just plan on doing it to work out all the kinks for your next endurance triathlon. I drank enough on the bike, but didn't on the run and this contributed to my downfall. You can even run with your water bottle and fill it up accordingly on the route at aid stations.

All of this should be practiced before race day. When you come in off the bike, consume a bar or something to fuel you up for the run. I like Lara bars, they are easy on my stomach and have natural ingredients which make them easy to chew. They are moist and won't make you choke when you try to eat them in a hurry. Try eating prior to getting off the bike. Just remember you still need to consume little bits of nutrition along the run, and don't forget your gels. There's one more detail.

The last detail which saved us on future distance races like marathons or triathlons was the supplement factor. We so desperately needed endurance supplements to ward off cramps and heat exhaustion. Since that race I've been hooked-up to IVs on several occasions. Hotter than Hell 100 miler in Wichita Falls, Texas isn't called hotter than hell for no reason. Eric,

Pat, and I now use anything from Sportlegs to Endurolytes during races. Look them up on the website as each one has a little something different in it. A lot of times I will combine them. I take a few Sportlegs and a few Endurolytes every hour. These products are an Iron Chick's best friend, and I don't know how the body can make a long event without Endurolytes, proper liquid and proper nutrients. So there you go, save yourself, save the IVs for those in need, and have a successful race.

An article in **Psychology Today** July/August 2013, noted, *"Truly happy people seem to have an intuitive grasp of the fact that sustained happiness is not just about doing things that you like. It also requires growth and adventuring beyond the boundaries of your comfort zone. Happy people, are, simply put, curious."* The article titled, *What Happy People Do... Differently* is loaded with interesting information and strongly recommended. It goes on to note, *"Curious people generally accept the notation that while being uncomfortable and vulnerable is not an easy path, it is the most direct route to becoming stronger and wiser."*

Me with Matt Long. (THE LONG RUN)

Iron Nugget:

What do you think keeps the average "Joe" from doing a long race?

Why do you think people tell themselves "I could never do that!"?

20   Mr. Galloway, You Rock!

I decided to move from half marathons to a full marathon in 2004. It was on mile nine in the San Antonio marathon when I started to cramp up. Wow, I had 17 more miles to go. My right quad started to scream at me and pulled my knee out of place. There are times a runner thinks they are having knee issues, when it is actually a muscle attached to the knee that affects them. The cramping quad seared from the effort it took to hold my body upright and not tumble over face-first.

My husband was running with me and I told him to go on because I had no choice but to walk. A little further on, my knee actually locked up. I looked like a feeble old man crouched over not able to move. At one point, two guys came over to assist me to the side of the road where I massaged the area around the knee. I had cramped up and almost fallen on the course and they saw my distress and came to offer aid.

Mediocre runners are some of the best-spirited people around. We all want the same outcome: To complete this major feat, and we want others around us to succeed, too. Endurolytes would have helped me, but that would be three years down the road until I discovered that miracle. During my first marathon, I would walk, run a few feet, the leg would cramp up and throw my knee out of place, and then I would limp along until I could start a slow jog again. That vicious cycle went on for 17 brutal miles.

I was so afraid that I would finish after the cut off time and not receive a medal. It became my obsession to finish prior to the cut off time, and I wasn't going to do this bucket list event without getting a medal to show for it. No way. Someone was going down at the finish line if I didn't get a medal. "I'm gonna make the biggest scene, kick and scream, yell, throw a temper tantrum, but by golly, I'm getting a damn medal. Got it?" I was actually getting mad rehearsing in my head how I would get that medal if I came in too late.

"Focus," I told myself, "Run, focus. You can make it." A marathon is a lot like life, we can carry all sorts of burden and anger with us and continue to be "Worry Warts," or we can take action and carry on toward our goal with a positive outlook. As I came across that finish line, I was crying like a big ol' baby. Seriously! I had a catharsis and just cried from so much relief and satisfaction that I made it before I had to fight someone for their medal. It was such a relief, challenge, and a sense of accomplishment. A high like no drug, ever!! What drug lets you feel frustration, satisfaction, and a feeling of being on top of the world all at once?

I reflected after the race to try and figure out where I went wrong. We had a pre-marathon dinner with friends the night before when I learned from a doctor friend that if I trained with wine along the way I could have a glass of wine the night before. One, mind you. My friend, Janelle, has raced the Boston marathon several times and is married to a French man. Of course they drink a lot of wine, but Janelle's approach was "no wine the night prior to a marathon." When I was racing and doing so awful I kept thinking, "It was that damn glass of wine that caused me to cramp up and ruin my marathon!"

Truth be told, it wasn't. It was my lack of hydration prior and during the marathon that ruined my race and one other factor. We all talked about the marathon after the event to compare experiences. Melissa is a very tall gal and a busy doc, she doesn't have as much time to train as the rest of us. She stays on call and works long hours. How she finds time to train truly amazes me. Melissa rocked her first marathon! She smoked my husband and me regarding time. I just had to ask Melissa about her secret.

Melissa informed me that the year before she, too, had knee issues. She was training for a marathon, but had to back out due to issues with her knee. This is where Melissa shared the most amazing race detail with me. Are you ready, because this secret is the key to anyone being able to complete a marathon? Even if you are severely overweight!

Those of you using excuses that you work long hours and don't have time for long races, *Suck it up.* If Melissa can get up in the middle of the night, work all day, still find time for her family, and train for a marathon—wow! That woman is a super hero to me and the rest of you who work long hours and accomplish major feats.

Melissa shared the Jeff Galloway method with me. This dude is an old marathoner and has a remarkable book. I immediately went out and bought Mr. Galloway's book, but I lent my book to someone years ago and never got it back, so go out and buy it yourself to learn all the details. It goes something like this: You can actually have a better marathon time if you do a run-walk. In long distance races this is referred to as the "Galloway method."

I'll be doing a long-distance race and someone inevitably comes up to me and says, "Doing the Galloway? Me too!" We just smile, like we have some secret ammunition compared to the rest of the racers. It's like pro-cyclists who inject themselves with human performance-enhancing products. Our ammunition is better as it is legal and works with the body and not as a foreign invader! We run, recover, run, recover! It's actually fun.

The Galloway method consists of doing a five-minute jog and one-minute walk or a four-minute jog and one-minute walk or a three-minute jog and a one-minute walk. Commonly referred to as a five-one, four-one, or three-one, whichever you choose. This is only a small part of the method, so you need to buy the book to really understand the physics behind his method. It is a life-saver for us mediocre athletes. You can actually finish a marathon with a good time. Yes, I said good time.

My best marathon is around a 4:40, and that's not fast, but I enjoy myself along the route and don't stress my body out. Compared to my first marathon that is huge. I was like an hour slower on my first marathon and I tried to run the whole thing. I previously thought you should only walk as a last resort. I learned to relax during marathons and that people walk all the time. Don't ever feel like you have to keep up with the Jones.

After learning about the Galloway method, I decided to put a story component in my future marathons. I figured out it was about the experience, not the time. I would use the Galloway method, yell encouragement to others on the route, stop at Starbucks for coffee, and drink a sip of beer when offered along the course. Yes, I said, "Stop at Starbucks". I was doing a "Booyah, in your face!" to all the PR (personal record) racers. For all the hard-core athletes out there not taking in the scenery, who gives a crap that you ran your marathon in a 3:40? "Did you stop and have a soy latte, use the clean bathroom at Starbucks, or have a few sips of beer during *your* race?" I did, and I had a blast!!

I made it my goal to look for a Starbucks along marathon race routes. I like to go against the norm. If I can't be fast, I can sure have fun! I never drive the course ahead of time, so this is like a Hide-and-Go-Seek game during the marathon. "Where is that Starbucks?" It's amazing how an ADHD person can focus when it becomes a game. You don't focus on your pain, you just focus on the game factor. "Does this block look like one that might have a Starbucks? Hmmm... Keep going, not this one."

I hated it when the Starbucks was in the first five miles. My last marathon, I missed the Starbucks because it came too early and I ended up drinking a protein chocolate drink along the race. Wrong!! People usually say, "How do you drink a latte, don't you need to crap after that?" The answer is, "No, I don't." This probably goes back to Melissa's comment if you train with a certain drink or food then it's not as likely to make an impact. I drink a lot of coffee, and may have a cup of coffee before an afternoon run. I've had coffee before numerous runs. Usually the afternoon coffee is a soy latte with no extra sugar or flavor.

The next important lesson is "don't change anything on race day." Don't add new things to your list. This goes down to everything from new underwear, new shoes, new supplements, new nutrition, etc. I'll give you the protein drink example: During the expo the day before the race, one company was giving out boxes of their new chocolate-flavored protein drink. As I'm hypoglycemic, this product tasted good and had what I thought was a good ratio of carbs to protein. I drank some and didn't have any stomach issues, so I thought I'd tuck some away in one of my little 8 ounce bottles on my training belt.

I missed the Starbucks earlier so around mile 15, I was feeling a little low on blood sugar. I took out the bottle of chocolate protein drink and had some. At mile 17, I was sure I was going to have an accident and couldn't find a bathroom or Port-a-potty anywhere!! My brother was doing his first marathon with me during this event and just laughed that I had to crap, bad, and now! It's all good, I video-taped him coming out of a Port-a-potty at mile 21 where he had to stop and there was no toilet paper!

I managed to run/walk until I found a little airport on the backside of the San Antonio marathon. This was the part of the race where you had to use the bushes to take a pee, but I wasn't about to crap without any toilet paper. My hilarious friend, Betina, just had a mean case of poison ivy from crapping in the woods prior to an event. She evidently wiped with a leaf and somehow got "herpes-looking whelps" all over her butt and legs. She had to try and explain what it was when in public. Crazy Betina! I would rather crap in my pants and throw the underwear away. You laugh? It could happen.

Thank the dear Lord that I found the Stinson Airport Hanger just in time and was able to use a public facility that was clean—just what I needed. And thank the Lord that just past the hanger the aid station had little samples of trial mix, which settled my stomach and helped my low blood sugar get back to normal. I chalked up another marathon finish line that day without any nightmares running down my leg. Thank goodness.

Now for the don't change things like socks, shoes, or shall we say underwear on race day? The underwear issue happened prior to a different race. Janelle, Eric, and I were running another marathon and after dinner we all had gone to our rooms to sort out our race items prior to the next morning. Another detail: Always have everything you need laid out the night before as you get up very early on race day, and may forget something. You will only suffer as a result, so take the time to lay everything out and think through what you need. The night before this particular race, I noticed I had totally forgotten to pack my race-day underwear. Victoria's Secret underwear wasn't going to cut it for race day.

In fact, if I were to wear it, I would probably have ended with cuts. It's amazing what those fancy panties can do to your privates during a long race. You probably want to invest in some anti-chaffing cream to apply to groin areas, bra areas, inner thighs, and under the arms. You are likely to end up with severe-looking rug burns if not. Plus, the chaffing hurts.

If you cycle it's a no-brainer. You must, I mean must, invest in some anti-chaffing cream or you may not be sitting on your bike seat for quite some time. You can find them at athletic stores. Names like Butt Butter, Chamois Butt'r, Body Glide, Egg cream, etc., are out there. Vaseline works to an extent, also. I'd rather spend a couple more bucks and get the good stuff. Privates are not an area you want to gamble with!

When I discovered the night before the marathon I forgot to pack the appropriate underwear all I could do was go buy some. It was 8 p.m. by the time Janelle and I ventured to the mall— this was late. Marathoners need to get in bed early, watch a little TV, and just relax prior to the race. You have to make your body think it's late, so you can get in bed early and get a decent night's sleep. We went to the closest department store, Macy's. There wasn't an athletic store around, and Janelle wasn't about to travel all over town to find a stupid pair of panties with me.

I found some athletic-type underwear that looked like it was made out of appropriate material and wouldn't leave me all scarred up. I wore them during the race, and it did turn out to be a miracle. The moral of the story is, if you forget the appropriate supplies, or underwear for that case, you may just want to invest in a pair similar to what you've been using. Victoria's Secret was not a marathon garment, and I wasn't going to gamble. I'd rather lose an hour of relaxing downtime and find something similar to my regular race underwear than have Victoria up my backside on race day!

With cycle pants and tri shorts, you don't wear underwear so there's nothing to worry about. Except for the anti-chaffing cream down there, don't forget that. I like to wear jog skirts which have built-in underpants, and I just didn't bring them on this race. It was cold outside and the CWX running pants I had were older and a little see-through. Going commando wasn't as appealing to me, besides the cotton liner in the pants was messed up so it didn't absorb anymore. Who wants to run with sweaty crotch? I retired those expensive running pants, but they sure served their purpose of keeping the muscles energized during long runs. Compression tights are the best during cold runs!

I'd rather have people look at my panty lines in back of me than look at my fat, white rear end. If you have been cycling for any period of time, you know what I mean. Those spandex cycling britches get thinner and thinner with every wash. We all have witnessed someone with britches that show their crack line when you are behind them. You may put them on in front of the mirror, turn around and check them out, but until you're on the bike when they are stretched out, you have no idea how bad it really is.

Point in case, I had a pair that were getting worn down from a bike seat I had a crash on. The seat got messed up on the right side and would rub my bike shorts. I noticed it when I put them on, but it wasn't until my friend, Tami, came up behind me and said, "I see your hiney, all bright and shiny!" that I knew it was time to fix the seat and throw out those bike shorts. I had no idea. Tami said it looked like my bike shorts had seen better days.

On another occasion, we were all out for a ride and Pat was with us. Pat just loved his Ironman bike shorts and would wear them on long rides from Kerrville to Fredericksburg and back. On this ride, Linda and I came up behind Pat and noticed *his* hiney, all bright and shiny. I'm sorry to say, we just giggled and continued on our way.

I feel really bad now as he is most likely to hear about this story, get embarrassed, and say, "Girls!! Why didn't you tell me?" Why? Because Ironman athletic wear is expensive and hard to come by. You usually buy it at the Ironman event and hold on to it like it was your favorite Superman pajamas. I didn't want to disappoint our friend and say, "Buddy, it's time to retire that $150 pair of bike shorts." That's basically what we would be saying if we let him know we saw the "full moon".

Back to the Galloway method, according to Jeff Galloway, some speed work goes a long way. Galloway advocates training with a friend using his "cat and mouse" method. Start with an easy 10 minute warm-up, then take turns leading and speeding up and slowing down, your friend has to stay on your heels. Do these for three to five minutes then take a one to two minute walk recovery together, and switch leaders. This pattern will go on as long as your run takes. It's fun, and it's a great way to boost your run times. Someone once asked Jeff Galloway if it was OK if they never did any speed drills. His reply was, "Sure. While speed work will make you stronger, many runners never run outside their comfort zone, and that's perfectly fine." On the opposite end of the spectrum, Galloway tells runners when doing speed work they should never run at top speed or they could injure themselves. (www.jeffgalloway.com)

Fueling up: I gave you some tips on ways of eating earlier, but now that you have read this far, you obviously are an athlete or contemplating being one. Hoorah for you and boo for those losers who put the book down after the dysfunctional stage. Some people just live off of others' drama. I commend you for being an "inspirationalist"—for being a Christopher Columbus and setting off on a new journey. I promise you, you won't be disappointed, and you will have so many new stories to tell.

Iron Nugget:

Why do you think it is important to set goals?

How have you gotten thrown off course from goals you've set?

What is your definition of a winner and a loser?

21   A Half Marathon A Month

I never thought in 2008, when my husband came home to tell me he just became the master of **my sport** and signed up for Ironman Wisconsin 2009, that I would ever do a full 140.6 Ironman event myself. The words Iron-Chick was nowhere in my vocab. Leave that mess to Iron-Chick Allana, in town, who had already done seven Ironman events on her own. To top it off, Alli is diabetic. Whoa! That makes my hypoglycemia look like Mamsy Pamsy Land. Never think you can't do something because of a disability. I've seen many like Alli doing Ironman races, along with those with cancer, lost limbs, and in wheelchairs doing marathons.

What was my hubby thinking? Was he crazy? He was the state-level tennis player who couldn't swim worth a hill of beans, NOT an Iron dude!! I kindly pointed out to him that I had to save his ass at Water World when the wave pool started 10 years ago. Then there was the time in Cancun when he said I may need to assist him while we were snorkeling since the boat was "pretty far away."

It's amazing what a little confidence and practice in the water makes a person THINK they can do. I admit, I was Dana Downer the whole time he set off on his adventure, but I was afraid for him. Afraid he may have a heart-attack and die. OK, just a little piece of me was jealous. I was the swimmer in the family, and I started doing triathlons more than 10 years ago. It was my sport, not his.

Sure, I'd let him tag along at events like the time I showed up at one of the half marathons with my shirt that read: "Running shoes $89, race entry fee $45, crossing the finish line before my husband, **Priceless.**" I took pride in being better at something than him. He was a much better tennis player and in better shape than me, so I needed something to be better at than him. Didn't I? Plus, I didn't want to be a widow at my age and have to quite running or doing triathlons for fear of my daughter losing the only parent she had left. I prepared myself while Eric prepared for his race that year.

I prepared to call the doctor for more anxiety meds. It only makes sense, if he dies and leaves me, I would need to get some strong prescription pills to see me through this. I wouldn't be able to handle it all alone. I prepared for the dating scene and not falling for those controlling men who are single for a reason in their 30s and 40s. I also made him take out a decent life insurance policy. You think I'm kidding? Not in the least! He did, and I planned on how long that would last me.

If I was frugal it would last about five years. I could start dating after 5 years, "but don't settle or fall for any man prior to the five years because I would still be weak and needy," I thought. I needed to know what was out there, spend time with my daughter, and experience life as a strong widow and not one who falls for the first man who comes along to rescue this damsel in distress. No, sir!

After I did the emergency planning, I had to make a comparable athletic plan. I wasn't going to let him show me up leaving me all womanly and weak. A woman needs to stand up to a man and take the bull by the horns. Let them know whose boss; we are strong. OK, so I wasn't willing to do it Ironman wise. My 2009 New Year's resolution was to do a half marathon each month with a few Olympic triathlons and end the year with a bang, the San Antonio Rock'N'Roll marathon in November. I would ring the New Year in with the Boerne Duathlon in December which is a 5K run, 20-mile bike race, and 5K run.

My challenge was there. "Let's see if he can do all this in one year," I thought. I got into a pissing contest without even knowing it. Following is my journal entry:

A half marathon a month.... '09 is mine!

Last week was my second half for the year, exactly three weeks apart. Each year I set some sort of goal for myself, as many others do, but this year is different! You see, my husband and his friend, Pat, got this wild hair to take on a full Ironman!! What does this have to do with me, you say? Well, I'm a competitive person and although I have done two 70.3 Irons, I cannot see myself going through the trauma of an Ironman. The time, the dedication, the ...MONEY! So, I had to get original and ask myself what would be challenging but achievable. Here I am, on my second half marathon, last weekend in Austin with beautiful, cool, sunshine outdoors. The excitement in the air during races cannot be duplicated. You meet the obsessive ones as you arrive just before the start, which are coming back from their 15 minute warm-up already sweating and always with a stern look on their face. You know, kind of like the man who walks into Wal-Mart and looks right past everyone he passes. No expression, just more on the scowl side than positive side. These are your P.R. people. Always wanting a personal record!!

Most of the people who race are fun and friendly. This is what I love! I meet so many new people and we just talk. Before the race, during, and after! My husband and friends all agree... our racing events are ALL ABOUT THE STORIES. So, here I am on mile six or seven having a pity party. You see I have an old injury—a hairline stress fracture on my right metatarsal from '06 that tends to act up at times. This is bad alone, but two weeks prior to my half marathon in January I did something stupid. My buddy, Janelle, is a P.R. person. She does not qualify with the scowl on her face, but I guarantee she is warming up with a stern look on her face on race day and not meeting strangers until after the race.

So we were at Janelle's for Christmas and noticed she had a full-length mirror by her treadmill. My husband, Eric, and I laugh..."What? Do you like to look at yourself while you run naked?" She didn't appear amused! She informed us that she watches her gait while she runs and makes herself more efficient, etc., if needed. Wow!! That's why she gets those PRs. That Janelle, she's one smart cookie. Me, I just like to have fun! If it includes writing down numbers and splits, forget about it.

Because of Janelle's comment about watching her gait, I thought I too would put a mirror by my treadmill. There was just one problem. The mirror I had was 1/3 the size of hers. Because of my old stress fracture, I am well aware that I run too much on my forefoot rather than a good heel-to-toe strike. (Research shows the old heel, toe strike is not exactly the best either. Somewhere in between would be best.) I decided to give it a try so I'm running and actually bending down to try and see what my feet look like in this short mirror and snap... I feel something snap on the top of my left foot. Now you get the picture. I have both feet to deal with injuries instead of one. Confucius say... Never listen to friend who likes to run naked in front of mirror!

My first half marathon was horrible with just the one foot injury. I dealt with it and was only five minutes slower than usual. The last half marathon was already paid for, so I was not going to back out. I figured I would run until my foot gave out. Here I am, on mile six and seven, and both feet are literally killing me. The funny part? The right foot had an underside forefoot injury, while the left foot had a mid-foot top injury. Can you just imagine what I looked like? You know how a pelican waddles? Yep, that's the picture.

During my pity party, I started talking with God. As I always do during long runs. I thank him for allowing me to have the ability to do what I do and how I wish so much with all my heart other people would be able to enjoy what God has given us. Many go through life so unhappy and down. Science has shown with exercise alone, we can increase the serotonin, endorphins, dopamine, etc., in our brains and not be so unhappy. I came up to an older wheelchair participant just as I was thinking about how I wish more people would get outside to exercise. I started talking with him and I noticed his hands were wrapped in tape that was literally disintegrating. He had bruises on his upper arms from the wheelchair. I told him he was hanging in there and doing a great job. He told me I was doing better than him, as I was passing him and laughed.

I tell you God talks to us through people like him. I have tears in my eyes as I think of him. I was complaining about my small foot injuries and here is this man with tattered hands, bruised arms, and no legs giving his entire God-given strength to make it up the hill. I did not see my friend after the race, but I keep his spirit, drive, and dedication with me just as I do others I have met on the race route.

Your health tip for the day is to stop what you are doing, take a deep breath in through your nose while counting to eight and hold your breath counting to five, then release the breath slowly through your nose. Add some spice to this deep breathing exercise by grabbing a piece of rosemary outside. Crumble it up in your hands. Now do the deep breath with your hands cupped over your nose and take a deep breath in. Ahhhh. Go Green, get outside and exercise!

My third half marathon was in San Marcos in the freezing cold with an active gas leak in the air that made many of us running the course physically ill. To top it off, when the highway was closed down for two hours, I couldn't get back to my crappy Howard Johnson motel room in New Braunfels. The owner's didn't speak much English and tried to make me pay $25 before they would let me in my room. I tried the nice, professional approach to let them know there was no way of getting to their roach motel in time as the roads to New Braunfels were shut down for more than two hours.

Because of my upbringing, when a disagreement arose I learned to lash out or to keep silent and guard my true feelings. This was one case when lashing out actually worked for me. During stressful times the old Dana comes flying out on a broomstick. Not as often, I'm still working on it! Part of my problem during that race was my lack of water before the race and during because it was so cold out. Water is not just refreshing to our bodies, it's necessary. My mother wouldn't have all the debilitating issues and take a purse full of pills if she just would have added water to her daily regimen years ago. She has every health risk related to aging Americans one can have most likely due to only consuming soft drinks and eating processed foods. This was not a part of God's plan for us.

Water has been proven to ease one's everyday debilitating physical ailments. It's so sad, I hope the young readers take heed and just add water and proper nutrition to their diets before it's too late. Research is leading to the fact that this American generation may be the first generation to die before their parents. That's just sad that I may outlive your child because I chose to take care of the body God gave me. To fuel it with natural God-given products including water, fruits, vegetables, beans and whole grains.

If you have extra weight on you, water has been proven to boost those fat-burning cells, to recharge your immune system, and to fight off infections. For those with dry, dull skin, water has been proven to improve the lymphatic fluid and boost your skin cells. Dehydration or lack of appropriate water creates a brain fog. Your brain is 3/4 water and the lack of water can lead to an impairment of executive skills— the skills that solve problems and reason with others. If you are prone to arthritis pain and/or headaches, yep, might want to up that water intake and see if it makes a difference.

Check out the National Institute of Medicine to see how much water you should be drinking daily. You might be surprised how many physical problems can be prevented just by drinking the correct amount of water daily. You too can do a half marathon a month by taking care of your body. I went on to complete my mission that year and felt on top of the world.

Iron Nugget: I'm going to give you another assignment. This one is to check out two different short films. These films changed my life and supported the hunches I've had for years as a personal trainer and health nut. The first film is, **"Fat, Sick and Nearly Dead."** This story is a remarkable story about a man who was taking around nine to ten prescribed pills a day and was on his way down death row, but he wasn't in prison. He was a perfect candidate for a heart-attack or stroke due to his condition. Google his short film and learn about his adventure. He's been on a life-changing journey these days.

The next short film addresses health and the percentage of those inflicted with cancer. Find out how much cancer is related to genetics and how much is related to our diet. This next film is called **"Forks over Knives."** Both of these films are available on Netflix.

Look at the website: www.forksoverknives.com, along with www.fatsickandnearlydead.com

A plethora of information follows: Beets are supposed to increase your VO2 max. Beer has properties that may reduce post-race infections. Drink chocolate milk after long sessions—it brings your blood sugar back to normal and the protein in the milk contributes to improved lean muscle mass and loss of excessive body fat. So, by all means, go run or cycle hard for more than an hour and replenish with a low-fat glass of chocolate milk.

22   A Close Encounter of the Blind Kind

I find Americans don't want to see the problems right in front of their faces. Perfect case in point is my almost fatal accident, recently on my bike ride. Yes, I said fatal a little too easily, but I definitely would have been maimed if not killed. My morning started off late as usual, when I plan on leaving at 8 a.m. it turns out to be after 9 a.m. I like to move slow and enjoy my morning coffee while watching the beautiful redbirds come and feast in the backyard through my screened-in porch.

I gathered my water bottles early so I wouldn't forget them on my 52-mile bike ride. As I got on my bike, I did my usual prayer to God, asking him to protect me and send Angels to keep me safe while venturing through and out of town on that day's 52 miler. I have about 6 miles of in-town traffic before I head out of town. Wouldn't you know, I was only 3 miles into the ride when this happened? Studies show that many accidents happen when a person is only 2 miles from their home. I guess that applies to bike accidents, too.

I was headed east out of town on a nice straight away road just down from our local courthouse. Jefferson Road has many perpendicular roads, so a cyclist has to be alert for cross traffic. I had just cleared a cross road and my attention was directly in front of me when this car came up on the opposite side headed west toward me. He didn't have his blinker on, but he started to turn into the auto parts store directly in front of my path, across my lane. I let off my speed which was 15 miles an hour and put my hand up in the air to say, "Stop! See me! I'm right here in the road, don't cut me off or we'll crash!"

His car stopped as its nose entered my lane. It appeared he saw me, and I started accelerating my speed up again to get past him before he turned fully across my lane to enter the store. As I'm back up to 15mph, his 1999 Tan Mercury Sable just starts across my path a few feet in front of me. My two choices were body-slam my bike and body into his older model car and across his hood, I thought that might cause too much damage to his car, or brake hard and veer left to avoid him.

If I went right he would slam into me instead of me into him. I know the accident scene is hard to visualize, but stay with me because the next part is not hard to visualize. I braked and went left and my body went up over my handle bars as my bike went down. I caught myself on the palms of my hands and on my knees. Luckily there wasn't any skidding or I would have had a lot of road rash and bloody cuts to deal with.

Let me tell you, if you have fallen on a bike as many times as my husband and I have, you start getting good at it when something like this happens. You snap out of those clips that hold your shoes down on the pedals like nobody's business. It took me a lot of falls still clicked in my pedals as I went down with my bike to learn that lesson.   It pretty much came naturally, now, to click out as I was being thrown off the bike.

The man stopped in the middle of the rode as I was falling just a few feet away from his car. I immediately jumped up after getting myself untangled and ran over to his passenger window which was down. He was an older, pot-bellied gentleman with coke-bottle glasses.   Here's the visual... I ran up and said, "What the @#$*s the matter with you? Are you a @#!$ ^& idiot? You almost #$ *ing ran over me!!" He started in broken English, "I'm sorry, Laaaadeeee! I'm sorry, Laaaaadeee!" I replied to him, "You shouldn't be on the *&$^ing road!" Again he replied, "I'm sorry, Laaaadeeee. I sorry, Laaaadeeee. I didn't see you."

I continued to rant and rave like a total lunatic in the middle of the road with my hands making gestures back and forth, "Well, then you need some new %$#@#^& glasses!" First of all those were really, really thick glasses he had on, and he was pretty old and disheveled looking. He then said to me, "Laaaaadeeee, my heart is beating so hard, like this" and he took his hand to his heart and made a thumping sound. I was starting to hear him, but still yelling at him.

It wasn't until he said, "Laaaaadeeeeee, what can I say to you that you will accept my apology?" That's when I saw Cher from the old movie Moonstruck say, "Snap outta it!!" as she was slapping someone's face. I stopped, and like nothing had happened at all I told him, "I'm so sorry I was yelling at you like that. It's not like me to yell and curse at people, but we just had a cyclist friend killed on her bike, and I pray to God to protect me each time I get on my bike. I pray that God will return me home safely to my daughter and husband."

No sooner was this was out of my mouth that Robert from the Plant Haus across the street came up to me to ask if I was OK. I just started crying to Robert that this man cut me off and almost crashed into me and "all I could think of was our friend Debra getting killed and how I know we take our lives into our own hands each time we get on the bike." Robert just said all the right words to offer encouragement as the old man was parking at the store.

Robert agreed that too many times we have people on the road that maybe shouldn't be driving because of their age or whatever. He was like my Angel, there at the right time. I met Robert more than 10 years ago from the tennis days. He's this tattooed dude who used to have big holes in his ear lobes, but can play some mean tennis although he doesn't look the part. He doesn't look like the sweet, gentle soul, but he is. He's a perfect example of "don't judge a book by its cover." He appears more like a cussing motorcycle type than the quiet type, but he's quite the opposite. Robert told me he saw me go by and then heard something directly after. I recall I said, "Yeah, I wasn't going real slow, but then I wasn't going real fast. I was going about 15 mph." I point this out, because I found myself almost apologizing for my bike speed.

As if I shouldn't be a cyclist on the road. Like maybe I was going too fast, but I really wasn't because the speed limit is actually 30 mph on that road (ha, ha). Robert's reply to my comment about going 15 mph was, "And as you should." I recall, because he confirmed that I didn't do anything wrong.

It's so hard being a cyclist sometimes. So hard doing what you love. I've had full soda or beer cans thrown at me while cycling. I kid you not, people yell at cyclist to "get off the f**king road," I've had a grapefruit or large orange thrown at me, trash, cigarettes, and then the stupid, dumb-ass, redneck who drives his big truck and revs up the engine real loud as he comes up behind you on the road. By the way, I always ride on the shoulder, but there are areas in town when there's only a fine white line. I try my best to ride that fine white line. Like a tight rope.

Some rednecks find some sort of pleasure out of intimidation. My theory is they have "little penis syndrome" and drive those big trucks to compensate. Enough said—you get the picture. Idiots!! Because I still have to work on my impulse control, it's those guys I wave my middle finger at as they pass by. Then I look up to God and say an apology prayer. An issue I have to work on, I know.

This brings me to forgiveness. I felt so bad at what I said to that man that I was going to write something up in the paper to tell the man who cut me off and almost killed me that I was sorry for yelling all those obscene, potty-mouth words to him. I prayed to God for his forgiveness as I'm sure I traumatized the old man with coke-bottle glasses almost as much as he traumatized me.

I had bruises and swelling on my hands and wrists, along with a large knot on my right shin and right knee with a few boo-boos on the left knee. My whole body ached for days. It's amazing what being thrown does to the body. I feel sorry for football players now. Yikes, that's some trauma. Or bull riders. The day wasn't over. A police man pulled up as Robert was comforting me and asked if I needed an ambulance. I guess someone else saw me go down and called the police. I told the police officer that I would be OK and I think I straightened it out by calling the old man every bad word I could think of.

I ventured down the road 15 miles to Center Point and went up past the river bridge where I usually get in for a dip on the way back. There were cars everywhere and I couldn't figure out what was going on. I took my back way behind the main road and figured out that people were waiting for a parade to start. Hm… interesting. As I came up to the main road in front of the high school, I saw people lined up all along both sides of the road. I thought, "Good, it hasn't started, I'll hurry up down this road before it starts."

Not knowing which direction the parade was starting or going. This stretch was only a mile or two, but down the road I came up on the parade. I was headed east and it was headed west. I stayed on the far right side of the road trying to stay out of the way of the parade and the people lined up, but it was really awkward. Llike the old man earlier that day, I couldn't think straight and just thought, "I gotta get out of this mess." It didn't make sense to turn back around and look like I was a clown on a bike in the parade, so I just hurried in the opposite direction. That's when a gaggle of people on horses started yelling at me, "Slow down, get off the road!!" I was so embarrassed. I know I was at fault and looked like an idiot for the second time that day.

Like the old man, all I could spit out was, "I'm sorry, I'm sorry," as I worked my way past the parade. Most of the parade occupants just laughed at me but those rednecks. I guess they really hate cyclist. It was a lady who kept screaming at me. I guess she thought I'd spook the horses, which I totally understand. I was at fault and had no idea a parade was scheduled two weeks after the 4th of July. I still have no idea what that parade was for! I posted my coke-bottle glasses experience on Facebook and my sister-in-law's response was, "Hey, by the way, were you on your bike in Center Point this afternoon?" Oh my!

Iron Nugget:

Describe when you have had blinders on?

How did you find a way to see?

23 Live Life to the Fullest

"Life has less to do with what happens to you than it does with how you deal with what happens to you." Anonymous

Are you ready for another tidbit of information? Did you know that the Statue of Liberty, which was given to us by the French, needed a base to hold it and the American government couldn't fund the project, so they enlisted the help of donations from American citizens? Now, that's not the interesting part, the interesting part is that those who donated to the project were to have their names listed in the New York paper back then, and 85 percent of the funds came from children. I learned this in church one Sunday.

I was reminded that if we raise and educate our children properly they can go on to accomplish amazing things, even things as grand as the Statue of Liberty which defines what the American Dream is. Don't settle for people telling you what you can't do, settle for those who build you and your dreams up.

Pastor Ray's sermon addressed the Ark that Sunday. He pointed out that there were Cherubim's protecting the Ark. Apparently the Israelites would take the Ark with them into battle. It was the Ark that protected the Israelites, not the soldiers. When I pray to God to protect me and send me special Angels during a time I need them, it works. It actually works. I may make horrible choices along the way while I'm under his protection, but once I snap out of it, I realize I'm protected by God and his Angels.

I recognize I should make better choices from that point on. It's a vicious cycle. I'll correct my ways, get off the beaten path I'm on, notice the obstacles in my road, then tell God I'm ready to get back on the right path and to please forgive me for going astray. Funny thing? God still chooses to protect me, even with my many imperfections. He loves me, imperfections and all, and he loves you, too. Ray pointed out that God desires that God's presence not be contained in the Ark. God wants us to have faith in him and live our life in fullness. Not like the person who tries to act oh-so wonderful and perfect at get-togethers. Ray pointed out in his sermon that "this means making mistakes, and who cares about people thinking you are making a fool of yourself."

I admitted I made a mistake when I aggressively yelled foul things at the poor old man who almost ran me over, but I'm human. I make mistakes. The important part to me is that I tried to make it right by apologizing to him before he left and I never saw him again. I'm reminded of the song that says "dance like no one is watching." Live life to the fullest and keep God close and just love. Make mistakes.

As a teacher, I've always told parents that research shows we learn from our mistakes. If you don't make many mistakes, you haven't learned much on your journey. Ray pointed out that God is offered to us through faith. My philosophy is that there is so much more to those three words: Faith, Hope, and Love. Faith – Hope – Love, live your life this way. Life happens! Move forward through your faith, your hope, and your love. Leave the crap behind you.

Recently, a client came in with a lot of anger and marital issues. She had numerous failed relationships, three children, and she was only in her 20s. She was about to end her latest relationship with the father of one of her three children. She said, "When I close that door, it's over. Closed!!" She commented that she would NEVER love that man again. Period!

How sad. You people out there who can't live your life with **faith** that people do change, with **hope** that someone who is led astray will find their way home someday, and with **love** to accept people for their differences. People talk about how the universe works. "Put it out to the universe and it will happen." Silly people, that's just **faith** at work. Good things come to those who live their life with Faith, Hope and Love. To succeed in faith and hope, one must learn to love thy self, first. One of the many problems teens face these days is the inability to satisfy their need for love. As a result they end up with all sorts of problems like drinking at young ages, using drugs, using sex as a tool, and thriving on drama. Somehow they think this is what love is about. They are so far from the truth.

No matter what a person accomplishes in life or obtains, it cannot take the place of our basic need, love. I have known women who are attracted to men with money. They end up getting what they think will make them happy, the money, and then live unhappy lives because the men they marry love their money more than they love their women. The need for love begins with your need to love yourself. You cannot move on through your journey of life without loving yourself. You get stuck! Those mud pits will continually hold you back and keep you drawn up in the muck! Talk to someone knowledgeable who can teach you how to love yourself if you feel you are unlucky in love.

If you are looking to attempt an Ironman or endurance triathlon, you must get your mental outlook set in the right direction. Too many people throw in the towel when they get discouraged with the swim. God forbid I give coaching lessons to anyone in the Ironman arena; however, I have been there so here are a few simple pointers to getting in the right frame of mind.

In the water think, body rotation. Many forget to roll the body when they rotate the head, the body is attached to the head and it has some rotation too when breathing to the side. Don't try to stay flat and straight and then turn your head, you will end up lifting your head and screwing up your whole stroke. NO Bueno. Not good. I roll to the left as my right arm is out front and about to start pulling down toward my right upper thigh as I breathe in and return my head to the water.

When you return your face to the water, you may think you are pulling the water back behind you with your opposite arm. It's a feeling, not a technique. Like the groove of running. I used to teach children by doing something I called the wheelbarrow in the water. I held their legs and had them work solely on their arms and breathe technique, before they added legs. Your legs should not be the strong point of your swim. Save the legs for the bike and run. Pay attention to your hips, don't drop them. Have someone hold your legs in the pool if you need to practice your breathing. Learn to relax. When you add the kick, keep it light and think of your legs as just trailing behind you, not as power. I do drills with my upper body only and let the legs just drag. The upper body is the key to a long distance swim. If all else fails install a floatation device, get silicone breast implants!

Iron Nugget:

Are you living life to the fullest?

What set backs do you encounter?

24   Wisconsin Ironman

I had so much fun training with my husband and Pat for their 2009 Ironman race, I didn't want the event to come. We would swim in the river on Wednesday nights and on weekends. I would go on shorter bike rides with them, but nothing more than 50 miles. Pat, Sheri, Eric, and I would have a lot of "training parties," as we called them. This basically meant we all got together over several bottles of fine wine and told stories.

Sheri, Pat's wife, is a marathon runner so she can tell some great stories about running. I remember Sheri's "Sondra story." Sheri is so funny when she gets on a roll with her stories. She's a beautiful lady in her 40s with shoulder-length, straight dark hair and really blue eyes. Her dark hair and olive skin tone really show off her blue eyes. Sheri has the cutest little laugh when she tells a story, and we all tend to listen. Me, I'm loud to start with and get louder when I tell a funny story. It doesn't sit well for the punch line, but oh well.

Sheri had competed in the San Diego marathon on one of the days Eric, Pat, and I were out doing a triathlon. She had flown in to see an old buddy and was basically by herself doing the marathon. We were the Three Musketeers at the race, and she was feeling a little like the Lone Ranger once she got out on the marathon course. Pat and Sheri have a great relationship, and always boost each other's confidence by doing an event together or having the other one present. This was hard for Sheri as she flew across the U.S. to do a marathon solo without her partner. High-Ho, Silver, away!

Sheri started having a little "pity party" along the race when this well-built black woman in front of her kept getting cheers. Her name was Sondra. Sheri said she started getting jealous that Sondra had so many friends and family there to cheer her on while Sheri had no one. Sheri's two teenage boys were not there, her husband was not there, and evidently her friend she went to see was not there. Man, that would be hard—I need encouragement on race day! I want to feel like a rock star and hear some cheering out in the audience!! Something to help me go from mile 15 to 26.2.

It's at mile 15 that our Id, Ego, and Super Ego start arguing with each other. "What were you thinking? I told you, you couldn't run 26.2 miles. Are you crazy?" The other part is saying like the little red engine, "Shut Up! I think I can, I think I can!!" And so goes this dialogue for 10-plus miles. Sheri pointed out, "I'd be in the middle of having a hard time and someone would yell out, "Go Sondra," Sheri told us she had an idea after the pity party started getting old. Sheri is a glass half **full** type of gal, and I mean this in more than one way as she is a connoisseur of wine. We wine lovers love our glass full to half full, never half empty. Sheri looks at life this way. Make lemonade when life gives you lemons.

Sheri commented, "I just told myself, I shall be Sondra!" She said her step got lighter, and she picked up her pace. Sheri became empowered when she was running through the crowd and they started cheering for her, "Go, Sondra! Go, Sondra!" Many of us have taken this story and turned it into our own during a race. We have laughed that we raise our hands in the air and say, "I'm Sondra, and I am woman!!" Sheri's Sondra story lives through us when races start to conquer us, and we chicks fight back and become personified as **Sondra**! It's become such a source of inspiration to local chick athletes that Sheri has made a line of jewelry by the designer name of Sondra—designs by Sondra has a nice ring to it. Maybe she will start a website with her inspirational jewelry.

After a year of the four of us doing long runs and getting ready for the guys to participate in the Iron event, we headed off to Madison, Wisconsin the second week in September 2009. Madison weather is funny. It can be 40 degrees in September or in the 80s. Most of the time, it's somewhere in between 50 and 70 degrees in September. This lends itself to perfect weather to do 140.6 miles in less than 17 hours. The weather was just gorgeous ranging from the 70s to low 80s that week in 2009.

Sheri and I got a few runs in around Madison, not together as they had their two sons and Pat's parents with them. Eric and I left our daughter behind because she generally didn't enjoy racing "stuff." The University of Wisconsin in Madison is just beautiful. The lake on the campus is so serene and soothing. The campus and State Street remind me of the University of Texas and 6th Street in Austin only cleaner, older, and more respectable. Sorry, that was just my impression. It lacked the smell of marijuana and the bums sleeping down 6th Street. It made me think, "Man, I wish I were in college, again. I'd love to come to this university and live in Madison!"

The Iron event takes off from the Monona Terrace, which was one of Frank Lloyd Wright's architectural visions for the city of Madison. The convention center links the shores of Lake Monona to the State Capitol which looks a lot like the Texas state capitol, but with prettier landscape. Eric and I loved walking to and from the Ironman site and staying a block away from the state capitol. There were shops everywhere, farmer's markets, fine foods and, of course, a Starbucks. It was a vacation for Sheri and I, but probably not so much for Eric and Pat as their nerves were trying to stay focused on the upcoming event.

The day of the big event finally arrived and our guys were off somewhere among 2, 700 other Ironman competitors with blue swim caps. Sheri remembers one old man telling his wife, "There he is, there's Joe, the one with the blue swim cap!" Seriously? All the men age groupers had on blue swim caps, the women red, and the pros had white on. So that man thought he saw his son in thousands of swimmers? Not likely. Pat and Eric were in a washing machine of people, literally. These people were swimming into, on top of, and underneath each other at the start. Ironman races start with a cannon firing, which deafens your ears and then the slapping begins!

It sounded like bats coming out of the Congress Avenue bridge by Town Lake in Austin. It was freaky watching the competitors take off and to hear that loud sound. Slap, slap, slap—the sound of swimmers' hands hitting the water as they return to front propulsion. I wondered if it scared anyone in the water. I was scared just watching and listening to it from the top of Monona Terrace which was numerous stories high.

I left the crowd and went for breakfast on the square. It was nice to relax for a moment before the guys came out of the water. The spectators get as nervous as the competitors on race day. People are passing some mean nervous gas, and they hold their breath while trying to look for loved ones. Some look like they are going to pass out, but perhaps it's just the carbon monoxide in the air causing them to look faint. It's almost comical.

Sheri was somewhere in the morning crowd, but I wasn't about to fight the group of 2, 000 plus and find her. We had agreed to hook up later for Tapas on State Street to watch the guys during the last leg—the marathon. I was volunteering in the women's transition area and

Sheri's family was volunteering on the run course before our scheduled Tapas date. We gals were taking it easy while the guys were living the most challenging day of their life.

If you desire to become an Iron Chick, you need to volunteer for at least one Ironman race prior to participating in the event. At least go watch an Iron event all the way through if you don't volunteer because it is the most exhausting and rewarding day any person could have. The athletes tend to be so humble and thankful when you help them. Some are just in a hurry and rude, but most are very considerate even when their brain is focused on completing this mind-boggling event. They say things like, "I really appreciate your help. You rock!" when you are thinking, "No, you rock!"

Helping the women in transition change from their swim clothes to their bike was a rewarding experience for me. Let me tell you, there's a lot of nakedness in that changing tent. The volunteer helps the athlete with her transition bag, by arranging things for her while she changes. There's not a lot of room in the changing section, so you may have as many athletes as volunteers all standing in a small area over the athletes who are sitting on the chairs trying to get socks, shoes, etc. on. As we all are squeezed in, there aren't any privacy booths and many athletes change from their bathing suits to their bike gear only inches away from your face.

After volunteering and helping the female athletes get from the swim to the bike start, I was outside by the bikes when my Honey came out to get his bike. He looked so happy at that moment; he was obviously enjoying himself, which is another important factor when you are doing an Ironman event. Right behind him was Pat. How could it be? How amazing that these two guys amongst 2,700 people came out of the water at similar times. This just shows you that whoever you train with makes a difference on race day. If you train by yourself or with those much faster than you, you probably won't see them, but if you train with someone who has similar times it can really lead to a successful race. It did for these two guys.

Pat and Eric started off on the bike together and would take turns taking the lead. They finished the bike in similar times and there they were as I was working outside the second transition station. I saw them mount their bikes at current times, but who would think I would catch both of them together 112 miles later? The dynamic duo started their swim, bike, and run off together.

 Sheri and I yelled encouraging words and told them they looked great as they started off on the run, together! You don't realize how this boosts your mental outlook, to be with someone to encourage you and talk to you during this event that messes with your mind at times. They looked so tired and happy at the same time as they took off on the run. One of Pat's eyes was blood shot. Eric said later that Pat lost a contact during the swim when someone knocked Pat in the head and his goggles came off. The bike ride made it worse. Regardless of the bloodshot eye, they had smiles from ear-to-ear with a little gimp in their gait from being hunched over for 112 miles on the bike. I was so happy for them.

Sheri and I met for Tapas shortly after the guys were on the marathon course. We would catch them at mile 12 and 14 along our own route—our Tapas route. The day turned out to be hot for Wisconsin. It was 83 degrees that day and the sun was full blast. Many of the Yankees were sub coming to the heat, but not our Texas boys. They had trained in 100 degrees heat earlier that summer and were well prepared for what Madison offered that day. Sheri and I giggled and laughed while we drank Sangria with fresh fruit. It was yummy, and I lost myself in my own sentimental journey. We waited in excitement. Unfortunately, we weren't prepared for what we saw when the guys came around the bend at mile 12.

They were hunched over and looked gaunt like zombies. A scene from Dawn of the Dead came to mind, or Half Ironman 2007. Eric was having a hard time keeping his eyes open and he said with a smoker's voice, "I can't keep my head held up straight." It just wanted to fall over he kept saying. He walked like an old man with a horror film shuffle and I think Sheri said Pat was having some bad leg cramps, *again*. The guys went on and our excitement changed to one of fear and concern.

Let's talk about STRESS. Stress on the body from doing an Ironman is a powerful thing itself, but stress alone on the body really compromises the body's natural rhythm. Stress may ruin your health. Taking on an Iron event is thought to be a stress-relieving journey from our daily stress of home, health, and work, but when people let the Iron event consume their daily life it can have the opposite effect. Stress alone is said to be a major contributor to heart disease which, as I mentioned previously, is a major killer of Americans. Stress tends to elevate blood pressure, speeds up breathing, and increases the amount of adrenaline flowing through your body.

Stop and think about what doing such a life-challenging event like an Iron event can do to your body. This is exactly why I was a "naysayer" when my hubby and Pat said they were going to do the Iron challenge. I worried about the stress on the heart and their body, not to mention the stress one puts on themselves to achieve their goals. To top it off, prolonged stress keeps the body in a constant state of tension and excitement, the fight or flight syndrome, forcing the heart to work even harder than normal.

I bring this up because many of you reading this book surround yourself with unwanted and unneeded stress. Yes, there are things in life we cannot change, but there are so many other things in life that we *can* take control of. If you are in a very stressful relationship or work environment, seek help. Find someone to talk to at your church, school, or work. Look for someone away from the situation that can give you an unbiased view of things. Talking to your mother-in-law about your husband's lack of interest in the home front is probably not the best person to talk to.

The medical community acknowledges stress can interfere with the immune system's functioning. Have you ever paid attention to how stress-related illnesses sometimes follow traumatic events like a divorce or job loss? My mother and aunt are both examples. My mother's health plummeted when my father left her for another woman. I truly believe if my mother would have received appropriate counseling almost 20 years ago, she would not have had all the weight gain and needed all the surgeries due to falls or health related issues like osteoporosis and a lack of muscle tone. Yes, my mother should have added some exercise and appropriate eating in there, but the lack of dealing with the stress that bombarded her life ultimately killed her chances of living an abundantly happy and healthy life. She chose to live in pain.

Many of us don't really start living until we turn 40!! The teens are a survival mode just figuring out how this thing called life really works, the 20s are figuring out how the job field works and how we can get the career we desire. The 30s surround us with molding that career and raising a family, while the 40s, well, baby, that's a ride in the amusement park! The 40s are about taking a fun ride and dealing with bumps and bounces that come up, but enjoying the ride for the most part. Wooohoooo!!!

My poor mother saw her life starting to go downhill at the end of her 40s and by 50, the writing was on the wall. I wish she would have done something about her stress back then, even if she chose to do something now, it would be such an uphill battle to tackle. Don't get me wrong. Those of you who maybe 300-plus pounds and lacking appropriate diet can fight that battle, but it will just take a little longer. It's worth it though. The body is a miracle factory. God created us so that when we do decide to fill our bodies with healthy foods and liquid it repairs some of the damage we created years ago.

Self-awareness and changes in your behavior can protect your body from stress-related problems. A body that is constantly weakened by a poor diet, stress, and lack of sleep just needs a change in diet, appropriate sleep, and counseling. **To be yourself, you have to be able to see yourself!**

Taking on too much can stress your body, also. If you decide to add an endurance race, there is a fine line. The training will most likely relieve stress in your life so enjoy the training and race. Don't let it consume your life. It's when you let it consume your life that the event becomes a Catch 22. It creates the stress in your life. As with Pat and Eric's training, it was all about the stories, having fun. Once the event hit the run part, all hell broke loose. They had not planned for this part to be so stressful on their minds and their bodies.

Wake up, people! **Life is an Iron event!** We look forward to some event like a new school, a new job, a new relationship, a new event, a vacation, and then **BAM** something comes up that we didn't plan on and we fall apart and let stress consume our mind, health, and body! It's so easy to see someone fall apart in an Ironman race, why can't we see it in our daily lives?

I'd like you to just sit back and think of a time when your life was going as planned and then a stressful event popped up and consumed you. What did you do? How did you handle it? I think I'm a good example as my life has had so many ups and downs, stressful situations, and challenges, that I know something is going to pop up at some time or another. I tend to deal with things better these days. Why? One, because I take meds (OK, that's a funny excuse) but two, because I have seen that reacting to stress rather than working through it is not the answer. Hear me out.

I can react to something stressful with my fight or flight syndrome and go *balls to the wall*, but if I stop and think the situation through with someone to talk to, appropriate diet, appropriate exercise, I'm most likely to work through the problem than react to it. There are times in our life when things are going smoothly you don't even notice the dissatisfaction until it slaps you in the face.

When we are younger we take for granted that we will always be in shape and healthy. Then we have kids and life becomes wrapped-up in raising the babies and taking care of everyone else. We reach a point where we are forced to look at what we have become or the lack of what we have become. It maybe weight issues, or just to get healthy again, but many of us choose to get healthy once the children are in school or even later if we forgot to set the "better look in the mirror" alarm.

You may get involved with new friends who have the same health interests and develop significant bonds with these people who share the same athletic outlook. When I first wrote this book I was in the throes of having to really look at those relationships and writing a book caused me to lose some of those friends I was deeply bonded to; however, I was tired of the slaps in the face regarding a few relationships that didn't work and felt I needed to write it down, not to hurt the person who provided the slaps, but for others who may get to a similar situation in their life.

Let me see if I can give an example to better explain. You may have developed a bond with a group who competes in the weekly 5k run or a tri-group or another group, but there will ultimately come a time when you let the OCD person in your bubble. You know the person who shows up to a race an hour early to get their fartleks in. Fartlek, which means "speed play" in Swedish, is a training method that blends continuous training with interval training. The person who needs to work out at 4am to get all the training in that consumes their life.

The person who puts your relationship after their training and PRs? Or the person you consider a great friend who is so busy climbing the social ladder that doesn't even give you the time of day at social functions because they are too busy networking and trying to get potential business connections your relationship takes second stage. The point being? It's not until these people continue to slap us in the face that we step back and think, "With friends like this who needs enemies?"

If you choose to become an athlete you definitely won't regret it, you'll just need to be aware that athletes come with a multitude of issues, too. The only difference is you will be the smart one working through your issues, others get so wrapped up in thinking they have to be perfect, they miss the boat all together. Just give those people room or you might go down with the Titanic.

Back to the stress of my husband's Ironman and my lack of control over the stress. I started feeling ill the moment Eric came by looking like he was going to pass out or die. My heart started beating out of my chest. My speech started sounding like it was on speed. I became irrational and told him, "Why are you putting your body through this, you can just stop, you know. Maybe you should stop? You made it this far."

Who cares about this silly old race? (Who cares that you trained for a year?) I told him he looked like shit and something could be seriously wrong with him. OK, that was NOT the thing to say, but I was reacting to my stress and not thinking it through. I had not been prepared for the hand of cards I was dealt at that moment. There I was sipping Sangria with Sheri and eating Tapas expecting a King of Hearts to show up, but I was given a Joker! I didn't want a

Joker! I didn't want that pathetic card. I might lose this game with a Joker, I needed a King! I wanted the strong powerful King to come into my view, not a zombie-like Joker!

I didn't plan for this in the strategy session. I thought Sheri and I would be along the race route for moral support yelling, "Go, Honey, you look so strong!" "You ROCK!" "You're the man!" All those wifely things we say to our man when he's out there racing. My husband just smirked with what little smirk he could manifest at that moment and said, "I feel like s**t. I can't keep my eyes open and my head up." When I pleaded with him to stop if he needed to, he agreed that he would if it got that bad, but at the moment, he would continue with one foot in front of the other—"baby steps." Well said. This man who was experiencing the most physical pain of his life was actually processing the pain and handling the stress better than his hysterical wife. Our men continued on with baby steps moving like little old Jokers with a crippled walk, but with King of Hearts souls.

I chuckled to myself wondering if I should go to the drug store down the street and get them each a cane to help support them, but thought that would violate the Ironman rules and could get them disqualified. It would have made for a funny story though. Visualize two 40-year-old men completing the Ironman with canes coming across the finish line. Talk about a buzz kill! Here Sheri and I were having our own celebration party looking forward to our men becoming something comparable to secret agents or Navy Seals. Crossing that finish line when all of a sudden our celebration became what seemed like Mission Impossible and worrying if those agents would be able to survive the mission they were on.

Sheri went back to her hotel to round up her kids and in-laws, while I went back to my room to get my running shoes on. I may be needed to run mission support. The black miniskirt, tank top, and rhinestone flip-flops were thrown on the hotel floor within a matter of seconds. I needed to change out of celebratory gear into athletic gear. I had my own race to run—the race of a partner in support of her Ironman. I was getting suited up, putting my game face on, but my heart was still beating furiously. My mission was not helped when Janelle called me from back home in Texas. She was glued to the athlete tracker. Let me explain the athlete tracker. The Iron website has a live Iron web feed. If you know your athlete's name or number you can track them along the race.

Janelle called to inform me that at mile 17 the guys just stopped. "It looked like something serious happened. Are they out?" They were averaging so slow a pace that they wouldn't complete their mission if they stayed this course. I, being without a car and not knowing the city, had no idea where mile 17 was. I couldn't help my man. I was out of control of the situation in more than one way. I couldn't control my anxiety at the moment or help on mission control. I remember getting off the phone with Janelle and just standing by a telephone pole along the run course. Like looking at every person that passed was going to help me help Eric? I was using mental telepathy.

I started willing each one of those hurting athletes to make their deadline to complete the mission. I became distracted after a while and just cheered each person on by their number. "Go number 1152, looking strong, almost there!" I'd make funny comments to get their mind off of their pain, "MMM, MMMM that's what I'm talking about! Now that's a boooodddddyyyy!!" They'd laugh and keep shuffling on. Let's talk strategy: As an athlete who has raced, I know people lie to me on the race route. I don't know if they know they are lying to me and other racers for positive performance reasons or if they are clueless about where they are standing at the moment. Case in point, there have been marathons where someone yells out to me, "Almost there, just two more miles!" Sorry, but this is bull!

I've had times where I'm 5 miles from the finish line. Don't tell me I have 2 miles left, and don't make me start picking up my pace to get this thing over with. I actually believed the idiots on my first race, picked up the pace, and then almost died when I still had 3 miles left to go. So, here I was telling these guys the same thing. The difference? They did only have a few miles left, they were almost there, but if they were like me in previous races, they were probably thinking, "Yeah, right, lady. Shut up! The fat man 5 miles back just told me I'm almost there. That the finish line was just around the corner." That's a spectator favorite: "Almost there, just around the corner!"

By the time Eric and Pat came back around my telephone pole, they looked like new men. Turns out the time when Janelle called to say they weren't moving helped the guys. That was the time they were hitting the wall and had to stop to process and rethink if they were going to make the mission. The strategy sessions evidently helped, as each man had different times when they hit a low. Eric would stop and process with Pat when he was not functioning or focusing and vice versa. This is why I say training with someone at similar speed is so important. It was foreshadowing something that would play a huge part of my success or failure to come.

Eric Cardwell, IM

Eric and Pat had a small loop to complete as they rounded past me. I cut across the loop running to the finish line ahead of them. The guys were actually running and had big old smiles on their faces. When I saw them approach the chute before the finish line they did a little jig and jumped in the air. "What?" I couldn't believe this burst of energy! Wow, what the mind can do!! They went from old men who couldn't walk before mile 12, to stopping around mile 17, to running and doing a jump in the air at mile 26.1 of the marathon, or mile 140.5 of the day. They were about to complete their mission, alive, and with smiles on their faces!

The mind can do amazing things. When, by all means and purposes, the body was not meant to complete 140.6 miles in one day and in less than 17 hours. It's amazing what we can do if we put our minds to it. This goes for losing weight, overcoming relationship issues, and even fighting life-threatening illnesses. How many times have you read about a person beating cancer by defying the odds? These people usually have a remarkable mind-over-matter solution. They don't let the news or issue affect their outlook, and they make their mind up that they are going to conquer this challenge and *do it*!

As Pat and Eric came across the finish line, I ran up to the barricade and gave my husband a long, wet kiss (I don't usually do much PDA). I have never been so happy to see someone alive than I was at that moment. I was so afraid he may die doing the Ironman race that I had him up his medical insurance and take out a nice life insurance policy. I could relax because all that worrying was over. Eric was alive and made it. Mission complete!! After the men received their congratulatory kisses, I made my way over to the Ironman finisher tent where the guys were. Sheri had her two sons and Pat's parents so it wasn't as easy for their crew to sneak in behind the finisher line.

I was able to go behind the scenes with my Ironman volunteer shirt on without any resistance. As I approached the guys in the recovery area, I will never forget the seven words spoken to me for the rest of my life. There was so much meaning and power in those seven little words. Those seven words would change my life **forever!**

Pat looked over at me with total excitement and total exhaustion. I wish I could describe how gaunt, dehydrated, and excited these two guys looked at that moment. Their cheekbones were protruding out of their faces, and their eyes were sunken in and had dark spots underneath. The only description I can accurately describe would be men released from the concentration camps with the damage to their bodies and the excitement on their faces of being released. I know, an extreme visual, but Pat and Eric's bodies looked emaciated and puny while their faces had smiles beaming from ear-to-ear.

Eric and Pat - Ironman

The seven words were from Pat. His first words to me after becoming an Iron Dude were, ***"You don't ever want to do this!"*** He was serious when he said it. I *saw* it more like "these guys are alive, and what a challenge!" I *heard* in my head, "What, you think a chick can't hang? That this mission is too tough for a woman? That women are too weak to do this (excuse me) mind-fucking event? That we are the weaker sex?"

What went through my head after Pat first said those words was some more Freudian talk—the Id, Ego, and Super Ego—the part of the mind that talks to itself. The part that says what is rational, what isn't, and the kid that says, "Let's go for it!" "Let's go balls-to-the-wall crazy!!!" Well, at that moment the little bug was implanted and the rest is history, as they say!

What drug were these guys on? They looked like crap and they pushed their body to the extreme, yet they are still smiling and they found enough energy to dance and jump at the end? Now Pat tells me, "You don't ever want to do this!" Oh yeah? What secret you got? I'm an athlete. I love a challenge. I love pushing my body to extremes, but I don't want to die doing it, and you guys didn't die!! Wow! What an ultimate challenge! To top it off, you think you will spare the little chick the misery of going through this? You guys know the saying, don't you? "What doesn't kill you only makes you stronger!"

This is the part where I should have told myself, "Sit down, hold on, and shut up, Dana, you're in for a bumpy ride!" After the celebration died down—when I say celebration, I mean it. Our town only had a couple of Ironman finishers that we knew of and, ironically, they were both chicks. We were friends with Allana who defied life's challenges by being diabetic and a seven time Iron chick. Allana had helped train Pat and Eric during their Iron journey. The other Iron chick was Kay, whom I didn't know but had heard about. Kay, at a young age of 26, decided she wanted to tackle the Iron event and became an Iron Chick on her first try, but DNFed (did not finish) on her second attempt. She was still an Iron Chick, no one could take that finish away from her.

When the guys got back as Iron Dudes, we had several parties in honor of them. To back up, we had a celebration dinner at Franciso's downtown a week prior to the race. Paco, who owns the place, has the best eclectic restaurant on the star with wonderful southwest cuisine. Paco had opened up his restaurant on Sunday night to allow the two Wisconsin Iron Dudes and other 70.3 Iron participants to host a pre-race celebration. One of the 70.3 Iron gals, Claire, was so humble to host the event, and I believe she paid for all or most of the food. We love you, Claire!

I remember having such a wonderful time at that meal. We celebrated life and the ability to do things that the majority of people in the world do not do for one reason or another. The anticipation in the air and excitement of the moment was to never be duplicated. All this played an important part in my future decisions. The mind can dwell on the pain of having a baby, or it can focus on the excitement of that precious miracle in one's life. I was noticing the miracle of the bond we established with our friends and the fear and the excitement we were all going through.

Eric and Pat became hometown heroes. There were newspaper articles written about them and there were friends inviting us over to hear our stories. We were wined and dined. People wanted to pick their brains. There was excitement in the air, and then it happened.

Iron Nugget:

Do you get excited and motivated when others succeed? Or do you get discouraged? Explain?

Where would you do an Ironman race? What state or country? Why do you like that place?

25   The Sherpas

Roget's 21st Century Thesaurus, 3rd Ed., 2012, lists the definition of a Sherpa as a tour guide—synonymous with a chaperon, escort, or guide. In training for an Iron race, we refer to those who are there to help us with the journey or on race day as our "sherpas." I have had the blessing of encountering many Sherpas who got me to the place I am today.

Look further on the Internet and you will find that a Sherpa is an ethnic group found in the Himalayan Mountains, mostly in the Tibet and Nepal areas. Approximately 30,000 Sherpas live in the area. Since the 1950s, tourism is the main source of employment for the Sherpas. Their services include assisting and guiding climbers who come to the area to climb Mount Everest and other mountain ranges. The Sherpa's boast the record for holding the most times summited for men and women on Mount Everest, along with the quickest ascent and descends, and the youngest climber to reach the summit of Everest (www.peakfreaks.com).

How ironic that a Sherpa helps people basically reach their spiritual journey? Everyone I encountered along my Iron journey had some part in my spiritual goal. Setting out to do a 2.4-mile swim in the ocean, a 112-mile bike ride in the hot blistering, wind, and a 26.2-mile run in less than 17 hours is definitely spiritual, whether you admit it or not.

There are times during the race that your mind plays freaky games with you and your body basically refuses to cooperate. The spirit prevails if you finish. The Sherpas are a big part of that finish line! No one comes across that line without having someone guide or bless them at some point of their journey.

Not even a month after Eric became an Ironman, I decided, like a kid who was going to attempt their first roller coaster ride, **I would do an Ironman event**. There was no question about riding that train alone—I would find friends to join me. I never once thought of inviting too many friends. My philosophy, *back then*, was that I loved a party, and the more the merrier. I called up four gals I thought would be able to hang in an Iron event.

The first one I called was Tamra. Tamra is a local M.D. who is a *killer* tri-athlete. I had competed against her in several triathlons and she had kicked my ass in all of them. Tamra raced with a big old smile on her face and appeared to put little effort into what she was doing. She was a natural at triathlon, so it was obvious I would call her first.

Each one of the women I called was a social friend, not a friend I hung out with all the time. Janelle was out of the question as she was claustrophobic in the water, and you have to be able to swim 2.4 miles in an Ironman event. Sheri was out of the question as she previously mentioned she had no desire to bike or swim. She was a runner—that was her thing—and I honored that.

My decision was to compete in Ironman Cozumel with Florida Ironman as a backup. Tamra was excited, took the bait and said she would talk it over with her hubby. The problem with inviting an M.D. is they are a little too smart at times. They may overanalyze the situation. Like say, the fact that we would be doing a life-challenging event in say, Mexico, which is not known for their wonderful medical facilities.

I didn't care. I cruised to Cozumel several times a year on cheap Carnival cruises. I have been to Cancun, Ixtapa, Zihuataneho, Montego Bay, Ocho Rios, and the Grand Caymans, but Cozumel is my favorite locale. Period.

I have a favorite same motor scooter shop and I go to it each time. Roger always gives me a half-price deal when I remind him how often I come to Cozumel just to see him. I go to the same beach—Paradise Beach—to enjoy all the toys, food, and excitement it provides, and I go to the same mercantile shops to buy vanilla or tequila. I'm a creature of habit, so when I decided to do an Ironman event, I wanted to see the fish down below while I swam. And I wanted to go to somewhere I love and visit regularly. Cozumel is one of the few places with perfect visibility for swimming. Doing a 2.4-mile swim could get old and my ADHD could kick in. I might have focused on the pain and not the fish if I competed in a place where I couldn't watch something to distract me.

I've spent many hours swimming in Cozumel, chasing the little sword fish, Nemo and Dory. The sword fish aren't really that variety, they just resemble the big sword fish and will actually swim with you as you swim in the ocean. The little Nemo and Dory guys swim from you, so you get to chase them for fun. The only reason I picked Florida Iron as backup is the fact that it tends to have warm water. I can't even attempt to swim in cold water as I get the chills and shake uncontrollable, which makes for a near-impossible swim. Cold for me is no Bueno!

The Florida Ironman is a two-loop course where you get out of the water at mile 1, run 25 yards on the beach and get back in. The positive part of the Florida swim is it breaks up the 2.4 mile ocean swim, you are able to get something to drink and eat a gel as you run down the beach, then get back at it. The negative part is the run on the beach can be tiring to your legs, the ocean swells are challenging—not one time, but two times. It all works out in the end as each Ironman event has its pros and cons.

Tamra hashed out all the pros and cons then called me back to say she would be open to doing Ironman Florida, but not Ironman Cozumel. She didn't want to be in Mexico if they needed medical help, and her parents were not fond of traveling to Mexico. She wanted her children and family to be there as support on this journey. Before Tamra got back with me, I had called three other gal friends.

Linda was second on the list to call as she was a fast runner. When I met Linda, had just had her daughter, Gyselle, and I only knew her as a stroller walker. Baby Mama. She spent several years dedicating her life as a new doctor and mother to Jon and Gyselle. Jon is about 3 years older than Gyselle, so Linda was a busy woman with a private practice and two children younger than 3 years of age when I met her.

It wasn't until Gyselle was 4 years old that I started to take notice of Linda's athletic skills. Linda started racing 5K races and was starting to make a name for herself at local events. Linda is a beautiful, short and slim, Latina woman with a big smile. Somehow those little legs have the fastest turn over I've ever seen. She smiles as she defeats her opponents during local 5K races. She tends to be quiet and blends in with a crowd.

Previously, Janelle had been the fastest female racer locally. It now became a game of "I wonder who is going to take home the top female on this race, Linda or Janelle?" The local races were fun for me, as I'm not part of the PR competition, but I love to watch others duke it out in a boxing match. Don't you like a good fight? I do, especially when it **doesn't** involve me.

Linda and I started talking about her new-found skills. Turns out she had done marathons and some triathlons back in college. She had a lag in her speed work and endurance races, so she hired a run coach who was a professor at the local college. He had coached many runners and even some pre-Olympian collegiate athletes down in the valley. Dr. G thrived on working with Linda, as she takes direction well and runs with it!

While Linda was checking off PRs on her list, I was getting slower and slower at my 5Ks. I had never been one to do speed work. Why? Look at the name alone. It has the word **work** in it. I never liked to use running, cycling, and swimming with the word work associated with it. Remember? My motto is "It's all about the stories." I thought you couldn't have a story, stop and smell the roses, if you were working toward something. It's a Carpe Diem kind of attitude. Seize the Day. Whatever happens will happen; it's race day. Every race is a different race, no two are the same. Go with the flow. I'm just here for the party and to meet new characters!

However, there was something enticing about Linda's new-found speed. I knew her as Stroller Mama, not kick ass and take names Mama. I kind of liked what she had become. I wanted a piece of that kick-ass skill. I had never had that. Maybe, just maybe, this coach could do something with me? I know I would never have the VO2 max that Lance Armstrong has, but maybe I could get a little faster?

I trained with Dr. G. a few times and then Linda invited me out on a long run with them where Dr. G would follow behind in his car. I thought this was a little creepy. Why does he have to follow? She said that we were going to be on Bandera Highway headed toward Bandera and he wanted to keep clock time on her and make sure she was OK. Still, a little creepy, but I was up for the challenge. I wanted to put my newly-learned skills out there on a long run. What better way than running with a speed demon?

I hate having pressure on myself to perform and, in fact, this is usually my downfall as I do too much negative self-talk. "What's the matter with you? You can't keep up with her. You are slow, remember. Hello? Are you kidding yourself?" I then give in to the negative self-talk and have affirmatives like, "Yep, that's it. Taking it easy is the only way to go. What do you have to prove anyway? Nothing, right?" This mentality has hurt me one too many times.

On this day, I was excited. I knew I wasn't racing and was just going to practice what Dr. G and I had been working on. Linda and I started off together, just talking about life, racing, and stuff. Before I knew it we were 5 miles down the road. Linda asked if I knew what pace we had been holding. I told her I hadn't. I don't even look at those things. I just run. Like Forrest Gump, "I think I'm gonna run. Hmmm, I think I'll stop now." There is no formula in the way I run. Why does she think I hired this middle-aged man driving behind us watching our rumps bounce up and down as we run? I did mention a little creepy, didn't I?

As Dr. G. followed along, Linda informed me that we had been keeping a high seven-minute mile pace. "Say what, what??" Linda laughed and told me, "Yep, you have been holding a pretty fast pace, girl." It was my mind and the lack of stress Linda provided that kept me from over focusing on what I thought I wasn't capable of doing. Somewhere between mile 5 and 8 I had to pee, as usual, and told Linda I needed to find a bush and then continue at a slower pace. She just smiled and said something about it being fun and carried on effortlessly as I traipsed through the long weeds off the two-lane highway to find a decent sized bush. I was hoping old Dr. G would go ahead and pass me and not watch as I peed—he didn't need a moon shot this early in the morning.

I motioned to him that I was going to head over to a little tree and to go on past me. He did. After our run, I remember smelling ammonia in my nostrils. It's amazing when you increase your speed and change your breathing rate how it affects little things. I probably had been yapping so much on our run that I didn't take time to breathe the way I should have.

As an avid yogi, I run with the same principle I do yoga. A deep breathe in through the nose, and if I'm going too fast to breathe out my nose, I take a deep, long breath out of my mouth, but never mouth to mouth! Never mouth-in and mouth-out breaths. People who do this generally breathe out of their chest and not through the abdomen. By taking deep breaths in through the nose from the belly, you actually help the mind focus and give the brain oxygen it needs during endurance races.

I called Linda to join me on an Iron journey. She was such a great runner; she would just need to perfect her bike and swim. Linda didn't have a bike, so that would be the first agenda. Linda talked it over with her husband who works long hours. He would have to be in favor of the race, because with Linda training this would mean some long "Daddy duties." Her hubby supported Linda and said, "Have at it."

The next two gals turned me down. One was Kathy, my twin. She was Tamra's neighbor. I didn't realize that Tamra had inspired Kathy to do some triathlons and runs. I just thought she was a haphazard athlete like me, in it for the fun. I'd thought she would be a perfect mix. Kathy just laughed when I asked her and said, "Dana, (with a west Texas drawl) now why in the world would I want to do an Ironman race?" That one was off the list.

The last person was a gal named Sue who has a sweet disposition and is always smiling like Linda. I met Sue a few years back during Conquer the Coast bike race in Corpus Christi. The race had a special tribute to Sue's father that year. He had been killed while doing what he loved—cycling. There was a point on the time trail dedicated to his memory when participants were asked to race with his memory soaring on Angel's wings. I must say it had to be very inspiring, yet soul searching for Sue during that event, but she always had a smile on her face.

I had talked with Sue and I knew she wanted to do triathlons. Sue is a hard-core cyclist, like her father, and I knew if she could do the 112 miles of an Iron event, the rest would be gravy. I called Sue just minutes after calling the others. I just dialed those numbers of the four gals with preparation in convincing them that they needed to become an Iron Chick like I was going to be. Woman Power! Chick Power!

We were going to be the dynamic duo, trio, quadpro, quintuplets. OK, something along those lines. I didn't really stop and think it through. I just figured, out of four gals who I knew had the potential; at least one was surely to say yes. And they did, two of them.

As we had the three inexperienced Musketeers gung-ho, we needed some sound advice on this journey. I called up Pat who just finished Iron Wisconsin and was starting to find himself with nothing to plan for the next year. You have to sign up for an Ironman event a year in advance as the event sells out right away. You might even miss the boat when trying to sign up on the computer. I knew this was the case with the popular Florida Ironman. It's one of the faster courses with warmer water, and many people choose it due to the fast and flat bike course.

I planned on working the upcoming November Florida Iron event as a volunteer to secure a slot. I convinced Allana as I told her she might as well jump on the chick bandwagon, because we would be calling her for advice along the journey, anyway. I told Pat what an opportunity for him. He could race with four women and use his recent skills to help us make sound decisions. He took the bait.

Allana called up her old buddy, Kay, because she knew how the last Iron event took a blow to her self-esteem and asked her to join us. Kay agreed. Linda and I flew up to Panama City Beach to volunteer for Ironman Florida 2009 together and stayed at the local Holiday Inn, while Kay and Allana got a cool condo. The Panama Beach Holiday Inn was directly on the beach, and the pool was a lot nicer than Allana and Kay's condo, but their condo was roomy, new, and beautiful.

Allana had the inside scoop on a good seafood restaurant and we all ate seafood and toasted with glasses of wine the night before working the Ironman event. Allana said the swim start is just gorgeous, so we all were signed up to volunteer at the race start, UNTIL, I heard you have to get there at 5:30 a.m.!! Damn, that's really early!!

I told Linda I was going to switch to volunteering at the women's swim transition, because you didn't have to get there until 7:30 a.m. Just in time to watch the start of the Iron swim and then head to the volunteer tent to help the pros who fly out of the water in less than one hour. Linda said that sounded good to her and we switched volunteer stations.

The start of the 2009 Ironman Florida was beautiful with a cool morning and some choppy waters. I remember it was cold, because Linda lent me her athletic wind gear. I hate being cold and was probably complaining out loud, not meaning to, so Linda told me she wasn't cold and for me to wear her light jacket. I didn't argue. I was warm and happy!

The women came out of the water immediately complaining about how turbulent the waters were that day and how they felt like they were in a washing machine. Some of the women complained of throwing up during the swim and some talked about people dropping out of the swim because they started to panic in the rough ocean swells. I was both excited and scared at the same time.

I knew each race was a different day, so having swells one year didn't mean it was going to be the same the next year. We saw way too many boobs and bushes that day, again, but carried on. We later met Allana and Kay for burgers which were provided for volunteers. Allana, Kay, Linda, and I all sat on the sidewalk and ate our much needed lunch. We talked about the morning event with excitement and anticipation in the air.

We would go back to our places and change, hang out by the beach and pool for a while during the bike event, then head back out to experience the run when it started. Allana said we had to stay until midnight to watch the last person cross the finish line. It's an exhilarating experience, she said. I didn't get to watch the midnight finish at my husband's Ironman Wisconsin. We were so tired and went back to the hotel after Eric ate some pizza and drank some Gatorade.

Linda and I changed in our room which overlooked the beach. As we looked out on the balcony, we saw swimmers swimming laps out in the ocean. The water had calmed down from the morning's swells, and the water was a clear blue-green just outside our hotel. We looked at each other and I can't remember who said it first but we said, "Hey, you want to go swim some laps on the beach before the other two girls get here?"

We were excited. We almost ran down the beach like eager beavers, pardon the pun, to get in the water. The temperature had warmed up and there was no cool breeze like there was that morning. We got in with our wetsuits and started swimming up against the tide so we would be able to swim back with it. At one point something really large brushed past me. It freaked me out! I told Linda, "Hey, let's not go out any further and swim back a little closer to shore. We can swim parallel to the beach." She agreed.

I wasn't about to tell her that something really large skimmed past me until we were back on shore. I had huge goose bumps from the experience and was trying to calm my breathing down. There were little jelly fish everywhere which we had to swim around. This wasn't freaky, it was the thought of the big thing that might take a large bite that freaked me out.

As we came back on shore, I told Linda about my experience. She said she saw some manta rays when she was swimming, so it was most likely a manta ray, not a shark. It wasn't until our beach encounter with the other girls that Allana informed me there was a code over the walkie-talkie for a school of sharks that morning at the beginning of the Ironman event.

Allana is an EMT and got to work more hands-on assisting swimmers with her volunteer duties. She was with a guy who was on the front line as an employee of Ironman. Allana said, "Code: Marine Life means sharks are in the area. It happens, and it was probably just nurse sharks who don't usually mess with swimmers." **I don't care!** I don't mind swimming with sting rays, manta rays, jelly fish, puffer fish—anything except sharks, they freak me out. I couldn't tell you which was a nice shark and which was a mean shark. A shark is a shark, and they all have big teeth that do a lot of harm!

Florida Sharks: According to the series Shark Week, Season 1, Episode 1, one year in Volusia County there were 79 shark attacks reported in a season on the Volusia Beach alone. The beaches had to be closed temporarily by the county. Once it was opened again, signs were placed in the vicinity that read: **Dangerous Marine Life in Area.**

I was glad to get our swim over for the day and didn't want to go back out in that Florida water until the same time next year! We hung out by the pool. Linda had just bought her wet suit so we took pictures modeling our wet suits. A wet suit really makes your stomach suck in so we felt almost a little sexy in our wetsuits.

I started to relax in the lounge chair by the pool when Allana said, "Well, ladies, we better get dressed and head back out for the run." I was exhausted and our race hadn't even begun. Even though our shift did not start until 7:30 a.m., Linda and I woke up at 5:30 a.m. to get our coffee, eat a bar, and walk 2.5 miles to get to the starting line. As we walked to the starting line that morning, this meant walking back from the event. Besides a lack of sleep the night before, I had already walked 5 miles so far and did an ocean swim.

To top it off, we had competed in a dance contest and Hula-hoop contest around the pool. I had just settled in to chill! So much for chillin'—this was an Iron event. Little did I know how tiring being a spectator could be? Linda and I got ready for round two of the day. We met the other girls at a destination and walked a good part of the run course to find somewhere we could hang out without all the people screaming in our ears. As we were walking, I decided this was a party so I got a drink.

I found an Asian market and decided on hot sake and a beer. Not a good combo! The next mistake was that I did not eat appropriately all day. We were busy and I wasn't watching my hypoglycemia. It hit me sometime that night when Allana started yelling at me. I guess the two alcoholic drinks revved me up because Allana and I were talking about some man on the run. We were disagreeing on something. Odd, I can't even remember the topic, but I remember the situation. I guess I was talking fast and loud because all of a sudden she just started yelling at me, "Would you just shut up and listen!!!???"

"Seriously, you're yelling at me?" I flipped her off and walked away. Yes, a little passive-aggressive. I ended up going up the road a mile or two in the dark and cheering for the racers under a street light. Anywhere I could get away from Allana at the moment. t was nice and serene where I stood for an hour cheering people on.

I regretted my actions as I didn't agree with Allana's behavior, but why did I have to react to her? Allana gets along with men better than women and there have been several occasions where she has laughed at me or made dumb blonde comments my way. When she started yelling at me like she had control over me, I reacted, and later regretted it. Dang impulse control got in the way again.

Linda walked up to me about an hour or so later and said, "There you are, I was wondering where you went off to." I told her about Allana pissing me off and she offered a very logical answer. As Allana is diabetic and I'm hypoglycemic she said, "Don't you think you two could have been experiencing some sugar issues and are just reacting to your lack of proper nutrition today?" Ahh, good point, especially since I told her I was feeling dizzy and had to get something to eat right away.

Once I'm down that path I don't process well. In fact, I don't even remember what I ate after that, but I do remember just praying to God to make it back to the Holiday Inn during the 2.5 mile walk back. I thought I was going to faint, and I couldn't see where I was walking in the dark. Unfortunately, this was some major foreshadowing.

I got something to eat prior to getting back to the hotel, but couldn't get my sugar level up to par, so I downed a bottle of Gatorade and tried to eat some peanut butter crackers in the hotel. It was late. Wait, I do remember going back to the finish line prior to heading to the hotel because I had a conversation with a gentleman who had competed numerous times in the Florida Ironman. He told me if the swim is rough one year, it almost always is nice, "like glass," the following year.

I exclaimed, "Ahh, I'm going to have glass for my swim. Amen!" Linda and I cheered the last lady on who was a larger set woman in her mid-50s. Just inspiring! I think we both had tears in our eyes watching her come in and hear Mike Rielly say, "Number 713, YOU are an Ironnman!" It was funny because 30 minutes prior to that, Miss Priss had crossed the line in all her glory living it up. Miss Priss was dressed in a sexy black running skirt with a sexy black running top and took her long flowing brunette hair down somewhere just before the finish line. She came prancing down that chute, throwing her hair around, and whooping it up for the crowd while men yelled out cat calls and she pumped her hands in the air for more. That was my new alter ego.

That was my Sondra! I was gonna do that when I crossed the finish line. I wish I would have kept that outlook, because things changed the next morning once I pushed that button to compete!

Iron Nugget:

Describe your Sondra.

Describe the perfect Sherpa.

26 Taking Care of Business

"Dread only one day at a time." (Charlie Brown)

When I got back to Kerrville, I was all business. Gone was the fun Dana. I was focused and had to get a plan together. Due to my incident with Allana, I wasn't looking to call her up for advice anytime soon. In fact, once you set off on this journey, you really need someone around to lift you up and support you. I felt that Allana thought I was a loud, hyperactive person and I had a hard time trusting if she would respect me and talk to me like the hyperactive, intelligent person I am.

Yes, I know, I get excited, talk too fast at times, bounce around with subjects, but I'm not stupid by any means, and when someone raises their voice to me like I'm a moron or 6 year old in the cookie jar, I get angry. OK, so sometimes I look like a 3 year old on the playground not wanting to leave when her mother says it's time to go, but I'm still not stupid! Don't talk to me like I am! I just get high on life—at least it's better than the alternative. Training started right away for me. I was scared. I was doubtful that I could do this. What had I gotten myself into?

Let's look at those boring people who aren't high on life. Did you know the person who goes through the same daily routine day after day is making themselves stupid? Seriously, when the mind does the same thing over and over without throwing in something new—a new task, a new mix, a new route—the brain does not receive a new challenge and so the synapses that are firing do not get a new challenge either.

It's the old "use it or lose it" principle. This is huge *people,* or should I say this is why people are huge. They are not only huge, but they are huge and stupid!! The brain tends to atrophy like the muscles do when you don't use it the way it should be used. A person needs to add new mixes, new hobbies, and new tasks into their regimen. Your brain will atrophy just like your muscles when you don't use them.

Haven't you known people who don't even get out of the city they live in? They stay landlocked. I know money doesn't grow on trees, but people need to add some periodic travel to their life to be able to live a full and abundant life. To see what is out there. God meant for us to see his beautiful world and meet his wonderful people, not to stay landlocked all our lives. Hence the term "nomad!"

It's like the abused youth I have worked with. Their minds are so messed up because they don't trust, they have been abused tremendously and their brains are functioning in one capacity, and that's through fear and lack of trust. These kids need years and years of counseling and training their brains to change that one dimension.

Women need to get out of the "little lady" role. We need to explore math and science. Don't leave it up to men who rule that field. Challenge your brains, people, and add a new sport or physical challenge. By adding an endurance race your brain transfers that workout through your whole body. You increase the little feel-good boogers in your head—serotonin, dopamine, and endorphins.

When your body gets stronger, your brain gets stronger, too. It's amazing how this works. I am not a scientist, but as a personal trainer and counselor, I have seen research which supports the idea that challenging your body improves brain performance. That's why I have advocated for years that youth with at-risk behaviors benefit from a challenging workout program.

I started the 5K mentoring program with youth years ago because I actually witnessed improvement in their executive skills and daily planning. They didn't take as many risky behaviors like getting in fights, running away, staying out past curfew, skipping school, and fighting with parents when they were involved in the summer training and summer 5Ks.

This principle needs to be applied to so many at-risk youth before they become adults and we, as a society, have to support them in the prison systems. Americans are truly lazy; we wait until *the shit hits the fan* to address severe issues, unfortunately. As a challenge, I will be donating $1 of each book sale to go to a running fund for at-risk youth to enter 5k races.

Some out there may use the excuse that you don't like to sweat and feel bad, well, let's look at the sweat factor. There are two different types of sweat. There's you're lazy sweat—apocrine sweat—which leaves your shirt yellow because it's laced with fats and proteins that nasty bacteria is attracted to.

The other sweat I will address is the feel-good eccrine sweat—the athletic sweat. People feel bad when they first have an exercise, eccrine, sweat because the mind and body revolt, but only at first. The mind says, "Whoa, buddy, what the hell are you doing? I want to sit back down, watch TV, and eat ice cream with fried chicken!! Stop, stop!" It's like an alcoholic going through withdrawal.

The alcoholic feels like crap, has sweats, gets sick, throws up, gets headaches, along with body aches and feels like giving up and going back to drinking at one period or another. It's not easy, the alcohol becomes like a nutrient to the body and the body expects that substance. So, as you know, the body goes through withdrawal!! Once the addict is through the bad part, the benefits outweigh the risks of being sober. It's common sense!

Exercise or endurance training is similar. You have to retrain the body to move through the killing stage. Your body has turned on you, it's killing you, and when you tell your body to get off its ass, it will talk back to you at first. It's like an alcoholic coming off alcohol. It's the same thing with the sedentary lifestyle. You are going to go through a little withdrawal stage from sitting around and taking it easy, but it's a Catch 22. While you sit and take it easy, you are killing yourself and becoming stupid! So, you can choose to get off your ass, go through a rough time of feeling awful, and become smarter and decrease your chance of killing yourself at a young age or take the alternative.

I already went through the withdrawal stage when I gained 15 pounds years ago by becoming cool drinking Diet soda, eating fast food, and taking the easy lifestyle. I will never, ever go back to that stage. I developed anxiety problems and always felt tired. Why, live like that? Besides the slug in my bug, I had aches and pains. Some studies show those with back and leg pains generally have it from the extra weight. I sure did and was only 15 pounds over my normal 5'6 130 pounds. You do the math. If you are carrying much more weight at a shorter height, you too likely have some aches and pains. Yep, it's probably weight related.

Think about it. I was pushed down a full flight of stairs, had surgery, and only experienced back and leg pain when I was overweight. The other years I was physically active and added weight training to my weekly workout regimen. I trained for Ironman in my 40s with a few right hamstring strains and a metatarsal foot injury, but no back pains. The hamstring injury came from a pull. Point being, I should have an excuse to have back pain and I used that excuse when I gained 15 pounds but, the pain miraculously disappeared when I lost the weight and got physically active, again. The more I worked out, the better I felt.

My blood work shows great cholesterol levels for my age, but I do have some low sodium levels due to extreme long bike rides in the hot Texas sun. I'd rather eat a lot of salt on my food and take sodium supplements than not be able to eat what I want for fear of dying from a heart-attack with high cholesterol. With the eccrine healthy sweat you don't smell, it's clear and odorless. Don't worry, once you get that "Hello, I'm lazy" sweat out of your system, your sweat won't smell. It will be like expensive perfume! Priceless and clear!

Little by little, my nerves started to calm down about signing up for an Ironman race. We had group rides at Tamra's house on Thursday evenings with beer and pizza afterwards so there was a party to look forward to each week. We swam in the river on Wednesday nights at 5:30 p.m. and sometimes followed it up with a short brick run down Guadalupe Street. Saturday or Sunday consisted of a long ride to Comfort or Fredericksburg with a get together at someone's home later that evening.

One day, we rode to Fredericksburg, had lunch and went to the wineries after our ride. Such fun! We all talked excitedly—we were high... on life. No one laughed at me for getting so excited, they were excited too. We all got our names after one long, excited bike ride. The 2010 Iron Florida crew consisted of an Eagle, Tigger, Lioness, Cheetah, and a Squirrel.

The only man on this journey was Pat, or Eagle. Pat tends to soar through life or his athletic events like a strong eagle. The Eagle is mighty and powerful watching others without them knowing, with the ability to swoop in to provide support, or a kill, when needed. Pat can help his teammates with his tough lawyer skills and knowledge about the Iron event, or he can overpower them on the bike when he wants to. He somehow earned the name Eagle.

The rest of us were given our names, but Allana who had done eight Iron events gave herself the name Tigger years ago. Tigger bounces along with a haphazard outlook on life. Allana has done so many endurance triathlons that she just takes off and bounces from event to event meeting new people along the way.

Tamra was given the name Lioness because she is our protector, our Momma Bear. She makes sure we are ready to go out on a long ride and gives us advice and encouragement along the way. She is a plethora of endurance information. Tamra and her hubby have been riding bikes for so many years, that if you are going through a bike issue, they have probably experienced it or seen it. Tamra will give you some sound advice to put in your bag of tricks. Tamra is the tough Lioness who protects and looks after her herd. If you are on a long bike ride, she's always at the lead, but will stop somewhere along the route to make sure everyone is OK. Once the last person has caught up, she will carry on. Tamra makes you feel safe.

On one of our Wednesday night evening swims Tamra's medical skills came in to play. We were headed out on the slippery dam to enter the water when we looked back and saw an older woman with her grandson slip as she tried to enter the water. She fell and then got back up and said, "Oh, damn, I just broke my arm!" All of us carefully waded back up the slippery dam to assist the woman. She looked and sounded fine, until two minutes later when she fainted and just slipped into the edge of the water. We got to her and the rest of us were a little frantic as what to do. One person dialed 911, but Tamra remained calm and just held the women's head up off the concrete until she came to.

When the lady came to, Tamra asked her the medical questions that people ask and told her to remain calm and help was on the way. After the ambulance arrived, we headed back out to swim. Tamra said the woman just had a vagal response which was most likely triggered by the trauma of breaking her arm. She should be fine.

The term is called a vasovagal response and referred to as a vagal response as short. Look up vasovagal response on www.wikepedia.com—quite interesting. Tamra is so encouraging in a no-nonsense type of way, she's known for not sugar coating issues. If she needs to tell you to "stop belittling yourself" she will with Lioness prowess. No pity-parties allowed around Tamra.

After one long ride, I was exhausted, and didn't want to go on a short 5K run. I told the group to go on as I couldn't. No, ma'am! Tamra made me go if only for 2 miles. She wouldn't have me sitting around. I was in pain, but she knew if I was going to become an Iron Chick I would need to learn to move through it, past it. I did that painful 2 mile run. Thanks, Tamra.

Tamra and Linda would bring me little items throughout our journey. I received a _**Believe**_ sign which is hanging in my kitchen and a little iron squirrel sitting on my kitchen window sill. What a metaphor. They are truly inspiring! Too bad Tamra makes more money being a doctor, because she would be an excellent coach. Both her parents were teachers, which must be where she got her patience and good teaching skills. Before our iron event, Tamra made sure we had some quality time with massages and a get together. Tamra knew how scared and nervous I was but told me, "Girl, you got me in this and you aren't backing out now." I cherish the note she wrote me just before my second Iron event. It read:

> Dear Dana,
>
> Enjoy the day! You are strong. I will be watching via Internet. I am sorry I won't be there in person, but know I will be praying for you. Remember your plan, stick with it! Eat even if you don't want to. Stop and rest if you need to. You have what it takes. I can hear the announcer saying already, "Dana Cardwell, you ARE an Ironman!" You are a beautiful person inside and out! I

can't wait to celebrate with you no matter what happens. You're a winner for even trying. Love, Tamra

Guys, this is the type of person you need to surround yourself with. Little did I know things would change in the future? Surround yourself with people like Pat, Linda and Tamra who make you soar on eagles' wings. Who make you believe that the world is a good place and you can conquer the most challenging odds. Be careful who you hang with, you can be with those who really push you and lift you up, or those who muddy the waters and make things a little hard to see. Ultimately, the challenge is yours to work through, and I know you can dig deep and push through any battle you are facing. Thank you Tamra, Pat, and Linda for giving me the pep talks along the way, you helped me see my way through the muddy waters.

The Small Texan Tri (Olympic) in Boerne,

Now there is Linda, aka Cheetah. A cheetah is sleek, quiet, and fast as lightening. While Tamra trucks along with power and strength, Linda starts off unassuming with little effort and patience to scope out the scene and then takes off with full speed. Linda is a neutral character, not an aggressive force. The Cheetah is friends with everyone and only gives advice if it is truly sought.

Linda listens, and then makes her point once we stop talking. I try to make sure I don't control the whole conversation like some of our other friends, but sometimes I feel Linda wants to tell me something, but doesn't. I tend to be hyper-vigilant at times. As you read with the poor little old man, I may get irritated and say things I shouldn't. Linda is encouraging and soft spoken. She gave me so many tokens and little "believe in you" items along the journey, and I started to believe I could do this event. I cherish the prayer and card she gave me before Ironman Florida.

Linda earned the name Cheetah due to her athletic prowess and her soft mannerism. Cheetahs are small in stature, but beautiful, and you don't think of them as hurting others in the jungle. They take their prey if needed, but for the most part they blend in with the environment and are not perceived as a threat. This is Linda in a nutshell.

Iron Nugget:

What business do you need to take care of currently to achieve a goal?

How are you going to go about taking care of the business?

27 Snap Outta It!

"Do not let what you cannot do interfere with what you can do." (John Wooden)

Fast forward to my Ironman Florida race which is the second week in November. Because we trained for a whole year, I started having concentration issues around September 2010. I couldn't focus. I got distracted and moody. I knew something was wrong, but I just chalked it up to the extreme training we were going through. I started pulling back from my friends and doing my own long bike rides because they were getting faster while I was getting slower. I told them I just wanted to train on my own. "I needed that."

Pay close attention, folks, because when your friends are going through issues they may say something but not mean it. By telling Linda I just needed to train on my own, that I do better that way, she heard it—I mean really heard it—like that's the way I am. And she heard it for the future. I just couldn't keep up with the other gals, so I didn't want to hold them back. I was doing it to save face because I was slow, and to not get in their way.

A tidbit of information regarding female athletes, *"At the recreational level as well as the elite level, recent studies have shown conclusively that sports participation generally leads to increased, rather than diminished, self-esteem for girls and women as well as for boys and men."* (The Athletic Personality Mere Myth? www.britannica.com) The article goes on to say, *"Although female athletes are increasing similar psychologically to male athletes, they continue to respond more readily than men do to encouragement and to react more negatively than men to admonition."*

I trained alone from September through November and my self-esteem suffered tremendously. I didn't have the camaraderie I was used to. I felt bad physically and mentally and became moody and frustrated with my performance and my feelings. I wanted to be Squirrel again. I'd rather people laugh at my hyperactive outlook than my angry and frustrated outlook. Remember, a fundamental principle: *We as human beings want to belong!*

What was wrong with me? I felt so alone and so sad. To top it off, my friends saw me as angry and pushing them away. When our friends are in the throes of something, they most likely don't know what's wrong either. If we think the relationship is worth salvaging, take that person out to dinner, coffee, or for a pedicure to do some soul searching. This is the time that they may really, really, need a friend. My friends were just respecting my wishes to train alone. They didn't really know something was going on. Either did I.

I tried to put on a new face at the airport heading out to Florida with all our friends, but something was different. Was this Iron training really a bad idea? We had so much fun until the last few months. I hadn't even started the race and I felt like I had hit the wall already! I told myself to **snap out of it**! In retrospect, there were two things going on—something medical and something mental. Yes, I was putting too much pressure on myself. I was sinking into a depressed state, but I should have had some blood work done when I noticed something feeling really off with me. This is why you have my book to learn from my mistakes, don't go through five or six months of feeling awful before you can't function anymore. Before you chase all your friends away and want to become a recluse.

I look back at my Ironman Florida pictures and see a forced smile—a nervous smile. We got to our condo and unpacked. Linda, her hubby, and daughter were staying with Eric, me and my daughter in one condo. The team of Tigger and Todd were staying at a condo across the street, Team Lioness and hubby were staying in a **sweet** penthouse with their families and team Eagle and Sheri (aka Sondra) were staying in our complex down the way.

We all were in different directions, but ready to head out on the same journey three days from then. Some of us were more prepared than others. Your mental outlook on the day of an Ironman event is so important. The funny part is that I needed my buddies then more than the whole year before, but I felt so alone and didn't understand why. I was having periodic panic attacks, losing sleep, and just plain tired. I literally made myself get out on long bike rides or long runs, but felt the lack of energy constantly.

I found myself with bad self-talk. *"You know, I can't do this anyway, what was I thinking?" "Why did I try to fool myself? I'm not a real athlete." "I just wanted to have some fun, but the fun is over. Why am I still here?"* In Florida I went for a short, 10-mile bike ride and felt exhausted. We tried to do some practice swims, but the tide was so rough we couldn't even **walk** through it. This became an area of concern to add to my current anxiety. *"How in the hell am I going to swim 2.4 miles through these waves?"*

Then it happened, without warning. A nasty cold front blew in. What? *"I hate cold water! I didn't sign up for a stinkin' cold-water swim. I get chills. I can't do it!!"* Oops, did I say *"can't"?* I think I did. Trying to get in that water with my sleeveless wet suit was near impossible. So the day <u>before</u> the Ironman, when the cold front blew in, I ran over to the Expo tent to see if they had anymore long sleeved wet suits to rent.

Some companies rent out wet suits, but most of the people renting them had done so three days before the race to try them out, etc. Sometimes wet suits get holes in them or have issues and a person finds themselves needing to rent a suit rather than forking $500 out at an already expensive race. The cost to rent is around $90, so much more affordable. There was one last suit and it was an X-small. "What? I'm not an *extra* small!" The guy helping was just what I needed. He told me it looked like it would fit and to try it on, "You may be surprised." I said a prayer, "Dear Lord, please let this fit. I don't want to not make the swim part. If I'm going to die at this race, please let it be after two hours and not within the first two hours during the swim." What do you know? God answered my prayers.

The wet suit fit like a glove. Not OJ Simpson's glove where he barely could get his hand in it and there was no way he could move it around. This was a casing that somehow made my body look curvy and sexy. I wanted pictures in that suit. I got one the night before and decided if I had $500 I would have bought that suit then and there.

Unfortunately, I remembered I would **never** be doing an Ironman, again, so why did I need a long-sleeved wetsuit? My unflattering sleeveless wetsuit with the long piece of extra material hanging in the middle of my crotch would suffice just fine.

If I didn't feel excited about doing the next morning's **freezing** cold *Ironman*, I did feel excited about how that wetsuit felt on my body and looked. I was as ready as I would ever be. Each day is a different race. The Florida weather in November is usually in the 50s-70s. Unfortunately for m, that morning it was a brisk 39 degrees outside. All the Iron buddies were meeting in Tigger's parking lot to have a 5:30 a.m. morning prayer.

5:30 a.m.? *"Are you guys crazy? Our daily food and supplies don't have to be there until 6:00 a.m. We are going to be out until past 12:00 am the next day, we need as much sleep as possible. We are only a half mile to 1 mile from the start. Why 5:30 a.m.?"* I just got one of those looks from the group and decided to exit the conversation for my own safety. I let Pat know, later, that I would pass on the group prayer, but please include me in the prayers and I would say a prayer of my own. Foreshadowing, again! This was one of my many mistakes!! The Bible says when three or more are joined in prayer... people, if you ever ditch a group prayer, you might just think twice!

Linda got up bright, early and bushy-tailed as cheetah's do. She had a look of excitement on her face as I was coming out of my room rubbing my eyes and looking less than ready to do 140.6 miles that day. I felt like the Grinch that morning and she was Cindy Lou looking forward to Christmas. Cindy Lou was getting ready to head out with her hair all cute in braids. I didn't wake up until 5:15 a.m., while she got up at 4:15 a.m.! It didn't even cross my mind that the early bird gets the worm. So many mistakes!!

My main question was, "How cold is it right now, and what do the waves look like?" Linda informed me that the water didn't appear to be too bad and that it was 39 degrees, but "it should warm up later." *There's* the glass half full, mine happened to be half empty. I needed coffee or some drugs, speed—anything. I'm not a drug user, but the Lance Armstrong thing did cross my mind that morning.

I really didn't feel *into* this race or excited. Just nervous and scared. We wished each other luck, and Linda told me she would be cheering for me at the finish line. How sweet. *"If there is a finish line,"* I thought. I stumbled straight to the coffee and proceeded to fuel up. I had to have enough coffee for my morning blessing. You can't start a long race without a good blessing. Kiss the day goodbye. Full intestines do not make for a good race. I was blessed, did my business, and got suited up while my friends were already approaching the site of the event.

Here's where my plan differed from my friends. They put their warm-ups and running shoes on and headed out to get their body markings. They would put their wet suits on at the event. Me, being lazy and wanting to sleep later, suited up at the condo and said "to hell with the body markings." How was it going to stay on in the 2.4-mile ocean swim inside my wet suit, anyway? I would put the wetsuit on and walk barefoot down the beach to the event. If I walked on the beach I would have a half mile walk compared to their one mile walk by taking the street route.

"I'm so smart and clever," I thought. I was a few feet down the beach and, being it was so freaking cold outside, my feet started to go numb. They went from numb to feeling like I was walking on knives. "Ouch, ouch, ouch!" I yelled out to my husband. "What's the matter?" he said. *"It hurts, it hurts! I can't feel my toes, and now it feels like knives are going into my feet! Shit! This really hurts!"* He was so sweet and offered to give me his shoes. I told

him, "No," then he would be in pain. I was the stupid one. I'd deal with it as I continued to yell out obscene words walking closer and closer to the cannon ball and all the Iron people getting ready for the big event.

As we approached the hotel hosting the event, Eric took his socks off and told me to at least put his socks on to help my feet thaw out. How sweet. I am married to a man who not only gives you the shirt off his back (which has happened), but the socks off his feet when it is 39 degrees outside. That's love! It worked, and my feet started to thaw out. I grabbed an FRS energy drink and tried to down it. I ate the FRS energy chews regularly on long runs or long rides, but never tried the canned drinks. Another mistake, if I never tried it before, I shouldn't have been doing anything new. I became desperate and felt like I needed a burst of energy. I was so tired and cold. I made my way through the crowd inside to the restrooms.

I ran into Allana who was frantically trying to down tons of energy gels. I thought maybe she had a secret I needed to learn about. I asked her, "What are you doing?" She said her blood sugar had dropped to like 68 and she didn't have her insulin pump. It was in her transition bag to be mounted on her waist after the swim before she set off on the 112 mile bike portion. Turns out poor Allana's blood went from too low to way too high in the 400's. Yikes. I asked her what she felt like at 400. She said, "A big, fat sloth in slow motion!" How does this woman do this? One Halloween, Allana showed up to the Hill Country Bicycle Works annual Pedal to the Pubs costume party as Wonder Woman. This is an understatement.

After the bathroom trip I saw Linda's husband, crouched under a little palm tree. "What the hell are you doin'?" I asked, "Hiding?" He told me that tree was his meeting place with Linda and he didn't want to miss her. He said he had been there a while and still hadn't found her, so he decided to walk toward the start with us. There was a bench just off the beach and Linda's hubby stood up on this bench around 3,000 plus people and started yelling out, "Linda, Linda!!"

He looked so funny. It was loud with all the excited people and you really couldn't hear him. We caught up to Pat and Sheri, eventually, and headed out on the beach. Linda finally found us and we all went by the American flag to stand for the anthem. It was touching. Pat and I had to pee so we waded out, like 500 other people in the shallow water, squatted and peed, yep, right there in our wetsuits. I must say, it did warm things up.

Linda stayed by the cannon. Pat and I were content to stay where we were, until I got a wild hair up my butt and took off to the front of the line for the start. I heard Pat say, "Hey, where you goin'?" I yelled back, "To the front!" There we were as Ironman Florida 2010 was about to start. Linda by the cannon, Pat somewhere in the middle of the crowd in 1 foot of pee water, and me at the front of the pack in waist-high water with waves splashing all over me. I could taste the salt water and started to get extreme butterflies.

We heard the song Iron man start playing and knew the cannon was about to go off. Poor Linda felt the cannon blast in her ear and part of the sparks from the cannon hit her and scared the crap out of her. It made for a fast race start for Linda, that's for sure. I took off when the cannon went off thinking that if I got a fast start I would be out of the water faster. This just meant that the strong men were going to trample over me. As I was swimming, I felt a large hand push me under. I started chocking between his big hand pushing me under and the waves that were splashing in my face. I went into full panic mode treading water while 1,000 people tried to swim into, over me, and around me.

I looked back to shore to see if I could make it back, get orientated, and take off again from the beach when the crowd passed, but there was no way to fight the crowd swimming at me. Besides, I'd have to make it a football field backwards to shore. Think the swim of the salmon. I panicked even more.

Finally, God sent me my Angel. She had this sweet smile on her face and asked me "You OK? Are you having trouble?" I told her, "*Yes, some man held my face under and now I'm having a panic attack and can't breathe.*" She told me to take a deep breath and she would be there to swim with me. "Seriously? We are kind of doing an Ironman here," I thought. My Angel told me to just breast stroke until I could get my face back in the water and try to get my breathing settled. I followed her directions, which were such a comfort. While this was taking place a guy swam into us and asked what the problem was. My angel told the curious man what was going on and he said he would swim with me, too.

This could only be a sign from God. Who literally stops in the middle of the ocean with huge swells, 2,700 people swimming into and over you, during a cut-off timed race, and offers to swim with someone? It's such chaos out there that you can barely tell where your own body and surroundings are. The swim start of Ironman is brutal. People kick you in the face, jab you with their elbows and, in some cases, push you under water. Some are just assholes and know they are trampling over people, while others are just going with their own anxiety and have no body awareness. I should have started off to the far right like Allana. *"Angels can fly because they take themselves lightly." (GK Chesterton)*

Regardless, I started breathing better and my Angel told me to try to put my head in the water and freestyle. She said, "Don't worry, I'll be here keeping an eye on you." I did it and the next thing I knew I started swimming. My breathing slowly returned to somewhat normal, if you can call it that, and I was moving along with the rest of the competitors. I looked up to see where my Angel was. Poof! She was nowhere to be seen. What a miracle. That doesn't happen. It just doesn't. If you have ever experienced a mass start at an Ironman event, you know what I'm talking about. If you haven't, prepare yourself and start behind the crowd or way off to the east or west of the pack. It will benefit your time in the long run.

You can't swim over the person in front of you, like that guy tried to do with me. It's like L.A. rush hour, you just have to adjust your speed and try your best to stay afloat in the pack. I got out of the water in one hour and 26 minutes. Not bad for having a full-blown panic attack, thinking I was going to die, and not being able to breathe for five to 10 minutes. The swells were there, but not as bad as the year before, and I didn't puke in the water like many others, thank goodness.

I ran out of the water praising God that the swim was over. I saw Linda in the swim tent, just a little ahead of me and yelled out, "*Hey Linda, nice swim!*" She just laughed and said, "Yeah, you too." We had this funny look like, "the sock is on the other foot now." Here we were on the receiving end with volunteers bent down with their heads sorting out our bags on the floor near our crotches. We were just trying to change with some privacy.

Was this really happening? All I could do was laugh! I don't think I can ever present this madness in the right words for you to appropriately visualize. It's funny. Just funny! There's more nakedness at an Ironman transition than there is at any strip club! Once out of the transition area, I ran my way over to the Port-a-potty. Even though I had peed in my wetsuit prior to the race, that was much earlier, and you can't head out on 112-mile bike ride without emptying your bladder. The toilets were just disgusting. Gross, from the morning craps that were in there. There was crap piled up to the opening of the commode. It stank and disgusted me!

I had my blessing (morning crap) back at the condo and did not have to use one of those gross facilities that morning, thank goodness, but now there was no choice and as a germ phobic I was having some issues. I peed without touching anything, but just knowing I had to touch the door handle to open it destroyed any appetite I may have had to eat some nutrition prior to the bike ride. I think I found some hand sanitizer lying around somewhere. This saved my day. I headed out and opened a power bar to eat.

My big mistake was the meal I put in my lunch bag for the 56 mile marker where everyone stops to consume a fast lunch. I packed Minute Ready brown rice and smoked almonds. Why? That's a real good question. I eat rice and almonds as an after bike snack and thought they would be easy on my stomach during the day. They were easy on the stomach, but trying to cram rice and almonds down in a hurry doesn't work. Have you ever seen a Chinese man scarf white rice? No, precisely my point, it clumps up in the bowl and clumps up in your mouth. You consume rice in small, chopstick-sized quantities. It's practically impossible to scarf rice.

I was trying to eat too fast and gagging on my food. The almonds were very dry and didn't go down in a fast manner. Rice and almonds were just the wrong choice for a race, and my tummy felt more issues from trying to eat fast. I hopped on the bike after what seemed like forever and continued down the road with 56 more bike miles to go. The Florida Ironman is the most depressing bike ride. You would think there is a lot of beach scenery on the ride, right? Wrong! There was only 3 miles of beach headed out of town, the rest is grass, tall pine trees, grass, more trees, more grass, and on and on and on! For an ADHD person, this is a very depressing course. I didn't have anything different to look at, oh, except all the people passing me on the bike.

I got to watch a lot of behinds as they passed me. "On your left, on your left, on your left," was all I heard for 100 miles. Not so much the last 12 miles, because there were only a few of us left at the back of the race. I might have even passed a few on the last 12 miles. Woohoo? Once I got off the bike and into the transition tent, I felt dizzy. I was so stupid and I didn't consume any food in the bike transition. Our bodies need nutrition to sustain us during endurance races, especially if you are hypoglycemic. A marathon follows the 112 mile bike ride.

My head was spinning from the cold ocean swim early that morning, and the cold air in my ears during the bike ride threw my equilibrium off. The day had warmed up considerably from the 39 degrees that morning, but I knew it was going to be cold again shortly when the sun went down. I kept my arm warmers on and thought the dizziness was just from my inner ears.

Iron Nugget: What have you had to Snap Out Of?

28   You Gotta Focus!

I was about to learn a valuable lesson and learn that my pea-sized brain could grow at a later date. I consumed some protein mix and water while in the transition area, then set off on my way. As I headed out of the chute I saw my Sherpas: Eric, Sheri, and someone else, Todd. I ran out of the chute with a new friend I met outside the disgusting Port-a-potty.

As my homies yelled in support of me, I did the most awful ADHD thing. I flipped the bird at them. They looked confused and puzzled. "Did she just flip us off?" one of them asked. I yelled to my husband, *"You got me into this!"* But, they didn't hear me, and Eric said they were really sad that I flipped my finger at them. It hurt their feelings. I felt so bad after I did that. I thought it was funny. Like a woman in labor says to her husband, "You bastard, you did this to me." I was just trying to find some amusement in my pain at the moment, but it didn't come across that way. Sorry, guys. I still feel really stupid about that impulsive moment. Won't happen again, I promise.

My new friend, Melissa, and I ran, walked, and talked. We were solving some serious life issues, and at mile 6, I couldn't think straight. I told her I needed to walk and I'd catch up to her a little later. There were aid stops along the way where I was passing up fruit because many of the volunteers were young, and I just knew they hadn't washed their hands when they cut the fruit. That was when I was still thinking straight.

It was getting cold again, and I was picking up a handful of pretzels and drinking chicken broth for the warmth and sodium. Little did I pay attention to the fact that I was not taking in any glucose. I forgot to pack sport beans in my pouch before I started on the run. The Sport Beans were in my transition bag at the half marathon mark, mile 13.1. My stomach was sloshing around from the gels and Gatorade. If I continued to run I thought I would puke all over the volunteers and spectators.

Turns out a buddy at a later Iron event did just that, projectile puke across a line of people watching the event. Nice!! Way to entertain the crowd, just not the people in the firing zone. I couldn't consume another cup of Gatorade or another gel pack, because it was going to come out one end or the other. I think you get the picture. Around mile 8, my home girl, Tamra, came up behind me, "I see a squirrel!!" "Hey, Dana Loo, how's it going?" That darned girl had a perky sound in her voice. It was dark by this time and I could not focus or see worth a crap.

All of a sudden the water faucet turned on. I just started crying, *"I'm dizzy, I can't see straight, I feel like I'm gonna faint, I'm not gonna make it!!"* Cry, cry, cry. Tamra, the caring doctor she is, said, "Oh, honey, your sugar is just low. Eat some sport beans or a gel." I told her while crying, *"I can't eat anymore gel cause it's gonna make me puke, and I left my sport beans in a bag somewhere."* The Iron event hands out protein bars and gels on the route, but not sport beans that also have electrolytes and glucose, which an athlete needs during an endurance race.

Tamra got out a handful of Sport Beans and said, "Here, honey, eat these. It will help." I remember holding my hand out and as I staggered back and forth like a homeless old drunk, she put the sport beans in my hand. A few of them fell on the ground and I swayed to pick them up, to actually eat them off the ground.

I was so out of it. I wouldn't eat some fruit earlier for fear of germs, but now I was going to pick jelly beans up off the ground where many athletes were just stopping and peeing as they continued on the road? Where the bottoms of those running shoes had graced the poop-filled Port-a-potties, earlier? Nasty. I recovered a few of the sport beans off the ground and Tamra went to help me up, "No, no, honey. I've got some more, here you go." Did I mention I was out of it? Like a really drunk friend who keeps saying, "I love you, man, I love you man." I was staggering along crying and not making much sense and trying to pick food up off the ground. Funny in retrospect, but not then!

Tamra lapped me, of course, and was on her way to become an Iron Chick. She wished me well as I stayed behind in my hellish nightmare. The sad part is the amount of beans she gave me was nowhere enough to bring my sugar up to a decent level. I know now as I have had similar incidents while training. I consumed two gel packets and a friend's bag of gummy worms to get me back to a decent level, recently. A handful of beans would not have been enough.

The next thing I knew, I kept seeing the ground and thinking, "I'll just pass out here. That looks like a soft place to lie down for a while." Shortly after, I found myself standing in the middle of a large puddle full of water. Looking back I hope that's what it was (and not pee), my running shoe was getting wet and my brain was saying, "Why am I just standing in a puddle of water?" It was like the synapses weren't firing correctly. I was in a fog, like moving through an amusement park at Halloween where they have those wacky houses and everything is distorted and you feel like you are moving in slow motion. Just an odd feeling. As I snapped myself out of my pool party, I saw Linda across the street going the other direction which meant she had already had her snack from her rescue bag at mile 13.1.

I told her how horrible I was feeling and didn't think I was going to make it. She said she also had tunnel vision, but when she sat down and ate a little snack at mile 13 she started seeing the light at the end of the tunnel. Her focus and mental outlook greatly improved. Must have, she looked fine to me. That must have been around mile 10 or 11, because by the time I came up to the aid station at mile 12, a lady working it saw me staggering around like a drunk person and said, "Miss, are you alright? Why don't you come sit down here for a little while?"

I just turned on the water works again and said, "I can't think straight. I think my blood sugar is low, I'm hypoglycemic." Sniff, sniff, cry, cry. She told me to sit down and she asked if she could call for help. "Uh-huh," I told her. I had no idea what was to come. The lady with her 13-year-old assistant brought me some oranges and banana slices. I ate, even though I didn't feel hungry. She told me help would be here, but they had a lot of people to pick up and it would take some time. I just ate and looked up at them with a blank stare. The lady asked the young man to keep an eye on me and get me anything I needed.

My new young assistant got me some Gatorade. I drank and ate my fruit. He was such a kind soul—so polite, so helpful. I don't really remember all of what he said or did, but he didn't take his eyes off me and there was a soothing look inside his eyes. It comforted me and with the little mental clarity I had at the moment I remember thinking, "This is such a nice boy. Why can't other boys this age be so nice, polite, kind, and considerate?" He really touched my soul, and I value the help he gave me at such a low point in my life. I felt like God had sent my Angel No. 2 for the day.

Clarity didn't return until after 15 or 20 minutes. Little did I know that I could have just got up and left? However, my husband once told me if your number is called in to the Iron event staff you are done. DNFed. Dreaded words: Did Not Finish! The lady who helped me called my number in over the radio and asked for me to be picked up. I may not have been ready to run after my sugar levels came up, but I most certainly could have walked and I had plenty of time to walk the last 14 miles. I just thought it was an Ironman rule that I had to go with the staff when the vehicle arrived. It never occurred to me that I could refuse the ride and say, "No, No....I won't go!"

So I stayed and waited for the dreaded SAG wagon to come get me. Amazingly, I felt fine by the time the staff dropped me off and told me to walk up to the medical tent. I didn't go to the tent because I was not dehydrated. I have had events in Texas like the Hotter N Hell 100-mile bike ride where I got overheated **and** my blood sugar got too low. I've received IVs and they do wonders. There wasn't any heat that day, so I had no idea that once my blood sugar came back up I'd be good to go. I would be able to laugh, walk, and talk. Maybe not run, but carry on, yes.

Where the hell was my new friend Melissa when I needed her? I let these Mamby Pamsy volunteers talk me into getting a ride? I had trained for a year to do 126 miles? To not hear my name across the loud speaker saying, *Dana Cardwell, you are an Ironman!*" It was hard watching my friends come across the finish line that day, but I was so happy for them. Besides, I probably wouldn't have written this book if I didn't go through the challenge of failing at the Florida Ironman race in 2010. I wouldn't have been able to clear the obstacles in the road and learn from my mistakes.

"For an in-depth look at the four main reasons why many people with an Ironman dream will never reach the finish line and how they can get past them and reach the Ironman finish line, visit **IronStruck.com**."(Ray Fautex. The Ironman Triathlon finish line: Reasons why so many never reach it)

The next day, I was in bed with the most horrendous migraine I have ever had. I felt like there was pressure or swelling on my brain. I lay in bed until 5 p.m. that day. The others were moving around, what was wrong with me? I came back to the Hill Country and immediately contacted Jack Fairchild at MANNA for some blood work. Turns out I had hyponatremia and hyperthyroidism. What a wonderful combination.

Hyponatremia is an electrolyte disturbance in which sodium concentrations in the serum are lower than normal. Exercise-associated hyponatremia is not uncommon, and some fatalities have occurred. It is related to excessive water intake that causes the blood-sodium levels to plummet to dangerously low levels. One report states that athletes may present with symptoms such as confusion, seizures, and altered mental status. In the 2002 Boston Marathon, Almond et al found that 13 percent of 488 runners studied had hyponatremia. Women were more prone than men to develop the condition.

Hyperthyroidism can cause some mental distress, also, like depression. The symptoms include irritability, impaired memory along with cold intolerances, weight gain, fatigue, muscle cramps, and hair loss. There are more related symptoms, but I had all the ones I just listed. Just lovely, this is why I recommend that anyone wanting to do an Iron event should have a blood panel done beforehand.

Know what is going on with your body before you start off on this journey. There could be one less obstacle in your road. If I had been given some medication for my thyroid prior to the race I might have had better results. I found myself always tired, cold, and irritable. I just thought it was the training, nothing else.

We made it back to Texas and everyone was on the down low back home since four came back with finisher medals and one didn't. I became the elephant in the room. I tried to keep an upbeat attitude, but I was just trying to survive this thyroid deal. I was having a lot of anxiety-related panic attacks before and after the Ironman event. I was put on a generic thyroid med at first, but then switched to name brand, and became much more stable.

Pat always says that an Ironman race *is* The Reward—you already passed the test with all the training you have done over the year. Relax and enjoy on Race Day. I wish I would have remembered that back then!

"The greatest fool of all is the man who fools himself." (Fortune cookie)

Iron Nugget:

How would you help a person focus when it seemed like they were drifting off course in life or on goals?

What is your reward? What test do you need to pass?

29 Cowgirl UP!

"Some people always have to be doing battle with someone, sometimes even with themselves, a battle within their own lives." (Paulo Coehlo)

"There are times in our lives when the winds around us seem too powerful to stand against. Yet in the midst of the storm, the presence of the Lord is stronger than ever." This was a card given to me by Linda prior to Ironman Florida the inside read: "Dearest Dana, Thanks for believing in me. God has a way of preparing us at every point of need. I have no doubt he put us together. It's been an amazing journey that I hope to continue long past November 6th. You've got IT to accomplish all of your hearts desires. Go get'em, Squirrel! Love, Linda" Little did I know my world was about to spin on a different axis than it had been on. Friends come and go in our lives, but one thing remains true...God.

Ironman Cozumel event is the last weekend in November. Once I started on the thyroid meds I decided to get back on that horse and try, try again. I immediately called up Linda and Tamra to see if they were in. Linda laughed and said she would love to do Cozumel. Tamra said she needed a break and was still not interested in going to Mexico to do an Iron event. Pat was already signed up to do Texas Ironman the next year.

So there it was, the Squirrel and Cheetah off on another adventure. In retrospect, I should have just kept it at this. I have kicked myself a thousand times after this happened, but I love a party and my philosophy used to be "the more the merrier." Not anymore, and never again.

Before I start, I need to clarify why I wrote this part of the journey. Some of my close friends, who decided after I put this information in writing that they were not as close to me as I originally thought considered me bitter, jealous, victim, etc. Let's just say after receiving a letter from someone I considered to be a very close friend, I came to the old Dr. Suess deduction:

Be who you are and say what you feel because those who mind don't matter and those who matter don't mind."

~ Dr. Seuss

The reason for the detail is that no matter what issues we have worked through from our past there are going to be relationship issues in our future. In counseling we say, "Are we, the counselor, working harder than the client?" I ask the same with your relationships, do you work at the relationship harder than the other person? I'm not talking about friends or lovers who are going through situational issues. That's to be expected. We are expected to support them and bring them up in the world. I'm referring to people with personality issues that just keep you hitting your head on a brick wall. The recommendation is that you look closely at that relationship and think twice if it continues to slap you in the face instead of lift you up on Angels wings.

There was another gal I had recently talked with at a party for quite some time and she had athletic desires and goals. Her goal at the moment was to do a Half Iron event. I had met her on two occasions, previously, and both times she was not friendly to me. I introduced myself at the Spring Fling festival while we were decorating cars, she didn't engage conversation with me when I tried to talk with her. I just went back to decorating and moved on with life. No hard feelings, no biggie. We all had busy lives.

The second time I saw her was during the Conquer the Coast bike ride when I attended with a couple of her friends a few years ago. A group of gals from our area would do the Conquer the Coast 65-mile bike event and gather for lunch afterwards. I was the newcomer that year and had met most of the women except this gal one time previously. As I sat at the end of the table with the ladies I came with, new gal stayed in busy conversation about a fall she had that day with the others.

I thought she was immersed in her issue. A year later we, both, were invited to a party. New gal actually talked with my husband and me. Looking back, I think it's because we became interesting to her. She knew we were training for Ironman. I'm not sure, but from not even given the time of day twice with this woman to hitting it off at a party makes me wonder in retrospect.

Hind sight is 20/20, so I didn't see anything at the time. I noticed how we seemed to have a lot in common. After Linda and I agreed to do Cozumel, I asked Linda if she thought we should invite this new friend. I must say I had a very long conversation with Linda about my two previous experiences with this gal. I talked about the fact that maybe she was just shy, Linda thought the gal may have been distracted as her son had an illness.

I remember thinking, "Well, so did my daughter, but I was not rude to people." Maybe Linda was right, different people handle stress differently and this was probably the case. Regardless, we asked our new friend if she would like to join us and after thinking it over, she was excited to come aboard. The new gal was a really fast cyclist, and I didn't realize she did most of her workouts before the sun comes up. Uh-oh! Big problem for me. Linda works full time, so it wasn't too hard for her to adjust her schedule to the early morning workouts.

The fact was either I get up before dawn to work out with them or workout on my own. I hated the latter, but I hated getting up at 4 a.m. even more. I did mention I'm mediocre and a tad bit lazy? Not lazy, I just like to have fun! Nothing about 4 a.m. is fun! I worked out alone. A lot. It became discouraging I thought this was the same journey as two years ago. I first said to my hubby, "I'm gonna do Ironman Cozumel!!" all happy and full of piss and brimstone. *"A good laugh and a long sleep are the best cures in the doctor's book." (Irish Proverb)*

The destination may not be the true goal. What happens along the way is more important. Are you missing out on the true journey by spending too much time focusing on the destination? Smell the roses. Enjoy the journey. If you choose to compete at an endurance level keep in mind some important facts. *"The disregard for one's health is perhaps the most important motivational difference between the elite and the recreational athlete. For the recreational athlete, a principal motive for sports participation is a desire to improve one's health and to shape one's body into closer conformity to contemporary ideals of physical attractiveness. For the elite athlete, the physical self is frequently jeopardized and sometimes sacrificed on the altar of sports success."* With the latter comes a unique personality trait. Are your friends the recreational type or the fast, elite type?

It turned into a different event when Tamra wouldn't agree to Mexico, well, all right, I can switch gears. However, being left alone while Linda and new gal worked out together strategized together, got faster together, made plans together. You get the picture. I have never been so alone and depressed in all my races, and then things started happening to make my outlook feel even bleaker.

In June, new gal was depressed because her hubby didn't remember her birthday, so Linda and I decided to take her to coffee to cheer her up. I went out and got her a daily devotional for women and items one might use at an endurance race to keep you going: Coffee beans, 5 hour energy, anti-chaffing Butt butter, bags of sport beans, different types of gels, honey, protein energy potion, just funny stuff to cheer her up. A sack full of surprises! It seemed to work, she understood we really cared.

Linda's birthday is in July and new gal makes nice jewelry for an occupation. She made a beautiful piece of jewelry for Linda in July. She asked me about the colors, which color would look best on Linda's olive skin tone. Which color pendant would Linda like the best? A lot of interest in what Linda would like and how Linda might react to new gal's gift. The two pieces she was deciding between were just gorgeous. Linda just loved the necklace. It was a gift of love and special.

In September Linda, new gal, and I signed up to do the Conquer the Coast 65-mile cycling event. My mother was going to meet us to pick my daughter up for the weekend. New gal was driving so we pulled up to the hotel to wait on my mother and drop Cami off. Linda, Cami, and I went inside to wait and new gal stayed in her vehicle. My mother pulled up right behind our friend, but new friend never got out of the car to say hello.

I chalked her lack of courtesy off as nothing. It wasn't until we were to pick my daughter up and meet my mother at Luby's for lunch that I really couldn't ignore her actions. Linda and I got out of new gal's vehicle to eat lunch while our friend decided she was going to pick up her bathing suit she had left back at her condo. Instead of getting the suit, new gal ended up getting Subway and eating in her vehicle outside in the Luby's parking lot.

When we walked out of the restaurant to get Cami's suitcase from my mother's car, my mother moved her vehicle over to where my friend was parked. My mother parked and got out of the vehicle hoping to finally meet my new friend who was going on the Ironman journey with Linda and me. Ironman is such an amazing challenge and my mother was impressed with any woman who decided to venture down this road. She wanted to meet a super woman in her book.

Our friend was on the phone and never got off the phone the whole time my mother stood by my friend's open, passenger side door. My mother looked at me, puzzled about my new friend and I just offered an apology to Mom. I told my mother, "I'm not sure what's going on. Sorry?" My mother said she has a friend "like that" and she understood. But it hurt, it hurt a lot. It was like a slap in my face. I was raised to introduce yourself to your friends' parents. It's the humble thing to do even if you don't really like them. Regardless, I gave new gal a "thank you" gift for letting us stay at her parent's condo during Conquer the Coast. I wasn't going to return one wrong with another just because I had hurt feelings.

The next week was my birthday. I picked new gal's son up at the bus that day when I picked my daughter up. I decided to help her out because she was running late. She picked her son up at my house and all I got was, "Hey, it's Dana's birthday, did you wish her happy birthday?" Her son said happy birthday and she left asking if I had any big plans that evening.

I remembered your birthday when your husband didn't and I don't even get a, "let's go have a cup of coffee?" Not even a "here's a Starbucks gift card to enjoy a cup of coffee?" Anything?

I figured I was not worthy of a custom piece of jewelry after new gal didn't respect me enough to meet my mother, but not even a cup of coffee? It's $3, for goodness sakes!

I even asked new gal on a cruise with me to try and connect with her. We had just gone on a beautiful, five-day cruise a month prior, in August. I showed new gal the Cozumel Ironman route. I thought we had fun even though she wouldn't go to dinner with my daughter and me while on the cruise. She didn't like the selection on the five course meal, so she ate a salad in the buffet line. My opinion, the five course meal is to die for!

What else could I do to try and connect with new gal? I'm sure my trust issues made me read into the matter more than it really was, but it hurt, a lot. I felt like new gal took my dream and my friend over. Do you have friends like this? Things they do and say for others are so much more than the way they act with you? Maybe we read the signs wrong, but maybe we don't. We may never know, but sometimes as adults we have to take care of *us* for the sake of moving forward.

You feel like the kid not picked for a kickball game. I realized I was not in control of her actions and we were never going to be best buds. The more the merrier may not be the way to go when training for an Ironman. I reminded myself of Linda's card given to me a year ago, *"There are times in our lives when the winds around us seem too powerful to stand against… yet in the midst of the storm, the presence of the Lord is stronger than ever."* I may have lost my Ironman Florida bond, but God's presence was stronger than ever.

Personality Profile for Female Athletes as reported in Psychological Parameters (www.montana.edu/olympics/physiology), *"As more women compete in sport, it is important to understand the personality profile of female athletes. The successful female athlete seems to differ markedly from the normative female in terms of personality profile. Compared with non-athletes, female athletes tend to be more: 1. Achievement oriented, 2. Independent, 3. Aggressive, 4. Emotionally stable, and 5. Assertive."* I hypothesize if you put a group of Ironmen women, yes that's an oxymoron, in a small room for a period of time, you will get a destroyed room with claw marks on the wall and there will be traces of blood!

I've finally figured out, at my age, that we don't need all the friends in the world. That it's OK to be selective and just stick with who you're comfortable around. Some mistrust issues protect us from the past. Hear me out. Socially, I will talk and have fun with anyone and everyone, but letting people in your inner sanctity is sacred. Some things are just not meant to be. After I wore my feelings on my sleeve and shit hit the fan. Linda and I had a long talk, she pointed out there were times I had pushed new gal and her away, too. I took ownership and agreed.

"One out of every four Americans is suffering from some form of mental illness. Think of your three best friends. If they're okay, then it's you." (Rita Mae Brown)

Most of my rudeness came right before Florida Ironman when I knew I was feeling odd and couldn't put my finger on it. My thyroid condition opened a whole new bag of nasty worms to me. I took ownership, but I felt like Linda made excuses for new friend. She said that our new buddy had opened up to her and that I was probably just misunderstanding the new gal. How was I ever going to understand new gal when she didn't give me the time of day? I had asked this girl on *my* journey!! She would have never done Cozumel Ironman that year if I hadn't asked her. The registration closes and she was just contemplating a Half-Ironman not a full one that year. She hadn't even done a Half Ironman, yet, or a marathon, or…..

Linda told me I needed to talk my issues over with gal friend, and I have to admit the friend was accommodating by coming over to talk with me one morning at my house. There was some truth in the conversation, but also a lot of excuses, like "I was making you something for your birthday." Yeah, right. Never saw it to this day. *"God is silent. Now if only man would shut-up."* (Woody Allen)

Even though I'm blonde, I do know an excuse when I hear it. I let her save face and just listened to her. We would be nice socially and have common friends, but the universe works in interesting ways and one can feel the energy when someone doesn't particularly like you.

Like Jodee Blanco said in her book **Please, Stop Laughing at Me**. *"It's the love you long to give that nobody wants. After a while, it backs up into your system like stagnant water and turns toxic, poisoning your spirit. When this happens you don't have many choices available. You can become a bitter loner who goes through life being pissed off at the world. You can fester with rage until one day you murder your classmates. Or you can find another outlet for your love, where it will be appreciated and maybe even returned."*

I found other outlets and other friends, but I was sad that mine and new gal's relationship would never work. I'm OK with Linda going in a different direction, I just mourn the fun we had a few years ago. I miss my friend, Linda, and I've had to face the fact that we have gone different directions, athletic wise.

John Gray, the author of **Men are From Mars, Women are From Venus** states in his book **What You Feel You Can Heal**, *"By fully feeling your emotions and expressing the complete truth about them, you will be able to heal the unresolved emotional tension and be free to love more fully." "Feeling your emotions and expressing them is the means to releasing them. However, this doesn't mean you should go out and dump all your negativity on your loved ones. Going out and indiscriminately sharing all your feelings could ruin your relationships and create even more trauma for you to deal with."* I find this paragraph to be like walking a fine line on a tight rope.

I believe in expressing what you are feeling with others, but it's how they accept it or how you deliver it that keeps you moving forward or falling flat on your face and losing the game. Dr. Gray goes on to say that *"to love a person doesn't mean you will always agree with them or even feel good about them. It doesn't mean you will like all of the things they do or don't do. Nobody is perfect."*

Iron Nugget:

Do you know someone obsessed with their performance?

How do you handle high energy, opinionated people in a social situation?

When have you found yourself having to put your big girl panties on?

30　Here Fishy, Fishy

"Today is your day.　Your mountain is waiting.　So, get on your way."　(Dr. Seuss)

When the Cozumel Ironman came along I told myself, "Have fun and make this a good vacation." The first night we were in Cozumel, the ladies went out to get our race bags. We left the kids with our Sherpa husbands back at the hotel. The men had already started their own party as the hotel was all inclusive. Inclusive is the way to go on a trip, I must say.

After we got our race bags, I suggested we each do tequila shots and have a drink ourselves while watching the ships sail out in downtown Cozumel. "We might as well celebrate two days out." We had a great time taking pictures and trying to stay out of trouble. It was hard with the attention we were getting in town acting crazy and all, but we made it home safely and with a lot of good pictures.

The next few days we did practice swims in the ocean and had some swells, but nothing too bad to discourage a 2.4 mile swim. I love the visibility in Cozumel, you can see for miles and miles in the ocean. The clear, blue ocean water is just gorgeous. Gal pal and Linda were so nice they even helped us pay for my daughter to swim with the dolphins, which was a dream of Cami's.

When we checked in to our hotel children were supposed to be free, but gal pal and my family got screwed somehow and were forced to come up with a load of money for our children to stay. My husband used most of his cash, which meant we were limited for the rest of the trip or he would max out his credit card. It affected our trip, and the budget was now much smaller than it originally was.

There are always solutions to dilemmas we face, and we just have to be open to a change in plans. A beautiful lady I know in town is an author and one of her books is titled **Plan A Woman in a Plan B World**. How true. In Debbie's book she *"unveils nine plan B land mines that, if left unchecked, can seriously injury a Plan A woman."* Debbie, like an Iron Chick, takes very good care of her body, mind, and soul for her age. It's amazing what being in touch with your mind and body can do for you. She's a wonderful Christian, so her spirit and desire to serve the Lord guides her.

When I do endurance races I'm technically tearing my body down, but it makes for a stronger body later. Hence the saying, "What doesn't kill you makes you stronger," mentally and physically. It's those small minutia tears that lead to a strong, powerful mind and body. There are so many lessons learned through hardships that make us a stronger person. I probably wouldn't go back in a time machine if I could to change the hard times. Yes, a loving father who told me I was pretty, smart, and wonderful would have been nice, but I wouldn't be here if that was the case. The hardships I endured made me a fighter!

Some studies show people who go through hardships handle it one of two ways. Many are unable to cope, may die of heart attacks or strokes, become violent, get divorced, or suffer from mental health issues. Another group of people actually improve their lives. Their health gets better, their careers soar, and relationships blossom. This group has the ability to treat crisis as an opportunity. They develop courage and motivation.

On the day of my second Ironman event, I woke up feeling better than I did the year before. Most likely because I was in my favorite place in the whole world and I woke up looking out at the ocean and a large Iguana on the hut across from me. It wasn't 39 degrees outside and this made a world of difference—I'm a warm weather gal. I was thankful to be by the crystal-blue ocean, and I knew my bike ride would include long stretches along the ocean.

Cozumel Ironman is a three-loop course, so I would get to see the back side of the island three times today! What a blessing. The wind wouldn't stop me, because the view was going to be breath-taking! I think that day was the only day I haven't minded getting up at 4:30 a.m. Anything prior to 6:30 a.m. is a train wreck to me. I don't know many people who enjoy train wrecks.

As usual, I was having two periods a month that came and went whenever they damn well pleased. Great, just one more thing to worry about, I thought. I put a few extra tampons in strategic places as I finished my morning business. I thought, "Note to self, get that period thing under control!" I tried to think on the positive side and referred to Debbie's idea of a Plan B. So Plan A would have been not having to deal with a period, guess I'd have to go to Plan B, totting tampons placed in strategic settings along my race! Murphy's Law was more like it.

To back track, I tend to have heavy periods, so a few years back I invested in the IUD to stop those unwanted heavy periods. The only problem was when I was having all those issues related to my thyroid, the year before I assumed it must be related to the IUD. I Googled everything I could find related to the IUD, and as with any medical science there were negative side effects related to the IUD.

I made an appointment and marched in demanding Tamra take that damn IUD out immediately. She laughed and told me, "Hold on, squirrel. Are you sure?" I informed her that I just passed the medical board exam, because I spent two nights researching the IUD on the internet. I was a plethora of information on the subject. My issues are the IUD! Tamra agreed that I had become an expert in the field and would honor my wishes, but "This is going to be a costly mistake, Squirrel, if the problem is not from the IUD." I had it removed and suffered the consequences a month later. I had heavy periods sometimes two times a month. I came to terms that I was not an Internet M.D.

So there I was, with my tampons and other necessities waiting for the bus to take us across the island of Cozumel to the Ironman starting line at Chakanab State Park. Eric was with me for support. That's a true husband to wake up before sunrise to escort his wife. The shuttle bus dropped us off bright and early just before sunrise and we didn't even have to wait long. I arrived to the masses at the park and it was a glorious day. The sun was shining, and the waves weren't too big—just normal small manageable Cozumel waves. I was actually getting a little excited to get this thing over with.

It was the run that concerned me. Would my nutrition fall apart again? Would I get overheated and need IVs? Would my blood sugar go low? Would I be able to run with this hamstring and messed up metatarsal? I knew I could do the swim and bike, but all hell breaks loose on the run. You either have it, or you don't. I'm not a fast runner, I shuffle even when I'm not doing an Iron event. I tried not to worry and reminded myself that the Anglo Saxon translation for worry is to strangle, to choke.

I shuffle even on a 5K—not a pretty sight. I don't really pick my feet up, and I just slink along like a fat lady with a big ol' butt. Waddle, waddle. That's me. No running, just waddling. I wasn't sure how I would waddle through 26.2 miles on that day considering all the variables I had to deal with and, of course, the dreaded DNF from last year that loomed over my fate. Would I DNF, again? (DNF = **Did Not Finish**)

The time finally came when the announcer called for all racers to enter the water. At the beginning of an Ironman race there are around 2,700 competitors entering the water at the same time. As you may suspect, it takes a while to get all those people in the water. An athlete can be treading water anywhere from 15 to 30 minutes prior to the start. This alone can be exhausting. Florida had a beach start, so there was no treading water. Cozumel had a pier entry where you had to jump 4 feet into the deep water.

The deep water didn't scare me. It was the jump from 4 feet that messes up your goggles and the water going up your nose. That wasn't exciting to me. I jumped in the cool, crystal-blue water and was able to swim to this "cage-like fence." Other athletes who entered the water early were already clinging onto the chain linked partition. We resembled a bunch of monkeys at the zoo clinging onto the tall fences.

Chakanub State Park has dolphins and other exotic mammals. There is a chain-link fence in the water to keep the dolphins from exiting the park enclosure. I grabbed on with a finger or two and just sunk under water to see if I could get a view of the fun-loving creatures.

Twenty-five meters away, I could see the dolphins. It was up-lifting. I felt like a kid at the pet store looking in through the glass with my nose pressed up to the window. I know this made for an exciting swim start. When the cannon went off I was sure to start way behind everyone and with a happy smile on my face. I can't even describe how far off to the right I ventured. I was going to make sure no one swam over me this time. It worked, but after I rounded the first buoy about a half mile into the race, it happened.

Shrek appeared. Yep, he was in a big red Speedo! The Ogre wouldn't get the hell out of my way. I'd strategically pass Shrek by swimming around him and then, "BAM!" he'd appear again in my path swimming, all 7 feet of him. I started cussing at him underwater. It's like he couldn't swim a straight line if it saved his life, he was cutting people off and I have no idea how he kept his pace with the way he was swimming.

At one point, when I tried to get past him, his big ole elbow knocked me in the side of my head and almost knocked my goggles off. "Ughh, you idiot! Watch where you're going!" I finally sped up past Shrek, or he continued on his path out to sea where I left him. What a nitwit. Where did he get that awful suit, anyway? He obviously was not from the U.S. with that attire.

I continued along my way and as I rounded the last buoy which meant I had only half a mile to go, I saw it. *Jesus Christ* on the cross under water!! Yes, sir! It was the most inspiring thing I've ever seen. There was this wooden statue with Jesus looking up to Heaven on the cross about 20 feet down at the bottom of the Cozumel ocean. It stayed underwater by being attached to a large concrete block. It was so amazing.

I felt God's presence that morning, but when I came across the sight of Jesus, I knew God was truly there with me. I continued on my 2.4-mile swim. Just past the sign that God was with me were scuba divers filming us. Cool! I remember swimming and waving at the same time while they were 25 feet below me. "Hey, guys, look at me! Hello!!" One even waved back, even more cool! The sights of the Ironman Cozumel swim can't be duplicated. It's just superb. I came out of the water all brimming with smiles from one end of my face to the other and my hands up in the air exclaiming victory. I even said, "Viva La Mexico!!" Like the other Mexican athletes were chanting as they exited the water. I wonder if they thought I was one of them. Nah, probably not. Oh well, it was fun. Arriba, Arriba!!!

All the spectators were cheering for us as we ran down the pier to the transition station. My time on this swim was 1:21. Five minutes faster than Florida, but I swam way off to the right to keep away from the crowd. Taking the straight line would have bought me five or 10 extra minutes, but I was happy. No panic attacks, and to see Jesus looking up at me was an extra blessing of the day.

I ran into the transition and just took my time. Way too much time, I believe my transition time was 18 minutes. I should have called for room service while I was at it. Transition is supposed to be quick, get in and get out, don't loiter and visit with all the volunteers. Someone in transition said that one swimmer was taken out of the race when they were attacked by a barracuda. Say what? I would be more prone to believe a shark attack, but a barracuda?

After hearing the latest news, I got my bike and hopped on. The first part of the bike is ugly— a straight away toward the backside of the island—plus, it's very hot and muggy. There was wind coming straight at me, but it did seem to cool me off a little. Luckily, I had my swim top on as a bra, so I was still cool from my suit being wet. I changed out of my swim bottoms to bike shorts to protect my privates for the next 112 miles.

My bike shorts had the latest diaper sewn inside it. This is what we call the padding inside bike shorts, a diaper; because when you get off the bike and walk around in them you look like a toddler with a big ol' poopy diaper. Sexy, huh? What's even less sexy are the scars you get if you don't wear the appropriate bike gear!

The first stretch of the bike race is about 18 boring miles and then it's all beach, baby!! Nothing but pure, open, white-sandy beach with crystal-clear blue waters and very few inhabitants. There was this bar and restaurant someone recommended to us that we got to pass on three occasions. We were going to have fun at that bar, Playa Bonita, the next day. It had *Dia de los Muertas* statues outside wearing Ironman bikinis with fake boobies. I laughed each time I passed the place, which is hard during a 112 mile bike race.

The back side of the island was where I would dismount and find a bush to pee by. You're missing out on the experience if you haven't squatted for a pee on a beautiful beach. Luckily, I didn't fall in the sand while I squatted or this would have made for some mean blisters in the sensitive areas. You don't want sand in your pants to begin with, but doing 112 mile bike ride magnifies all problems. I had made sure I applied plenty of Butt butter down there prior to getting on my bike. Hopefully the sand didn't blow up my backside when I was squatting.

The things you think about when competing in an Ironman are just mind boggling. You have a lot of time to talk to yourself during a 140-mile race.

I loved the local crowd in Cozumel when the competitors would bike through town and back out again. They were so supportive yelling, "Go, go!! ¡Tú puedes hacerlo! (You can do it!) This became my mantra! I love those people from Mexico!! On my second lap into town, I thought, "Oh, hell, I gotta go do this 33 mile loop, again?" I secretly started looking for ways I could cut through town to head back out and shave off a few miles but, there was security and spectators everywhere.

I had my Angel on one shoulder and the bad little guy with a pitch fork on the other. The Angel telling me, "Don't do it, Dana. You don't want to earn the title Iron Chick by cheating." And the bad guy screaming, "Do it, do it! No one will know. Find a place where there are just a few spectators. Tell them you have to find de baño! They won't know." I didn't give into the pitch fork guy. My luck, I would have to back track and end up adding on miles to my already long 112! Luckily, that day the good in me prevailed. Yeah!!!

Previously, during my lunch break on the back side of the island, at mile 56, I had a wonderful picnic with everything but the checkered table cloth. The break area was in the blazing sun and I needed out of the sun, so I found a closed little business just a few feet away that had some shaded steps under palm trees, just what I needed. I even took my shoes off, got extra ice from the break area to ice my swollen feet and sat and dined with my bag of tuna fish, packets of mustard, Wheat Thin crackers, and some protein drink.

It was nice, cool, and relaxing under those palm trees and the ice on my feet felt like a blast of cool air. I was in Heaven and didn't want to get up. A little mangy pooch even walked up to me and I shared some crackers with him, while I talked with him about icing my feet. Mangy pooch was a needed change of scenery. Unfortunately, I took way too long on my lunch break! It was like 30 minutes! Now my husband had good intentions when he told me to ice my feet during the event, but he didn't mean take a 30-minute break, for goodness sakes!

I was pushing my time limit without even thinking. Secretly, I think I thought, "Well, if there isn't a Starbucks on the route, I'll have a picnic!" I like to defy the odds and do things the hard-core athletes would never do or even think of. I like to say, "Oh, great job on your 12-hour finish, let me tell you about my race and the cute little pooch I met on the way."

> "We have to allow our child to feel loved again. We must please this child, even if it means that we act in ways we are not used to, in ways that may look foolish to others. If we listen to the child who lives in our soul, our eyes will grow bright. If we do not lose contact with the child in our soul, we will not lose contact with life." (Paulo Coelho)

It's all about the stories! If I don't meet new people or animals for that matter, I don't have any new stories. I continued 56 more miles down the road. By the time I got my dragging ass off the bike, I was on a time crunch. For the second time that day, I took way too long in transition trying to catch my breath from the heat outside. I was worried about the stripes of dried salt all over my shirt, shorts, and face. It wasn't from the beach. Unfortunately, heavy perspiration riddled with sodium meant I was becoming susceptible to the heat. I hadn't had to pee very much, so I drank a bottle of water and waited a few minutes.

I took a trip to the Port-a-potty, which, I must say, was much better positioned as there was a Port-a-potty right there in the women's transition tent. This meant the women had their own el banos and the men had theirs in their tent. Yes! The baño was not as bad as in Florida, but I came out and asked the volunteers if they had any hand sanitizer. They looked puzzled as they didn't know what I was asking them in English. An athlete yelled out to me as she was changing, "Ya, didn't see any either. I think you're out of luck there!" Darn, at least if wasn't full of crap piled high to the opening. I'd manage. I headed out of the tent toward the run.

Finally, I was on the run, but unfortunately because of my laissez-faire attitude, time was ticking and I had to complete this race in 17 hours. I got my protein drink and tried to consume it while walking. Once that was down, I tried to muster up a little jog. "Owww, what the hell is that?" I had the worst pain in my right groin. I had never had *this* issue. Where did this come from? What did I do? I couldn't run. My leg at the groin area was *not* able to move, it's like the area was stuck around the pubic symphysis, pectineus, gracilis, and the large rectus femoris. It wouldn't move and allow me to run, when I tried to push through the stuck muscle it felt like something was going to break or snap.

I walked at a fast pace the first four miles until I rounded the corner and saw my husband and daughter. They were excited to see me. My husband started walking with me and when he encouraged me to run a little I told him what was going on with my groin. My ankles were just killing me too, which was odd because I just got off the bike and don't recall using my ankles. In past races, my issues were with my right hamstring and my right metatarsal. My foot would turn black and blue periodically and it would go through the "pre-snap stage." That area would snap and it was like the old stress fracture would reappear during races at any given moment. Surprise, "Honey I'm home!"

I had two pairs of running shoes I brought to prepare for this issue, but the old issue wasn't there. All I could do was walk. I wasn't about to risk the muscles snapping, then I would really be out of the race. I just gimped along like on my first marathon. Eric was near me saying he was going to run back up to our hotel room, which I had just passed, to get something for me as I gimped along past mile four headed to the measly mile five, I only had 21 miles left to go. Woohoo! My outlook was bleak. Eric caught back up to me at mile six and had figured out I better kick my walk in gear if I was going to finish this race.

He was so supportive in his pep talks he gave me without saying what he was thinking, *"What the hell are you doing? Get your ass in gear, pick up the pace. You've come this far, you have to make this one. I know how this is going to affect you mentally if you don't finish this one. Everyone back home has been texting asking what is going on. Why aren't your times showing you as running, what is going on?"*

Sometimes the design of an Ironman course can be a mixed blessing of encouragement and cruelty. The run course was three loops. Each loop begins and ends near the finish line. This is nice because there are a lot of spectators gathered at the finish line. However, when you have to turn around and venture back into the total darkness for another mind blowing loop, it can seem cruel.

This is how it was on my last loop, heading back out into the abyss all alone while people were cheering for those finishing. As I turned to head back out, I caught a glimpse of Linda's expression, a worried look. I felt so defeated. I remember telling Eric, "There is no way. I don't have enough time to complete another 8 miles." He knew it would be close, but never would he acknowledge his own fears. Tears came trickling down my face, again. "Walk Dana, walk", I told myself. "Damn it! Don't stop. Faster, faster." Like Jenny in Forrest Gump, "Run, Forrest, Run!"

Eric didn't say any of those words he was probably thinking, just the "do one for the Giper" talk. "You can do it. You got it, keep going." When I mentioned earlier that Eric had no idea what was in store for him that day, I meant it. Eric was dressed in cargo shorts, old shoes, a cotton t-shirt, and jockey brief boxers. These are all the things we would never, ever, wear to do a marathon. Little did my husband know he was going to walk along the side lines doing around 22 miles that day, pretty much a marathon! He even ran some of those miles! At one point, he sent my daughter to walk with me for support while he ran back up to the hotel.

On the last run to the hotel, Eric went to get me some rice or potatoes from the buffet line of all things. I thought I needed some food for supplementation. I didn't want to have that same blood sugar issue like previously. Little did I know my secret weapon kept my blood sugar muy bien the whole time?

No, it wasn't rice. Eric came back with a cup full of nasty fried rice. Yuck! I couldn't eat that. "Thanks anyway, honey!" Cami was so supportive while Eric ran to the buffet line. I'm sure he looked like a maniac in that food line, running in the restaurant, peeking in at each item served for the day. Eric has been known for talking to himself on more than one occasion, "Will this work, can she eat this, will this work?' "Dang, I need a to-go container?" "Waiter, waiter, excuse me?" Such a good sherpa!

While Eric was at the hotel, Cami tried to support me by telling me what was going on that day, what she and the kids had done all day. I had not seen my sweet baby girl since the night before when we laid down to sleep. She was going to wake up that morning and head down to our friend's room. I didn't see her that morning except for her little head peeking out from under her covers while she slept in the bed next to my husband and me. I gave her a little peck on the cheek, but she never woke up when I headed out of the room around 5:15 that morning.

Cami told me she swam that day and played in the pool with the others earlier. She was feeling alone, later. She wasn't asked to dinner, so she stayed in the room and decorated it all for Ironman Mom. The parents were out on the course. Somehow my daughter got left out. She was feeling sad, and I was distracted by my own pain at the moment. "Join the club," I thought.

Eric caught back up to us and Cami jogged back to the hotel room to be by herself. I was so worried about her going to that room by herself. I think Eric said he got ahold of my gal friend's husband to see if he would bring Cami to the finish line. It appears the other kids had been taken down there a while back as their mothers were much faster than me. I hate that my child was left alone, to fend for herself in a foreign country. I'm not sure if that was a planning error on my husband's part, my daughter's part, or the part that she was secluded like she claimed.

I had to move on and finish that dang Ironman to be with Cami. Get'er done!! Eric informed me if I walked faster at a certain pace, I might just be able to make it. I had to stop and pee. I didn't see any Port-a-potties on the run, so I remember peeing in the lawn of a nice historical business, in the lawn of an Oceanside beautiful home, and in the bushes by the flood waters. I knew I had a deadline to make, but I couldn't help it. I had to urinate every so often.

Ahh, the flood waters. During the bike ride there was a down pour!! Our gal pal got the beginning drops of the downpour, Linda got the full effect of the downpour, and I got the end of the rain. Why so different? It had to do with our places on the island. Gal pal was smoking fast, Linda was somewhere behind her on the island, and I was most likely clear across the island way behind those gals and didn't get the full rain, just the end of it.

There was this area where competitors had to run through 2 feet of water, and no way of going around it. Many of the Ironmen were talking about that water being full of not only rain, but sewage. It was horrible, because when you came out of the 2-foot flood waters your running shoes were full of water and heavy, really heavy. It was almost impossible to run with a shoe that weighed three times what it had been.

It made for some really mean blisters, also. I had to take my shoes and socks off to change them somewhere along the way. This guy I talked to on the route told me he puts Vaseline on his feet to ward off blisters, which I did when I changed shoes and socks, but it didn't help. I looked like I had Swamp Fungus! My feet were gross with blisters and large areas of skin were peeling off the bottoms for weeks. It looked like I had leprosy.

Somewhere after the change of shoes and socks, I was able to start running again. The problem is it wasn't until the last 7 or 8 miles. This is the wall for most people. Most people can't run anymore at this point and are forced to walk if they want to make a marathon. Not me. I'm built weird, mentally and physically. I walked the first 18 miles and now was able to kick my butt in gear and do a little jiggety-jog.

I took off with a spring in my step and Angels on my shoulders. I literally felt like I had Angel wings lifting me up off the ground and carrying me forward. I had images of little white wings on my shoulder. It was amazing. For all intents and purposes I shouldn't have been able to run at this time, but I was. I give that to God and my husband's encouragement and guidance, plus my secret weapon.

Eric had run back up to the hotel for the third time after brining me my shoes and socks. He couldn't find me anywhere after this because I was running, so he hitched a ride with a Mexican native on a little motorcycle. It was hilarious. I remember running and across the road hearing, "Go, honey!!" Who was this guy on back of an old motorcycle? It was my hubby. Eric said he would meet me at the end, but somehow I convinced him to join me there. He got off the cycle and gave the guy $4 for giving him a ride.

I didn't know that he had his own chaffing going on. His nipples, groin, and feet all had some mean chaffing and blistering. Guess he didn't plan well and include his own Butt Butter. To top it off, he had the camera in his pocket, but ditched it in the hotel on one of his many trips back because it was throwing his back out. He ran with me and encouraged me. The next sight I remember made me teary eyed.

I had gained confidence in myself by that time and was jogging at a pretty good pace. It was around 11:00pm. Yes, you read that right. I had been racing since 7:00am and up at 4:30am. The only stops made were two in transition and one after the 56 mile half way marker on the bike for quick nourishment.

It was pitch black outside except for the occasional street light. As I neared the town, there were more lights and only a few spectators left along the course where hundreds stood earlier. We, Eric and I, were in our own little world. Me putting one foot in front of the other. Eric continuing his chant, "You've got this."

We were a 5K out—3 miles— just on the outskirts of town. As we approached the town, I saw Pablo beaming in all his glory. He was jumping up and down, waving his arms, "You can do it, Dana, you made it, just around the corner!!" Eric and I snapped out of the trance and I started to cry out of a sense of relief. I've done it, I'm gonna make it! Linda's hubby had just completed Ironman Texas, and he knew damn well I had a little ways to go. He started running with us, which gave Eric permission to walk, so he did. We ran! He was running at a fast pace. With only 1 mile left to go I said, "I gotta stop and get my breath a second. Just a minute." I walked a minute while my buddy ran back to meet me at the finish line.

I picked up the pace again and took out my Texas Flag which Allana had given us a year before for the Ironman Florida to raise as we crossed the finish line. I never crossed, so I held on to that keepsake which had the quote from Isaiah 40:21.

It was with me, a 2nd time, and I could feel the presence of God flying with me in the air as I lifted my arms in praise to God thanking him for his guidance in my life and on this journey. I was excited with tears of joy as I crossed that finish line at 16:42. I had fulfilled a dream!

My friends who came across the finish line three to four hours earlier where still there and freezing cold from being in their sweaty outfits. I know my gal pal that I had issues with was not thinking of herself at that moment. You couldn't if you were going to wait four hours in cold, sweaty clothes for someone else to cross the finish line. Poor Linda even dribbled in her pants because she couldn't find a Port-a-potty anywhere at the finish line. She said she was headed off to a tree somewhere and then the dribble just started coming before she found the tree.

When we got in the van to head back to the hotel it smelled and I thought it was just the Mexican water! I found out later that night it might have been Linda with the smell looming over her from her wet pants. That's true friendship. I would have said, "I'm leaving now. I'll see you all back at the hotel. I just peed in my pants and I'm not standing around here any longer!!" Not Linda, she was a trooper!

Iron Nugget:

What can you tell your inner child in trying times? How have you persevered during a difficult time?

31 You Are An Ironman!

"Most importantly, take the time to celebrate your success with your friends and family. Go out to dinner, eat ice cream, do all the fun things you may have been neglecting. Put your finish line photo on your desk." (Melanie Fink, IM champion) The next day, gal pal and I were up early while Linda slept in. Gal pal and I had mimosas to toast at breakfast. I still couldn't believe it. I needed someone to pinch me. With all my issues the day before, I actually finished. Dana Cardwell was an Ironman!

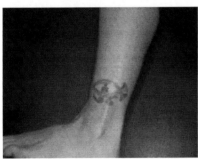

The year before was about getting the badge on my ankle, the coveted Ironman tattoo. The following year I focused on doing the Ironman race for me, not for the tattoo. My original tattoo design was a large M-dot (name athletes refer to as the Ironman brand) with the Icthus wrapping around the M-dot. After not making it during the Florida race, my priorities changed—it would be about the Icthus. My new tattoo design would be an Icthus with a small red M-dot inside my Icthus. It symbolized that I was a Christian first and Iron Chick second. God came first in my life, not some stupid race that a majority of the world would never do.

Only God led me to his clear, blue waters. He made sure I had what I needed in my life to do what I could. I would be a winner through him, nothing else. No Ironman event would make me worthy of being a better person. Only God could do that. I moved through the rest of the trip in a sort of fog. The only way I can describe the past two years was **preoccupied**. I was constantly preoccupied with what swim I had to do to make the 2.4-mile swim, what bike ride I had to do to make the 112-mile ride, and what run pace I needed to do to make the 26.2 marathon. It was the best and worst years of my life.

I had done it. It was over; I had nothing to be preoccupied with anymore. I felt weird. Part of me was relieved, but the other was confused. "What was I supposed to be doing?" I felt like I had lost a limb. Where did the preoccupation go? It had to be there somewhere? We went to my favorite place the next day—Paradise Beach in Cozumel. There are so many water activities at Paradise Beach like water trampolines, kayaks, floating pads, a plastic inflatable Iceberg to climb up and slid down, a challenging device to run across, a water see-saw, a lovely beach, a bungee, and a big gorgeous pool. Lounge chairs with umbrellas where the waiters serve you your own umbrella drink. No stress, just fun!

Eric and I rented motor scooters, while our friends rented a Jeep. We ended up at Playa Bonita Restaurant on the back side of the island after Paradise Beach. The food was good and the margaritas were some of the best. As we drank the Grande margaritas, we looked out at the crystal blue water. All of a sudden I saw a 5-foot manta ray or sting ray in the water. The patrons at Playa Bonita all went to look over the railing to get a glimpse of the beautiful marine animal. Not me. I whipped off my shirt and shorts and got out my goggles.

I was going to swim with this beautiful creature. I got in the ocean and headed over a few feet to where the large creature was, trying not to make a lot of motion in the water. I swam his direction and then stood up to see if I could see where he went. The crowd up above started yelling, "He went right, go right." So, I'd go right, "He just passed you, he went left." It became a funny game, until the big creature finally left the area. Darn. It was fun though.

My heart was beating out of fear and excitement at the same time. I loved that experience. I wouldn't trade that story for anything. I felt so excited to be able to swim with this lovely creature. If I swam up to him I was going to keep my distance! I just wanted to be near him, get a close-up view of him.

After some wonderfully strong margaritas, we dodged really big mosquitoes and sang, "¡Tú puedes hacerlo! ¡Tú puedes hacerlo!" all the way home. I was feeling no pain from the day before at that point and my preoccupation was gone, well, for the time being. I was an Iron Chick and life was good!

I felt the presence of God looking over our girls in this picture.

Giving my man a kiss for his love and support.

Iron chicks in cozy socks (given to us by Tamra prior to our trip). Tamra treated us to massages, fuzzy socks, and relaxing aromatherapy.

The beautiful backside of Cozumel Island during the Iron race.

"Dana Cardwell…..YOU….ARE….AN….IRONMAN!"

Many Americans look at Ironman as they do a Navy Seal; they could never become one. On the contrary. In the book _Fearless,_ Adam Brown worked through his dark past and became a Seal despite battling issues of depression, ADHD, and drug addiction. The odds were against him from the start. Many Americans can work through depression, weight issues, and their dark side through crossing the finish line of an Ironman. If two of the Biggest Losers can finish an Ironman, anyone can do it, even me. (At press time I met Tara from Biggest Loser doing Lake Placid NY with my hubby. He's finished three Ironman events now: Wisconsin, TX, NY.) It's our job as Ironman finishers to motivate Americans to stop wallowing in their drama and get active. Get Healthy! Choose Life! You only get one shot at it.

Iron Nugget:

What do you think you could never do? Why?

Describe your next challenge? Details! Details!

How do you think Tara worked through her weight issues and became an athlete? Do you think Tara ever thought she would be an Ironman or Marathon finisher when she weighed 300 pounds?

32   The Metamorphosis

"Do not be terrified; do not be discouraged, for the Lord, your God, will be with you wherever you go." Joshua 1:9

I read on my Facebook just recently where someone had posted, *"Don't expect everyone to understand your journey, especially if they have never had to walk your path."* You may be saying, "OK, you went and did this Iron event and became an Iron Chick. And?" And... I had a metamorphosis.

The metamorphosis didn't happen as soon as I completed the Iron event. Completing an Ironman is kind of like finding your way around the subway in Paris and not knowing the language. First of all, the subway is called the Metro, which is actually the bus system in many U.S. cities. Second, the streets are called Rues.

Technically, you don't know where to start or which direction you need to go. You may feel lost and alone even if you are with other people. Chances are those around you are feeling the same—lost and confused. Ironically, this scenario relates to those figuring out the Metro system in Paris and those who just completed an Ironman.

John 16:33 says, "I have told you these things so that in me you may have peace. In this world you will have trouble. But take heart. I have overcome the world." It's hard to believe that being in Paris or becoming an Iron Chick could present trouble in your path, but on the contrary. It's figuring out what to do once you get there that causes the trouble.

One of our Pastors, Bob, said, "God is messing with your head!" He then proceeded to tell us about how some soldiers in Vietnam were known for smoking their Bibles. "That's odd," I thought. Bob went on to tell us that soldiers would rip pages out of the Bible to use to roll cigarettes (or whatever else they were smoking). Bob pointed out that many of us choose not to open or read the Bible because we don't want to hear what it has to say.

Bob shared a story about one particular soldier trying to roll a cigarette in the midst of artillery firing, and having the paper fall into his lap. It happened to be Psalm 23, *"The Lord is my shepherd, I lack nothing. He makes me lie down in green pastures, he leads me beside quiet waters, he refreshes my soul. He guides me along the right paths for his name's sake. Even though I walk through the darkest valley, I will fear no evil, for you are with me; your rod and your staff, they comfort me."*

This is a perfect example of how God messes with our mind! God was sending this young man a SIGN! How many times have you been given a sign, chose to ignore it, and rushed through your life as usual? For those reading who are Christians, we just expect (or want) good to happen, unfortunately, it doesn't always work that way. *Life* IS *an* **Ironman**! It's the biggest high and the most trying experience. The catch? The reward and high don't come until you cross that finish line. Until you have worked through the darkest, lowest points of the race.

During an Ironman there are times when you just want to give in and give up. The race becomes too hard mentally to work through those places you never knew were hidden deep down inside. Places you don't want to look at or push through. It's almost easier to give-up than to go there.

If we learn how to push through an endurance race, I can promise this will transfer over into your daily life. It's an astonishing fact! Do you need to smoke your Bible or work through the Bible? Do you need to smoke your life or work through your life? The decision is ultimately yours. No one will make you turn your life around, only you. Invest in life experiences, not material things and stuff. You can't take stuff with you when you die, but you can take the experiences with you. Besides, it might just be the experiences that get you up to the Pearly Gates!

"Sometimes we recognize that the magic moment has passed and we've done nothing about it." (Paulo Coehlo) "We have to listen to the child we once were, the child who still exits inside us. That child understands magic moments." (Coehlo)

The destination of becoming an Iron Chick is a journey, and once the journey is over we become almost lost and confused. I felt so sad and lonely after my first Ironman when all the parties were over and all my friends went in different directions. Like a caterpillar in its cocoon, there's a dormant period after an Ironman. However, I realized God had a plan for me.

It was hard to go back to doing 5K races, half marathons, and bike races on my own. All alone! God's plan consisted of getting my message out to new people, to talk about the challenges in life, about getting healthy through endurance challenges. It's after that dormant period that a metamorphosis occurs and new wings help release us back into the community. "If we are not reborn- if we cannot learn to look at life with innocence and enthusiasm of childhood – it makes no sense to go on living." (P. Coelho)

My problem? I can never put down in words the metamorphosis or catharsis I had from completing a physical event that I couldn't complete the first time I attempted to conquer it. It could be a half marathon, marathon, or an Ironman. It really doesn't matter what physical test it is. It could be walking from one rim of the Grand Canyon to the other or climbing Mount Everest. It's the challenge of something that very few would attempt or even complete that is the re-awakening.

The Native Americans knew what they were doing years ago with sweat lodges. The sweat lodge experience is supposed to be a very spiritual journey. How is this different than an endurance race? On both journeys you are pushing your body to extremes and unnatural occurrences. I'm not advocating you should go find a sweat lodge because the new mamsy pamsy naturalists have been known for running sweat lodges and actually killing people from heat stroke or heat exhaustion. I think the true Native American forefathers are the ones who knew what they were doing.

A pal from yoga, Kevin Hartley, is a hiking guru and put together thoughts on his greatest challenge.

> "In August 2010, I did the Wonderland Trail, 100 miles around Mount Rainier. This was solo at age 58, shortly after my retirement. The trip was 11 days, and the trail climbs a total of more than 20,000 feet. The scenery is spectacular every step; everywhere there are grand vistas of mountains, glaciers, rivers, snowfields, and wildflowers.
>
> The biggest challenges were crises of self-confidence. At times I was dealing with anxiety, wondering what I had gotten myself into. The day I started I was afraid I was forgetting something important. By day three, I was afraid I didn't have enough food. By day four, I was wondering if the sores on

my feet would get bad enough that I'd have to quit. On day seven, I found myself rather lost on a trackless snowfield, after having gotten off the mapped-out trial.

The anxiety is common to most of us in such a challenging situation. This helps ensure we are prepared correctly. I can happily say I had done a pretty good job of preparation for this event. Though I had not done any backpacking of this extent for 30 years, I did do the Outer Mountain Loop in Big Bend National Park in 2007 (4 days) and a four-day trip into the Grand Canyon in 2008. The latter was a solo hike on un-maintained trails, where there, likewise, I had an anxiety crisis. These events were important preparation. I had to figure out my gear, but more importantly, I had to get my mind attuned to the challenges, though I didn't understand that at the points in time. Here's what was important as preparation:

Experience: As I hadn't done any recent backpacking the prior trips were really important, for my state of mind as much as anything.

Physical conditioning: I had done well-rounded strength building. I think yoga was also important for the flexibility.

Planning, very important: I read journals and everything I could on my gear, food requirements, and the weather. Due to the campsite reservations, I had to have a specific itinerary. On such a trip it is good to prepare for use of your spare time, maybe reading or meditating, and try not to get antsy and tempted to jump ahead on your route. My gear was pretty light; I saw some people suffering from heavier loads.

In 2008, I got training as a Wilderness First Responder. This was good for the knowledge gained, but more importantly this resulted in changes in my behavior and attitude on the trial. I knew some of the things that could happen through poor preparation and lack of attention. I would recommend the Wilderness First Aid course (www.nols.edu/wmi/courses) for every hike leader.

Since Mount Rainier I have done many other hikes. I may lead some hikes for Sierra Club; now that I have the self-confidence to lead others on some of these experiences. I'd like to hike around Mount St. Helens and should find myself with less anxiety and a more relaxed contemplative attitude. Happy hiking, Kevin.

For myself, I received my wings when I **owned** the fact that I finished an Ironman race. I survived all the pain I put my body and mind through. I came out of that journey a stronger, more confident, and healed person. I can conquer whatever it is I choose to conquer or I can lay down and DIE! I can give up and watch life pass me by. I say, "Hell No! I choose to live."

WORRY

Worry is like a cancer

Eating at your soul

Robbing you of happiness

And countless dreams untold

Why waste away this precious time

Allowed to you on earth

With thoughts of gloom

And "might have beens"

Told to you since birth

For life is a fleeting thing

Enjoy it while you may

And you'll find that things are getting better

Day by day.

By Suzy Shepard (My Mother)

For too many years, I went through unneeded worry. Kerri Wilt, at Grape Juice, spoke to me prior to the Ironman and said, "Dana, people will still love you, even if you don't complete the Ironman." Her words were a gift from God at that particular moment.

I spent the whole year being afraid that I would let people down if I failed at completing an Ironman again. I was so worried about what others would think if I **failed**. The fear of failure leads to so many issues with people: anxiety, aggression, anger, depression, isolation, and even suicide for some. I needed those words at that moment to tell myself, "As long as we put forth effort and perseverance in our lives, God supports us and people love us." I needed to hear that even if we have shortcomings, we are still loved, we still belong. Why waste away precious time worrying?

"There are many ways to commit suicide. Those who try to kill the body violate God's will. Those who try to kill the soul also violate God's law, even though their crime is less visible to others. We must pay attention to what the child in our heart tells us. We must allow the child to take the reins of our lives. The child knows each day is different."(Paulo Coelho)

You never know when God speaks through you to those who may be having a low point in their life or wasting time with unneeded worry. Keep your head held high and be that beacon to others who may be experiencing obstacles in their path.

The challenge. Here is the recipe to enter your own journey.

1. **Pain is your friend.** Hear me on this. The pain of carrying a shameful secret or 50 extra pound is not your friend, it is the opposite. The pain I'm referring to is the pain of getting healthy and challenging your body. EMBRACE THIS PAIN! The pain of pushing your body to its limits will only advance you in this world and help you deal with the psychological pain that gets stuck in your head. Hear me again. The psychological pain that is in your mind gets you stuck! You can't go anywhere if you keep spinning your tires in a bunch of muddy slop, can you? No, you need to get physical with the vehicle to get unstuck. Push the car out of the mess. Same thing with your life and getting active. I don't mean going out on a morning stroll, either. I mean get off your ass and get active!! Active to the point where it becomes uncomfortable. Pain is your friend!

2. **Break Your Cycle.** Like a caterpillar that drastically changes its whole appearance, you have to change your daily life. I challenge you to enter a 5K race if you never have done one. Walk fast if you can't run. Why you need to enter a race is because it is so easy to become lazy in our walks around the community and stay in our cycle (stuck). By forcing yourself to get the hell out of bed early on a Saturday morning and show up with a bunch of people you don't know, you are enduring some sort of pain. The pain in getting up early, standing at the start with other idiots, completing the event, and driving back home all sticky and smelly. That pretty much gets one out of their normal cycle. If you already compete in 5Ks, do a half marathon, a marathon, a triathlon, or something athletic that is different than what you are used to.

3. **Give yourself permission to take time for you.** You need to do something that gives you pleasure. I'm not talking about self-medicating and getting drunk or high. I'm talking about something just for you. Get a pedicure, manicure, massage, go to the bookstore and peruse with a mocha latte—anything to reward yourself for enduring the pain you endured this week. But remember, do the activity first then take time for you, not the opposite way around.

4. **Find Work You Enjoy.** Delaine Barnes, a theorist, says that "Work provides a means to sustain life. It gives one status, recognition, and affiliation with society. It is a source of friendship, a way to pass time, and it contributes to a person's sense of self-esteem and mental well-being." Too many people settle. If you find your work is contributing to turmoil in your life, look for a new adventure! Get that obstacle out of the way. Another theorist, Anne Roe, reports "an appropriate and satisfying occupation can be the bulwark against neurotic ills or refuge from them."

Where do I see us in a year or two? Completing this book and starting my next book with you in mind. I would like to hear from those who took on my challenge physically. I want to hear what you saw, smelled, felt, and learned on your first 5K run, endurance run, or triathlon.

Nothing beats a virgin story—the virgin triathlete, the virgin marathoner, and the virgin runner, etc. I want you to inspire people. What was the weather like the morning of your race? Was it hot, cold or rainy? Did the people around you look like hard-core runners or where most of them average?

Did someone smell really musty or like old, wet clothes during your run? What about the man who slathers himself up with expensive cologne to go out and run a race? Ugh, the strong cologne or perfume smell is almost as bad as the person smoking on the course when you run by. It makes you want to puke! But tell me all the details. Did you have a catharsis after the race? Did you find your inner demons weren't so bad after all? What were you able to piece together relating to your past and your present challenge? Details, details.

I'm available for public presentations and encourage you to email me with your story as I may use it, with permission, to inspire others on their journey.

Email me at: ironchickdana@gmail.com

I wish you the best, and I hope to hear from you soon about your new adventure.

I believe in you. *God Bless You*.   Dana L. Shepard Cardwell

Show the world you are strong and powerful. You are an Ironman!

Iron Nugget:

What terrifies you?

What discourages you?

References

Biscontinin, L. (2005). *Yoga Fundamentals I*. Northbrook, IL: SCW Fitness Education.

Blanco, J. (2003). *Please, Stop Laughing at Me*. Avon, MA: Adams Media (p. 139)

Bryant, R. (2001). *Walking Through Adversity*. Deerfield Beach, FL : Health Communications Inc. (pp. 30-31).

Chan, E. Hopkins, M., Perrin, J., Herrerias, C. & Homer, C. (2005). Diagnostic practices for attention deficit hyperactivity disorder: A national survey of primary care physicians. *Ambulatory Pediatrics*, 5, pp 201-208.

Foley, H, Carleton, C., Howell, R. (1996). The relationship of attention deficit hyperactivity disorder and conduct disorders to juvenile delinquency: Legal implications. *Bulletin of the American Academy of Psychiatry and the Law*, 24, pp 333-345.

Harlow, C. (1998). Profile of jail inmates, 1996. *Bureau of Justice Statistics Special Report* (Rep. No. NCJ 164620). Washington, DC: U.S. Department of Justice.

Hoza, B., Gedes, C., Mrug, S. &Gold, J. (2005). Peer assessed outcomes in the multimodal treatment study of children with attention deficit hyperactivity disorder. *Journal of Clinical Child and Adolescent Psychology*, 34, pp 74-86.

Gargiulo, R. (2008). *Special Education in Contemporary Society: An Introduction to Exceptionality* (3rd Ed.) CA: Sage Publishing.

Lodge, H. (2006). *Younger Next Year* (2nd Ed.) New York, NY: Workman Publishing (pp 67-69).

Molina, B. & Pelham, W. (2003). Childhood predictors of adolescent substance use in a longitudinal study of children with ADHD. *Journal of Abnormal Psychology,* 112, pp 497-507.

Monastra, V. (2008). *Unlocking the Potential of Patients with ADHD.* Washington, DC: American Psychological Association.

Pledge, D. (2004). *Counseling Adolescents and Children: Developing Your Clinical Style.* Belmont, CA: Thomson Wadsworth. (p 163).

Strydom, J. (2000). *Audiblox and Compublox: A Multi-sensory Brain Training Program.* Retrieved from www.audiblox2000.com on 9/7/2010.

Spring, B., Maller, O., Wurtman, J, & Digman, L. (1982). Effects of protein and carbohydrate meals on mood and performance. *Journal of Psychiatric Research,* 17, pp 155-167

Wesnes, K., Pincock, C., Richardson, D., Helm, G. & Hails, S. (2003). Breakfast reduces declines in attention and memory over the morning in school children.*Appetite,* 41, pp 329-331.

Don Winkley and I after Carraba's 1/2 Marathon June 2013. He's still at it!

Made in the USA
Middletown, DE
17 December 2021

54987168R10095